MW00608030

"Joseph Mudd carefully works with Bernard Lonergan's epistemology and metaphysics to achieve what the Jesuit foundational theologian only outlined with regard to eucharistic theology. The results should make for welcomed reading among Lonergan scholars and all concerned with philosophically grounding the fundamentals of Christian belief and practice."

> —Bruce T. Morrill, SJ
> Vanderbilt University

"In this book, Joseph Mudd brings the insights of Bernard Lonergan to bear on the field of sacramental theology, providing an appreciative but important critique of the significant achievement of French theologian Louis-Marie Chauvet. Responding to both old and new questions in that field, Mudd's work is satisfying and challenging. This book will more than repay the efforts of those who open its pages again and again."

> —Timothy Brunk, PhD
> Associate Professor of Theology
> Villanova University

"This book heralds a major step forward in sacramental theology and especially in the theology of the Eucharist. Mudd deftly proposes that the critical realism of Bernard Lonergan, opening on an ontology of meaning, enables an integration of the best of such hermeneutical approaches as that of Chauvet with a correct understanding of the metaphysical proposals of Aquinas. The dialogical and irenic approach that critiques Chauvet's work in the context of basic appreciation is exemplary."

> —Robert M. Doran
> Marquette University

Eucharist as Meaning

Critical Metaphysics
and Contemporary Sacramental Theology

Joseph C. Mudd

A Michael Glazier Book

LITURGICAL PRESS

Collegeville, Minnesota

www.litpress.org

A Michael Glazier Book published by Liturgical Press

Cover design by Jodi Hendrickson. Cover images: Dreamstime.

Excerpts from the English translation of *The Roman Missal* © 2010, International Commission on English in the Liturgy Corporation. All rights reserved.

Excerpts from Bernard Lonergan's *Insight: A Study of Human Understanding, Collected Works of Bernard Lonergan*, vol. 3, ed. Frederick E. Crowe and Robert M. Doran (Toronto: University of Toronto Press, 1992); and *Method in Theology* (Toronto: University of Toronto Press, 1990). Used by permission of University of Toronto Press.

Excerpts from Louis-Marie Chauvet, *Symbol and Sacrament: A Sacramental Reinterpretation of Christian Existence*, trans. Patrick Madigan and Madeleine Beaumont (Collegeville, MN: Liturgical Press, 1995); and *The Sacraments: The Word of God at the Mercy of the Body*, trans. Madeleine Beaumont (Collegeville, MN: Liturgical Press, 2001). Used by permission of Liturgical Press.

Excerpts from documents of the Second Vatican Council are from *Vatican Council II: The Basic Sixteen Documents*, by Austin Flannery, OP, © 1996 (Costello Publishing Company, Inc.). Used with permission.

Scripture texts in this work are taken from the *New American Bible with Revised New Testament and Revised Psalms* © 1991, 1986, 1970 Confraternity of Christian Doctrine, Washington, DC, and are used by permission of the copyright owner. All Rights Reserved. No part of the *New American Bible* may be reproduced in any form without permission in writing from the copyright owner.

© 2014 by Order of Saint Benedict, Collegeville, Minnesota. All rights reserved. No part of this book may be reproduced in any form, by print, microfilm, microfiche, mechanical recording, photocopying, translation, or by any other means, known or yet unknown, for any purpose except brief quotations in reviews, without the previous written permission of Liturgical Press, Saint John's Abbey, PO Box 7500, Collegeville, Minnesota 56321-7500. Printed in the United States of America.

1   2   3   4   5   6   7   8   9

Library of Congress Cataloging-in-Publication Data

Mudd, Joseph C.
    Eucharist as meaning : critical metaphysics and contemporary
sacramental theology / Joseph C. Mudd.
        pages cm
        "A Michael Glazier book."
        ISBN 978-0-8146-8221-0 — ISBN 978-0-8146-8246-3 (ebook)
    1. Lord's Supper—Catholic Church.   2. Catholic Church—Doctrines.
3. Lonergan, Bernard J. F.   4. Chauvet, Louis Marie.   I. Title.
    BX2215.3.M83   2014
    234'.163—dc23   2014001617

For my parents,
Margaret and John

Contents

Acknowledgments

It is a joy to be able to express my gratitude to the many colleagues and friends who contributed in various ways to this work. I owe a special debt of gratitude to the community of scholars affiliated with the Lonergan Workshop at Boston College. For the many conversations and insights we shared, I am especially grateful to Randall Rosenberg, Mark Miller, John Dadosky, Gilles Mongeau, and Jeremy Wilkins. For many years Timothy Hanchin has been a true friend and guide into the heart of the Gospel. Along the way, I was encouraged to pursue my insights by feedback from Robert Doran, Raymond Moloney, and Philip McShane, whose ideas have inspired my thinking for many years. This work would not have been published without the support and encouragement of my colleagues at Gonzaga University. To the team at Liturgical Press, Hans Christoffersen, Lauren L. Murphy, and Linda Maloney, thank you for bringing this work to completion.

I am deeply indebted to the mentors who shepherded this work through the various phases of dissertation writing. Charles Hefling, whose clarity of expression is unmatched among theologians writing today, encouraged me to say what I mean and mean what I say. Bruce Morrill welcomed me to Boston College and inspired my studies with his scholarly enthusiasm and passionate commitment to God's reign. Fred Lawrence showed me that theological scholarship is always a withdrawl into the world of theory for the sake of a return to the pastoral context of Christian discipleship. While his scholarly wisdom is without equal, Fred is a model of humility and Christian charity.

For her otherworldly patience with me and our three little boys, Henry, Quinn, and Tucker, I am grateful to my best friend, my lovely wife, Vanessa. We would be lost without you.

In many ways this work originated in my childhood home where the Eucharist was always at the center. There I learned the importance of eating gratefully and at the same time learned to love others as I knew myself to be loved. For so many meals and so much love, I am profoundly grateful to my parents to whom this work is dedicated.

Introduction

A controversy over how to talk about the presence of Christ in the Eucharist reemerged at the time of the Second Vatican Council. From the time of the Fourth Lateran Council (1215) the doctrinal tradition had identified the presence of Christ in the Eucharist in terms derived from scholastic metaphysics. Accordingly, in the Eucharist, Christ is present by way of a substantial conversion of bread and wine into his body and blood, or transubstantiation, and communion with Christ in the eucharistic sacrifice of the Mass operates as an instrumental cause to sanctify the faithful. These doctrines remain at the center of Catholic sacramental theology today.[1] But the language of the doctrines is increasingly obscure in contemporary

---

[1] See *Sacrosanctum Concilium*: "For the liturgy, through which 'the work of our redemption takes place,' especially in the divine sacrifice of the Eucharist, is supremely effective in enabling the faithful to express in their lives and portray to others the mystery of Christ and the real nature of the true church" (no. 2); "To accomplish so great a work Christ is always present in his church, especially in liturgical celebrations. He is present in the sacrifice of the Mass both in the person of his minister, 'the same now offering, through the ministry of priests, who formerly offered himself on the cross' [Trent, 22.2], and most of all in the eucharistic species. . . . In the liturgy the sanctification of women and men is given expression in symbols perceptible by the senses and is carried out in ways appropriate to each of them" (no. 7); "From the liturgy, therefore, and especially from the Eucharist, grace is poured forth upon us as from a fountain, and our sanctification in Christ and the glorification of God to which all other activities of the church are directed, as toward their end, are achieved with maximum effectiveness" (no. 10). Translations from Austin Flannery, *Vatican Council II: The Basic Sixteen Documents, Constitutions, Decrees, Declarations* (Northport, NY: Costello, 1996). See also *Catechism of the Catholic Church*, nos. 1076–1109; 1322–1405.

cultures, which are no longer familiar with medieval metaphysics. Furthermore, many hold the doctrine of transubstantiation especially responsible for corrupted liturgical practices. For example, George Pattison argues:

> The doctrine and the practices it gave rise to or endorsed led to the disruption of the narrative and historical integrity of the founding text of Eucharistic life, enacting an understanding of the Church that was ahistorical and hierarchical. Thus it effectively removed the chalice from the public rite, transformed the host into a visual object, reinforced the silencing of the accompanying word and mapped the spatial coordinates of the hierarchization of the Church's life by emphasizing the exclusiveness of the sanctuary and defining public space through a cult of processional liturgies.[2]

Others have argued that the Catholic understanding of eucharistic sacrifice has been subject to "massive misunderstandings . . . that have at times veiled rather than revealed what the sacrifice of Christ, and what authentic Christian sacrifice is really all about."[3] Still others might inquire simply: "Aren't these doctrines just plain embarrassing for Catholics?"[4]

In order to give a defense of the relevant doctrinal formulae, theologians have traditionally appealed to metaphysical accounts of substance and accidents, time and eternity, cause and effect. The question emerged in the twentieth century whether metaphysics is an adequate language to explain

---

[2] George Pattison, "After Transubstantiation: Blessing, Memory, Solidarity and Hope," in *Deconstructing Radical Orthodoxy: Postmodern Theology, Rhetoric, and Truth*, ed. Wayne J. Hankey and Douglas Hedley (Burlington, VT: Ashgate, 2005), 149–60, here at 149–50.

[3] Robert J. Daly, *Sacrifice Unveiled: The True Meaning of Christian Sacrifice* (New York and London: T & T Clark, 2009), 4.

[4] Bernard Lonergan, *Method in Theology* (New York: Herder and Herder, 1972). Lonergan refers to the embarrassment many contemporaries feel over the language of doctrine: "Doctrines that are embarrassing will not be mentioned in polite company" (p. 299). See P. J. Fitzpatrick, *In Breaking of Bread: The Eucharist and Ritual* (Cambridge and New York: Cambridge University Press, 1993), especially 178ff. See also Laurence Paul Hemming, "After Heidegger: Transubstantiation," 299–309, in *Sacramental Presence in a Postmodern Context*, ed. Lieven Boeve and Lambert Leijssen (Leuven: Peeters, 2001); previously printed in *Heythrop Journal* 41 (2000): 170–86 (published online 2002). Hemming argues that it is the very embarrassment that demands that we take up the question of transubstantiation again, especially in a postmodern context "after Heidegger," that is, after Heidegger's "critique has been carried out and is operative in discourse" (p. 308).

what is more than anything else a ritual practice and religious experience. Historically, metaphysical explanations of eucharistic change and sacramental causality have set the complicated world of religious experience aside as too subjective. Classical treatises also tended to extract the Eucharist from the rest of the liturgy with its complex ritual mediations of meaning. As a result, questions about the presence of Christ in the Eucharist were answered without reference to the liturgical life of the church. But the Eucharist does not exist in isolation. The emergence of liturgical theology as a distinct discipline encouraged new ways of thinking about the Eucharist as part of the prayer of the church, which took the performative dimension of ritual seriously as a site for theological reflection.[5] Categories like "symbol" and "sacrament" were recast in ways that responded to the subjective and performative dimension of religious experience.

A variety of approaches, some drawing on existentialism, others on phenomenology, and still others on postmodern thought, offered new ways of thinking about the Eucharist.[6] Edward Schillebeeckx, recognizing that sacraments are signs, and that bread and wine also function for human beings as signs, proposed thinking about the Eucharist in terms of

---

[5] See Aidan Kavanagh, *On Liturgical Theology* (Collegeville, MN: Liturgical Press, 1992).

[6] The various interpretations of eucharistic doctrine that emerged around the Second Vatican Council prompted Pope Paul VI to issue the encyclical *Mysterium Fidei* in 1965, effectively reasserting the classical doctrines promulgated at the Council of Trent despite the changes in the liturgy encouraged by *Sacrosanctum Concilium*. In the encyclical Pope Paul suggests that criticisms of the dogma of transubstantiation "are disturbing the minds of the faithful and causing them no small measure of confusion about matters of faith" (*MF* 10). He continues by referring to emerging interpretations of the doctrine of transubstantiation: "It is not permissible . . . to discuss the mystery of transubstantiation without mentioning what the Council of Trent had to say about the marvelous conversion of the whole substance of the bread into the Body and the whole substance of the wine into the Blood of Christ, as if they involve nothing more than 'transignification,' or 'transfinalization' as they call it" (*MF* 11). Since the promulgation of *Mysterium Fidei* a debate has continued among Catholic theologians over the best way to understand eucharistic doctrines. Further complicating our understanding of the doctrines is the fact that this theological debate is intertwined with an ongoing controversy over the shape of the liturgy in the post–Vatican II church. For a discussion of this controversy, see John Baldovin, *Reforming the Liturgy: A Response to the Critics* (Collegeville, MN: Liturgical Press, 2008).

"transignification."[7] Karl Rahner's theology of the symbol explained the presence of Christ in the Eucharist in terms of his category *Realsymbol*, arguing that unlike signs, which refer to something else, the Eucharist effects what it signifies.[8] Robert Sokolowski's theology of disclosure—grounded in Edmund Husserl's phenomenology—attends to the many ways in which Christ is present in the liturgy, restoring the phenomenal after modernity's assault on appearance as illusion.[9] Louis-Marie Chauvet elaborates a theology of symbolic mediation grounded in Martin Heidegger that identifies the presence of Christ in the Eucharist as absence.[10] Jean-Luc Marion criticizes theories of transignification for sliding into an idolatry of the collective subject and argues that the presence of Christ as pure gift is secured by the theology of transubstantiation, which "alone offers the possibility of distance."[11] Matthew Levering joins Marion in criticizing Schillebeeckx and others for advocating "eucharistic idealism," while offering a defense of Thomas Aquinas against his modern critics and an interpretation of eucharistic sacrifice grounded in Jewish tradition.[12] Each of these approaches is worthy of study, but the present work turns to the potential contribution of Bernard Lonergan's methodology for eucharistic theology.

While Lonergan rarely mentions the sacraments or the liturgy in his major works, we do find him exploring the area of sacramental and espe-

---

[7] See Edward Schillebeeckx, *The Eucharist*, trans. N. D. Smith (New York: Sheed and Ward, 1968).

[8] See Karl Rahner, "The Theology of Symbol," *Theological Investigations IV*, trans. Kevin Smyth (Baltimore: Helicon, 1966), 221–52. See also Stephen M. Fields, *Being as Symbol: On the Origins and Development of Karl Rahner's Metaphysics* (Washington, DC: Georgetown University Press, 2000).

[9] See Robert Sokolowski, *Eucharistic Presence: A Study in the Theology of Disclosure* (Washington, DC: CUA Press, 1994). See also Robert Sokolowski, "The Eucharist and Transubstantiation," *Communio* 24 (December 1, 1997): 867–80.

[10] See Louis-Marie Chauvet, *Symbol and Sacrament: A Sacramental Reinterpretation of Christian Existence*, trans, Patrick Madigan and Madeleine Beaumont (Collegeville, MN: Liturgical Press, 1995), 7; original French publication *Symbole et Sacrament: Un relecture sacramentelle de l'existance chrétienne* (Paris: Cerf, 1987). See also Louis-Marie Chauvet, *Sacraments: The Word of God at the Mercy of the Body*, trans. Madeleine Beaumont (Collegeville, MN: Liturgical Press, 2001).

[11] See Jean-Luc Marion, *God without Being: Hors-Texte*, trans. Thomas A. Carlson (Chicago: University of Chicago Press, 1991), here at 177.

[12] See Matthew Levering, *Sacrifice and Community: Jewish Offering and Christian Eucharist* (Malden, MA: Blackwell Publishing, 2005).

cially eucharistic theology in some important early works, for example, "The Notion of Sacrifice"[13] and "Finality, Love, Marriage."[14] As Frederick Crowe has noted, however, much of Lonergan's early work on sacramental theology is positive theology or collections of theological opinions on the subject for his students.[15] Although these brief works in sacramental theology hold some insights, it is Lonergan's metaphysics, theological anthropology, and Christology that will inform our interpretation of eucharistic doctrines. Lonergan spent most of his career laying the groundwork for bringing Catholic theology up to date by focusing on the question of method, both in cognitional theory broadly and in theological inquiry more specifically. For Lonergan this primarily meant jettisoning the logically rigorous metaphysics characteristic of a classical culture concerned with the universal and necessary as a point of departure. Instead, theology on the level of our era must attend first to method and only subsequently to metaphysics if it is to speak to modern cultures that are concerned with the particular and concrete.[16]

Lonergan laid out his program in brief when he wrote: "So today in a world whence classicist culture has vanished, we have before us the task of understanding, assimilating, penetrating, transforming modern culture."[17] However, Lonergan also recognized the challenge this task presents to theology:

> Classical culture cannot be jettisoned without being replaced; and what replaces it cannot but run counter to classical expectations. There is bound to be formed a solid right that is determined to live in a world that no longer exists. There is bound to be formed a scattered left, captivated by now this, now that new development, exploring now

---

[13] Bernard Lonergan, "The Notion of Sacrifice," *Method: Journal of Lonergan Studies* 19 (2001): 3–34, repr. with the original Latin in *Early Latin Theology, Collected Works of Bernard Lonergan* (CWBL) 19, ed. Frederick E. Crowe and Robert M. Doran (Toronto: University of Toronto Press, 2011) 3–51.

[14] Bernard Lonergan, "Finality, Love, Marriage," 17–52, in *Collection*, CWBL 4, eds. Frederick E. Crowe and Robert M. Doran (Toronto: University of Toronto Press, 1993).

[15] See Frederick E. Crowe, *Christ in History: the Christology of Bernard Lonergan from 1935 to 1982* (Ottawa: Novalis, 2005), 41. Lonergan was responsible for teaching sacramental theology to seminarians in 1942–1943.

[16] Bernard Lonergan, "The Future of Christianity," 149–63, in *A Second Collection: Papers By Bernard J. F. Lonergan, S.J.*, ed. William F. J. Ryan and Bernard J. Tyrrell (Toronto: University of Toronto Press, 1996), at 161. See also in the same volume "Theology in its New Context," 55–67.

[17] Bernard Lonergan, "The Future of Thomism," *A Second Collection*, 43–53, at 44.

this and now that new possibility. But what will count is a perhaps not numerous center, big enough to be at home in both the old and the new, painstaking enough to work out one by one the transitions to be made, strong enough to refuse half measures and insist on complete solutions even though it has to wait.[18]

Nowhere is Lonergan's observation more incisive than in the area of eucharistic theology. Since the Second Vatican Council a scattered left has offered a variety of ways to move beyond the restrictions of medieval and Renaissance eucharistic doctrines by appealing to contemporary philosophy, historical criticism, and ritual studies. On the other hand, a "solid right" has stepped in to restate the traditional doctrines and even to argue for a "reform of the reform."[19] The center is not numerous, and the transitions remain to be made.

The goal here, then, is to assess the contemporary theological context and to execute some of the transitions needed in the area of eucharistic theology. I turn to Lonergan because his philosophical and theological investigations hold untapped resources for illuminating the meaning of Catholic eucharistic doctrines.[20] His work helps us to answer these systematic theological questions: (1) What does it mean to say that the bread and wine of eucharistic worship are converted into the body and blood of Christ through transubstantiation? (2) Why is the Mass called a sacrifice? And how is it related to Christ's sacrifice? (3) What does a sacrament, especially the Eucharist, "do"? How does it "make" human beings holy?[21]

---

[18] Bernard Lonergan, "Dimensions of Meaning," 232–45, in *Collection*, CWBL 4, ed. Frederick E. Crowe and Robert M. Doran (Toronto: University of Toronto Press, 1988), at 245.

[19] See, for example, Thomas M. Kocik, *The Reform of the Reform? A Liturgical Debate; Reform or Return* (San Francisco: Ignatius Press, 2003).

[20] I am not alone in making use of Lonergan's work to illumine questions in liturgical theology. The works of Stephen Happel and Raymond Moloney have provided invaluable insight into the questions that drive the present work. Others who have contributed important studies of Lonergan in relation to sacramental theology include Philip McShane, Giovanni Sala, Margaret Kelleher, Peter Beer, and Michael Stebbins.

[21] Note that questions of presence, sacrifice, and grace are treated together. As with a knot, if we pull on one thread without attending to the others the knot will only get tighter and more difficult to loosen. We treat the three questions together in order to avoid the perils that too-exclusive attention to one thread can cause. See Joseph M. Powers, *Eucharistic Theology* (New York: Herder and Herder, 1967), 42, where Powers

In order to clarify Lonergan's position by contrast, I begin in chapter 1 with Louis-Marie Chauvet. Chauvet offers "the first radically different sacramental theology to come out of Europe since the existential-phenomenological transformation of neo-scholastic thinking wrought by Rahner and Schillebeeckx over thirty years ago, and for that reason alone it deserves serious attention."[22] In addition, Chauvet's influence among theology faculties has grown since the publication of *Symbol and Sacrament*, as has his postmodern critical exegesis of classical sacramental theology. Our particular concern in this work will be with Chauvet's methods, especially whether his appropriation of the Heideggerian critique of onto-theology offers an accurate account of the tradition and a fruitful way forward in eucharistic theology.

In chapters 2 and 3 I turn to Lonergan in order to discover a metaphysics capable of bringing Catholic eucharistic theology up to date by offering a method for transposing traditional eucharistic doctrines into categories that communicate to a contemporary culture. These chapters build on J. Michael Stebbins's article "Eucharist: Mystery and Meaning," where he argues that "for all its shortcomings, the idea of transubstantiation rests on a valid insight into what we mean when we affirm that bread and wine become the body and blood of Christ. The problem is to re-capture that insight, but to do so within the context of a metaphysics grounded in a verifiable account of human knowing."[23] Stebbins refers to the metaphysics presented by Lonergan in *Insight*, where he proposes a derived metaphysics that avoids the onto-theological problematic that Chauvet, echoing Heidegger, rightly criticizes. Lonergan's critical groundwork attends to the problems of bias and the polymorphism of human consciousness, leading to a heuristic

---

argues: "the [Council of Trent's] disparate emphasis on real presence, communion and the sacrifice of the Mass as three rather unrelated values in the Eucharist set the tone for the theology of the Eucharist and Eucharistic piety for several centuries." The key to understanding the doctrines of the Eucharist is to explain how they relate to each other. See also Edward Kilmartin, *The Eucharist in the West: History and Theology*, ed. Robert J. Daly (Collegeville, MN: Liturgical Press, 1998/2004), 170: "The teaching of the council on [transubstantiation] was presented in such a way that it merely affirmed this real presence without situating it in the context of the whole Eucharistic event."

[22] Joseph Martos, "Symbol and Sacrament: A Sacramental Reinterpretation of Christian Existence," *Horizons* 23/2 (Fall 1996): 345–46.

[23] Michael Stebbins, "The Eucharistic Presence of Christ: Mystery and Meaning," *Worship* 64 (1990): 225–36, at 226.

metaphysics rather than a tidy conceptual system. That heuristic metaphysics is articulated in chapter 3, which makes the turn from cognitional theory and epistemology to the elements of critical realist metaphysics.

Chapter 4 deals with two issues: (1) theological foundations and (2) categories of meaning. When Lonergan treats the functional specialty "Foundations" in *Method in Theology* he explains that the foundational reality is religious, moral, and intellectual conversion.[24] If there is confusion today over the meaning and relevance of doctrines it is partly due to a failure to come to terms with the importance of intellectual conversion in theological reflection. This is especially the case in sacramental theology, which can veer off in the directions of either magic or skepticism. Attending to the roles of conversion and authenticity as foundations in sacramental theology will help to make sense of the doctrinal statements of the church about the Eucharist. Lonergan's elaboration of the categories of meaning facilitates a transposition of metaphysical terms and relations employed in eucharistic doctrines into categories of meaning without abandoning metaphysics.

Chapter 5 proposes an understanding of eucharistic doctrines grounded in Lonergan's critical realist metaphysics and transposed into categories of meaning.[25] Rather than separating eucharistic presence and eucharistic sacrifice, I will treat them in an integrated fashion in order to get at the meaning communicated by the rite. There has been a tendency historically to understand the presence of Christ in the sacramental species as the condition for the possibility of eucharistic sacrifice. In this way of thinking the priest first confects the sacramental presence of Christ, the spotless victim made present by the miracle of transubstantiation, and then, by breaking the bread, reenacts the sacrifice of Calvary. This interpretation does not agree with the tradition, especially the theology of Thomas Aquinas, who clarifies that the presence of Christ in the Eucharist is the presence of Christ at Calvary—the presence of the sacrifice. Having clarified the doctrines of transubstantiation and sacrifice through an application of Lonergan's metaphysics and Christology, I propose understanding sacramental causality in terms of mediation of meaning.

---

[24] Lonergan, *Method in Theology*, 267.

[25] Neil Ormerod has laid out a general strategy for the transposition in "Transposing Theology into the Categories of Meaning," *Gregorianum* 92, no. 3 (2011): 517–32.

A Note on Method

While assessing a contemporary shift in the area of Christology, Lonergan once remarked: "In an age of novelty method has a twofold function. It can select and define what was inadequate in former procedures and, at the same time, indicate the better procedures that have become available. But it may also have to discern the exaggerations or deficiencies to which the new age itself is exposed."[26] Sacramental theologians today, Chauvet chief among them, often attempt to deal with eucharistic doctrines in new ways with new methods. Today we find certain "exaggerations and deficiencies" in contemporary sacramental theology that present an opportunity for further reflection on the methods that will lead it into the third millennium. Moving into the third millennium involves coming to a renewed understanding of the dogmatic statements that form the tradition of Christian teaching. Today some theologians pronounce certain dogmas meaningless; nevertheless, the questions those dogmas attempted to answer are meaningful questions, and they continue to be asked by the faithful.

There is indeed much in the history of theological doctrines on the Eucharist that is inadequate and in need of further development, but there are also genuine insights in the tradition that can be transposed for a new age. Accomplishing that transposition will take time. The sacramental doctrines of the past were conceived and communicated according to categories derived from a logically controlled metaphysics. But Lonergan argues, and I agree, that "in our time of hermeneutics and history, of psychology and critical philosophy, there is an exigence for further development. There are windows to be opened and fresh air to be let in. It will not, I am convinced, dissolve the solid achievement of the past. It will, I hope, put that achievement on a securer base and enrich it with a fuller content."[27] Establishing a "securer base" for the "solid achievement of the past" demands a new philosophy, and enriching the past with a "fuller content" requires that we attend to interiority and religious experience. In his own time Lonergan recognized that scholasticism was on the way out, and that neoscholasticism was a dead end. He wrote:

---

[26] Bernard Lonergan, "Christology Today: Methodological Reflections," 74–99, in *A Third Collection: Papers by Bernard Lonergan*, ed. Frederick Crowe (New York: Paulist Press, 1985), at 74.

[27] Ibid., 89.

It remains that something must be devised to be put in their place. For what they achieved in their day was to give the mysteries of faith that limited and analogous understanding that helped people find them meaningful. Today that help is not forthcoming. The bold pronounce the traditional formulations meaningless. The subtle discern in them an admixture of Christian doctrine with a Heideggerian forgetfulness of being. Nor is there any general consensus to expound and vindicate them, for the theological and philosophic basis for a consensus no longer seems to exist.[28]

Lonergan hoped to identify that basis by attending to the concrete performance of the subject. Understanding what Lonergan had to say about theological and philosophical foundations may help us answer some fundamental questions in eucharistic theology on the level of our time.

The Eucharist is at the center of the church's liturgical life. It is a profound mystery. But inquiring minds want to know. Is there anything we can know about this mystery? Does the eucharistic mystery, more than any other Christian mystery, simply require a sacrifice of the intellect to the demands of blind faith? If so, how does it mean what it means? Can we articulate a fruitful analogical understanding of this mystery that can illumine faith? Having learned from both Chauvet's critique of metaphysics and Lonergan's development of a critical metaphysics, we hope to offer a fruitful understanding of traditional eucharistic doctrines that is able to respond to some contemporary problems and shed some light on the great mystery that stands at the center of Christian worship.

---

[28] Lonergan, "Questionnaire on Philosophy: Response," 352–83, in *Philosophical and Theological Papers 1965–1980*, CWBL 17, ed. Robert C. Croken and Robert M. Doran (Toronto: University of Toronto Press, 2004), at 365. Lonergan refers to this shift away from an earlier consensus as a shift in the understanding of culture from a classicist to an empirical notion of culture.

Chapter One

Louis-Marie Chauvet's
Postmodern Sacramental Theology

Chauvet's work represents the most thoroughgoing criticism of metaphysical accounts of sacramental theology.[1] He embraces the challenge of thinking about the sacraments on the level of our time by undertaking a Heideggerian critique of onto-theology and elaborating a fundamental theology of sacramentality grounded in the symbolic. In a brief apology for his project Chauvet indicates why he takes a different tack: "If today we can think differently, it is not because we are more clever than they but because we have available to us tools of analysis and reflection which only the modern ethos at a certain stage of its evolution could supply."[2] The decision to take a new approach situated in the present cultural reality, Chauvet says, "unites us to Thomas Aquinas as much as it separates us from him."[3]

---

[1] See Glenn P. Ambrose, *The Theology of Louis-Marie Chauvet: Overcoming Onto-Theology with Sacramental Tradition* (Burlington, VT: Ashgate, 2012). For a biographical sketch of Chauvet, see Philippe Bordeyne, "Louis-Marie Chauvet: A Short Biography," ix–xiv, in *Sacraments, Revelation of the Humanity of God: Engaging the Fundamental Theology of Louis-Marie Chauvet*, ed. Philippe Bordeyne and Bruce Morrill (Collegeville, MN: Liturgical Press, 2008). In addition to *Symbol and Sacrament*, see Louis-Marie Chauvet, *Du Symbolique au Symbole: Essai sur les Sacrements* (Paris: Cerf, 1979); Louis-Marie Chauvet, *The Sacraments: The Word of God at the Mercy of the Body*, trans. Madeleine Beaumont (Collegeville, MN: Liturgical Press, 2001).

[2] Chauvet, *Sacraments*, 95

[3] Ibid.

Chauvet's goals are limited, in accord with the theological method he adopts. His purpose is not to offer a definitive statement on the sacramental mediation of grace but to articulate one way to approach the sacraments other than that offered by scholastic methodology. In fact, he rejects the idea that a definitive statement is possible, preferring instead a variety of approaches. The question that concerns us here is whether he has adequately portrayed the older scholastic methodology, especially as it is found in Thomas Aquinas. And if not, what has he missed?

This is not to disqualify Chauvet from the start but to alert the reader to two key problems that emerge in the following account of the methodological program of *Symbol and Sacrament*: (1) Chauvet's misreading of Thomas's theory of knowing, and (2) the empiricist understanding of causality that both prejudices Chauvet's reading of Thomas on sacramental causality and influences his notion of the symbolic speech-act as "revealer/operator." Again, these problems do not disqualify Chauvet's massive contribution to contemporary sacramental theology, but they do call for clarifications and further development. My exploration of his work here is therefore undertaken with an eye to his critique of metaphysics and his methodology, because it is here that Chauvet's treatment raises fundamental questions about how best to understand church doctrines on the sacraments, especially the Eucharist.

1. Symbol and Sacrament: Overcoming Onto-Theology

I begin by outlining Chauvet's presentation of what he calls the "onto-theological presuppositions of classical sacramental theology."[4] Under this heading he raises his central concerns with traditional eucharistic doctrines insofar as they are indebted to onto-theological foundations and formulated in terms of scholastic metaphysics. After examining his criticism of classical sacramental theology, I will move on to explore his appropriation of Heidegger in his attempt to "overcome" metaphysics. Chauvet's use of Heidegger leads to a discussion of mediation through language and the body, or the symbolic—the key to Chauvet's sacramental theology.

---

[4] Louis-Marie Chauvet, *Symbol and Sacrament: A Sacramental Reinterpretation of Christian Existence* [= *SS*], trans. Patrick Madigan and Madeleine Beaumont (Collegeville, MN: Liturgical Press, 1995), 7.

1.1. Destruction as Therapeutic: Overwhelming Metaphysics with Difference[5]

At the center of Chauvet's critique of classical sacramental theology is what he calls the "ontotheological presuppositions" that inform traditional Catholic sacramental doctrines. Chauvet's concern is that these doctrinal formulations and the onto-theo-logic that supports them undermine the transformative power of the sacraments in the lives of Christians. Instead, he proposes a theology that "bases itself upon [the sacraments] as *symbolic figures allowing us entrance into, and empowerment to live out, the (arch-) sacramentality which is the very essence of Christian existence.*"[6] Thus he proposes a sacramental reinterpretation of Christian existence, or a foundational theology of sacramentality.[7] Chauvet avers that his project is simply a matter of "trying to understand what we *already* believe, immersed as we are, through baptism and Eucharist, in *sacramentality.*"[8]

In order to achieve his goal of a sacramental reinterpretation, Chauvet undertakes to free sacramental theology from the constraints of a metaphysics of cause and effect. He proposes a "radical overturn of the classical approach" that "ultimately strikes at the unexamined presuppositions of *metaphysics* and its always-already onto-theological profile."[9] Chauvet uses the first part of *Symbol and Sacrament* to criticize these "unexamined presuppositions" on the one hand, and on the other to develop the categories through which he will elaborate his theory of the symbolic in later chapters. He admits that the "*theological* reflection proposed here can stand only if we have first made explicit the *philosophical* position which undergirds it."[10] The philosophical work of the first part is therefore essential to the later constructive theological effort.

---

[5] See Martin Heidegger, *Being and Time*, trans. John Macquarrie and Edward Robinson (New York: Harper and Row, 1962), 41–45: "we are to *destroy* the traditional content of ancient ontology until we arrive at those primordial experiences in which we achieved our first ways of determining the nature of Being—the ways which have guided us ever since" (p. 44). Heidegger goes on to indicate the "positive" goal of this program: to uncover the assumptions that lie at the base of our approach to the question of being. See Sean J. McGrath, *The Early Heidegger and Medieval Philosophy: Phenomenology for the Godforsaken* (Washington, DC: CUA Press, 2006), 210–28.

[6] *SS*, 2. Italics in the quoted material are all original except where indicated.

[7] Ibid., 1.

[8] Ibid., 2.

[9] Ibid. 2–3.

[10] Ibid., 3.

Chauvet takes the disparity between the real and thought about the real as foundational for a theology of the sacramental.[11] The mistaken assumption of the metaphysical tradition, according to this view, is that when we employ the verb "to be" we transcribe the real into language.[12] While he recognizes that the best thinkers in the vast sweep of history have always "taken a *step backwards*, a step of humble lucidity before the truth, a step which has protected them from falling into the deadly dogmatism of confusing their thought with the real," Chauvet wants to take the disparity between the real and thought about the real as his point of departure.[13] The refusal of Western philosophers and theologians to recognize this difference between the real and thought, or discourse about the real, shows a "lack of interest in exploring the bias of their unconscious assumptions [that] gives these thinkers a 'family resemblance' and allows us to speak of *the* 'metaphysics' or better still, *the* metaphysical."[14] Chauvet dwells on the difference, resisting any totalizing claims of knowing on being.

The primary category Chauvet criticizes in traditional sacramental theology is causality, which he describes as "always tied to the idea of production or augmentation."[15] According to Chauvet, causality "presupposes an explanatory model implying production . . . a model in which the idea of 'instrumentality' plays a pivotal role."[16] There seems to be a radical discontinuity, however, between grace and the "instrumental productionist language of causality."[17] Chauvet wonders why "the Scholastics chose this idea, apparently so inadequate and poorly suited to expressing the modality of the relation between God and humankind in the sacraments."[18] That causality is "poorly suited to express the modality of the relation between God and humankind in the sacraments" would seem to depend on what one means by causality.

While Chauvet admits that, of course, causality served only as an analogy and his subsequent criticism may be directed at a straw man, nevertheless he asserts that underlying the scholastic use of the language of causality

---

[11] Ibid., 8.
[12] Ibid.
[13] Ibid.
[14] Ibid., 8–9.
[15] Ibid., 7.
[16] Ibid.
[17] Ibid.
[18] Ibid.

is "the never explicitly recognized or criticized assumptions that lay hidden at the foundation of the way they set up the problem."[19] Chauvet claims the scholastics were "*unable* to *think otherwise*" because of the "onto-theological presuppositions which structured their entire culture."[20] He believes the onto-theological foundations of scholastic theology constitute an "unconscious logic" that holds from the time of the Greeks down to the twentieth century. Despite the "many concrete, diverse, even opposed forms which the philosophical tradition inherited from the Greeks has taken over the twenty-five centuries of its existence" there remain, according to this view, "uncriticized assumptions lying at the base of all these systems" which can be discovered by studying their "family resemblances" or genealogy.[21] For Chauvet, as for Heidegger, these uncriticized assumptions make possible a total explanation of being.

What it would mean to explain the totality of being would depend on what one means by being. It is not true that all philosophers have meant the same thing by being, even though their formulations of being may have a family resemblance. Indeed, since philosophy develops, as do all areas of human knowing, later positions rely on the insights of earlier positions. But any genealogy of being would have to account for key differences as well as family resemblances if it were to do justice to particular theories of being. A full-blown genealogy is not Chauvet's project. He left that work to Heidegger, in whose thinking he finds resources for moving out of "foundational ways of thinking" that are characteristic of metaphysics.[22] But, perhaps with Heidegger, we should ask Chauvet, "What is metaphysics?"

The metaphysical is for Chauvet synonymous with "the onto-theological framework (that is, the always-already theological outline of metaphysics)."[23]

[19] Ibid., 7–8.

[20] Ibid., 8.

[21] Ibid.

[22] Debate over whether Heidegger's criticism applies to the metaphysics of Thomas Aquinas is ongoing. See, for example, John D. Caputo, *Heidegger and Thomas: An Essay on Overcoming Metaphysics* (New York: Fordham University Press, 1982); Jean-Luc Marion, "Thomas Aquinas and Onto-Theology," 38–74, in *Mystics: Presence and Aporia,* ed. Michael Kessler and Christian Sheppard (Chicago: University of Chicago Press, 2003); S. J. McGrath, *The Early Heidegger and Medieval Philosophy: Phenomenology for the Godforsaken* (Washington, DC: CUA Press, 2006).

[23] *SS*, 9.

In his way of understanding metaphysics this means "a *methodological* concept . . . showing a *tendency* or an attracting pole characteristic of Western thought since the Greeks; this attraction is characterized as the 'foundational way of thinking' and therefore as the impossibility of taking as the point of departure for thought the very distance between discourse and reality."[24] In opposition to the so-called metaphysical method, Chauvet proposes a method that takes the gap between discourse and reality as its point of departure and operates within it. Chauvet proposes an alternative method that operates within the difference between thought and reality. This is the way of language, or the symbolic.[25] Chauvet claims for his method not merely the status of opposition to traditional metaphysics but rather "*another epistemological terrain* for our thinking activity."[26] The shift to another epistemological terrain will enable Chauvet to develop a fundamental theology of the sacramental based on a theory of the symbol rather than on a theory of being or metaphysics.

The methodological opposition between the symbolic and the metaphysical is for Chauvet a *heuristic* one. Therefore, because his concern in distinguishing between the symbolic and the metaphysical is primarily methodological, Chauvet's critique of metaphysics will target what he considers to be the unrecognized foundations or schemes of thinking it employs. Recognizing the potential for a circularity in this critique of metaphysics, he defends his revision of sacramental theology via symbolic methodology by emphasizing that the symbolic approach is never fully achieved, thus constituting a transition to be done again and again, which shows "how little we have to do here with the mere substitution of a new conceptual system for an old."[27] To escape the gravitational pull of foundational ways of thinking, one's method has to be always already self-critical, and it is never fully achieved because it stakes its claim on the terrain demarcated by the disparity between discourse and reality. The foil for Chauvet's elaboration of a symbolic method is the metaphysical method of Thomas Aquinas.

[24] Ibid.
[25] Ibid.
[26] Ibid.
[27] Ibid.

1.2. Thomas Aquinas and the Metaphysical

Chauvet singles out Thomas as the chief representative of the meta-physical, even while admitting from the outset that his presentation of Thomas may be a straw man.[28]

First, he points to the *place* of the sacraments within the *Summa Theologiae*. Although he highlights the fact that they are alluded to briefly in his discussion of the virtue of religion, Chauvet objects to Thomas's placement of the discussion of the sacraments in the *Tertia Pars*, after his theology of the passion. Chauvet understands that Thomas's note on the sacraments in the prologue of question 89 of *Secunda-Secundae* indicates that they could be taken up within the context of ethics, thus confirming his assertion that "the sacraments are considered to belong to ethics" as "the principal expression of our moral relation to God, a relation authentically Christian because it is brought into being by Christ, who directs the offering of a sanctified humanity toward God."[29] In a way Chauvet seems to inadvertently explain why Thomas places sacraments in the *Tertia Pars* since they belong to the situation of relationship with God mediated by the Christ event.

The virtues of religion are general categories that include acts of religion outside the Christian sacramental economy. Specifically Christian acts of religion are established by Christ and derive their power from his passion. Nevertheless, Chauvet is disappointed with the ramifications of this arrangement of the text: "One may regret that Thomas insufficiently emphasizes, in the treatise contained in the third part of the *Summa*, the ascendant and ethical aspects of the sacraments touched upon in the question relating to the 'exterior acts' of the virtue of religion."[30] Placing the treatise on the

---

[28] Ibid., 8.

[29] Ibid., 10. This is an odd reference to the *Summa Theologiae (ST)* because II–II, q. 89, deals with oath taking, or invoking the name of the Lord. Chauvet might have pointed to the preceding questions, particularly question 85, where Thomas connects sacrifice and ethics at q. 85, a. 3, ad. 2m: "Man's good is threefold. There is first his soul's good which is offered to God in a certain inward sacrifice by devotion, prayer and other like interior acts: and this is the principal sacrifice. The second is his body's good, which is, so to speak, offered to God in martyrdom, and abstinence or continency. The third is the good which consists of external things: and of these we offer a sacrifice to God, directly when we offer our possessions to God immediately, and indirectly when we share them with our neighbor for God's sake."

[30] Ibid., 11.

sacraments in the *Tertia Pars*, "stressing as it does the role of the sacraments in the sanctification of human beings, is too heavily weighted in favor of the 'Christological-descending' aspect."[31] Chauvet is concerned that this arrangement severs the real connection between sacrament and ethics.

Second, after questioning the placement of the sacraments in the *Summa*, Chauvet goes on to assess what he calls its "major innovations," especially the relationship between sign and cause in Thomas's thought. Chauvet traces three key shifts in Thomas's thought on the sacraments between the *Commentary on the Sentences* and the *Summa Theologiae*. First, there is a "transition from the priority of the *medicinal* function of the sacraments to the priority of the *sanctifying* function."[32] This shift influenced the way Thomas employed different kinds of causality in his theology of the sacraments. The *Commentary* emphasized the role of the sacraments as disposing the recipient to grace, but in the *Summa* Thomas subordinated even the medicinal function as a mode of efficient causality to the sacrament as the efficient cause of sanctification.[33]

The second shift involves Thomas's use of the categories "sign" and "cause." Chauvet says that ultimately Thomas chose Augustine's definition of a sacrament, "the sign of a sacred thing," but added a note on the causal function, viz., "*signum rei sacrae in quantum est sanctificans homines*."[34] The key addition, "insofar as it sanctifies human beings," reveals the causal dimension in Thomas's understanding of the sacraments. Sacraments are both signs and causes; they effect what they signify. This development in Thomas's thought grows out of a distinction between dispositive and instrumental causality. If the sacraments merely dispose one to receiving grace they are cases of "occasional causality." Thomas objected that dispositive or occasional causality would make the sacraments mere signs of a potential grace, but instead he holds that "it is the consistent teaching of the Fathers that the sacraments not only signify but also cause grace."[35] On Chauvet's interpretation, sign and cause are incompatible.[36]

---

[31] Ibid.
[32] Ibid.
[33] Ibid., 12.
[34] Ibid., 15.
[35] Ibid., 16.
[36] Ibid., 17. "The 'sign' (*signum*), as it is presented by the celebrating Church, is the *very mediation* of the gift of grace. The whole problem consisted in *harmonizing two categories as completely foreign to one another as are 'sign' and 'cause.'*"

The question is whether a sacrament causes by signifying. Granted that sacraments do whatever they do by signifying, what could it possibly mean to say that something causes what it signifies? The answer is based on the analogy of instrumental rather than dispositive causality. Thomas's decision to discard the notion of dispositive causality in the *Summa Theologiae* reflects a shift away from Avicenna's notion of cause to Averroes's more Aristotelian distinction between principal and instrumental causality. According to Aristotle and Averroes the principle cause moves and the instrumental cause, being moved, moves.[37] Chauvet sums up the ramifications of this change: "With this one stroke, the sacraments no longer have to be considered as merely pseudo-efficient causes—only disposing—but rather as true causes in their own right, exercising their proper agency and leaving their mark on the final effect even if this action is always subordinated to the action of God, who remains the principal agent."[38] Because the principal cause of sanctification is God, any work of sanctification, including sacramental causality, is caused by the principle cause.

This subordination of all causation to the principal cause enables Thomas to suggest that sacraments can rightly be called causes of grace. Chauvet notes that the same schema is employed in Thomas's discussion of the incarnate Word in which the human nature of Christ operates as an instrument of divinity.[39] As the sacraments derive their power from the incarnate Word who instituted them, Thomas's sacramental theology follows from his Christology. In question 62 of the *Tertia Pars* he writes: "The principal efficient cause of grace is God, for whom the humanity of Christ is a conjoined instrument (like a hand), while the sacrament supplies an instrument that remains distinct (like a stick moved by the hand). It is thus necessary for the salvific power to pass from the divinity of Christ through his humanity and finally through the sacraments."[40] The proposition that the

---

[37] Ibid., 18.

[38] Ibid. This is a key insight for Thomas and represents an important change in his mature thinking. What Thomas recognizes in this change is the agency of God in the universe and the subjection of all other agency to the divine as secondary causes. This insight follows on the "theorem of the supernatural" which places God in a different entitative order and accomplishes what de-ontotheology desires but is unable to accomplish, i.e., thinking God outside of being.

[39] Ibid., 20.

[40] Ibid., here citing *ST* III, q. 62, a. 5.

sacraments derive their efficacy from the incarnate Word, in that they join the divine Logos to the finite human order—just as the incarnate Word was united with human nature—means that the sacraments are *"prolongations of the sanctified humanity of Christ."*[41]

Having surveyed the development of Thomas's thought on the sacraments from the *Commentary on the Sentences* to the *Summa Theologiae*, and having summarized the relation of sign and causality in Thomas's thought, Chauvet turns to a critique of what he calls the "productionist" scheme of representation.[42] Returning to and elaborating on the foundational critiques with which he began his study, he wonders: "To explain the specificity of the sacraments in comparison with other means of mediating God's grace, one must say that they effect what they signify. But according to what modality?"[43] For Thomas the most fitting analogy is with instrumental causality. Therefore the sacraments can be said to "cause grace." Chauvet claims that Thomas's explanatory framework, employing terms like "cause," "work," "produce," "contain" (though Thomas repeatedly cautions that these terms function analogically), serves "to build up an ever-present *scheme* of representation that we call *technical or productionist*."[44] This kind of representation is the result of "unconscious (and uncriticized) onto-theological presuppositions" that Chauvet attempts to overcome with Heidegger's help.[45]

There are three aspects of Chauvet's critique of Thomas. First, the placement of the sacraments in the third part of the *Summa* is symptomatic of the persistent separation of sacrament and ethics, paired with a potentially unwarranted presumption of holiness on the part of the recipient because of a guaranteed sacramental effect. Chauvet's remedy incorporates the ethical moment into his theory of symbolic gift exchange, so that ethical conduct

---

[41] Ibid. Chauvet hints here that he will return to this notion of sacraments as "prolongations of the sanctified humanity of Christ" in the final section of *Symbol and Sacrament*. At this point it is worth alerting the reader to his concern there, i.e., that Thomas's sacramental theology is affected by the "Christo-monism" characteristic of the Western theological tradition (p. 463). We will return to the question of Trinitarian relations in sacramental theology below.

[42] Ibid., 21.

[43] Ibid.

[44] Ibid., 22.

[45] Ibid.

becomes the fulfillment of the gift of grace in the liturgy of the neighbor.[46] The second is related to the first, namely, Thomas's putative understanding of the sacraments as containers or quantities of grace that can be earned or hoarded. This image enables a rivalrous vision of sacramental grace, leading to potentially disastrous pastoral consequences. Third, the conception of sacraments as instruments tends to emphasize a priestly intermediary between God and the believer in the manner of ancient sacrificial cults. As the one who applies the instrument, the priest becomes the mediator of sacramental grace, especially in the context of sacrificial offering.[47] Chauvet thinks these ethical, pastoral, and clerical distortions are rooted in an onto-theo-logic that promotes the human tendency to be satisfied with apparently self-evident half-truths about the divine-human relation. A contemporary sacramental theology should help people face the symbolic labor of restructuring their relationships with God and others as a result of taking symbolic mediation seriously. In order to do that, contemporary sacramental theology will have to move definitively beyond scholastic metaphysical explanations of sacramental causality. Chauvet turns to Heidegger to begin constructing an alternative.

2. Reconfiguring Foundations:
From the Logic of the Same to Symbolic Mediation

Chauvet summarizes Heidegger's argument about the forgetfulness of being characteristic of Western metaphysics as follows: "Being is thus presented as the general and universal 'something' or 'stuff' which conceals itself beneath entities, which 'lies at the base' of each of them (*hypokeime-non*), a permanent 'subsistent being,' *sub-stratum*, *sub-jectum*, and finally, as Descartes describes it, *sub-stantia*."[48] Because it confuses entity and being, "metaphysics believes itself to have produced an explanation of being, when

---

[46] See ibid., 265: "The element 'Sacrament' is thus the symbolic place of the on-going transition between Scripture and Ethics, from the letter to the body. The liturgy is the powerful pedagogy where we learn to consent to the presence of the absence of God, who obliges us to give him a body in the world, thereby giving the sacraments their plenitude in the 'liturgy of the neighbor' and giving the ritual memory of Jesus Christ its plenitude in our existential memory."

[47] See ibid., 259–60 and 308–9.

[48] Ibid., 26. See Heidegger, *Being and Time*, 123–34.

in fact it has only ontically reduced being to metaphysics' *representations*, utterly forgetting that nothing that exists 'is.' "[49] In attempting to find a "property common to the entirety of entities," metaphysics seeks a base, or foundation (*Grund*) in being and "from the moment it is conceived as at the base of all entities, being necessarily and simultaneously 'twins' into a unique *summit*— a *causa sui.*"[50] Thus Chauvet writes: "Through its status as a preliminary onto-theological interpretation of the relation of being to entities, metaphysics, far from preceding theology, proceeds from it in a fundamental, and not an accidental, way."[51] That metaphysics proceeds from theology is not especially a problem for theologians like Thomas Aquinas who already operate in a horizon of faith in a creator God. It becomes a philosophical problem for Heidegger because he wants an account of the being of beings that does not lean on theology for foundations.

Even Thomas's insistence on analogical predication fails to satisfy Chauvet. So while metaphysics expresses an onto-theological interpretation of reality, it does so analogically, only because "analogy is . . . *congenital to metaphysics.*"[52] Thomas's use of analogy simply reflects this congenital relationship, in which created realities participate in Being or the Good only in a deficient manner.[53] The ontological substrate, which is also the metaphysical within onto-theology, is the basis for attempts at total explanation of reality by means of universal and necessary causes beginning with a first cause. The god of metaphysics functions as a foundational cause blocking an infinite regress and thereby offering a totalizing account of being.[54] The metaphysical project manifests a desire to master being; it turns the truth into "an unfailingly available foundation, a substantial permanence, an objective presence."[55]

---

[49] *SS,* 27.

[50] Ibid.

[51] Ibid.

[52] Ibid., 28.

[53] Thomas's use of analogical predication does not treat created realities as deficient. The point of analogy is to preserve divine transcendence. See Denys Turner, *Faith, Reason and the Existence of God* (New York: Cambridge University Press, 2004), 179–83. See also Ralph McInerny, *Aquinas and Analogy* (Washington, DC: The Catholic University of America Press, 1996).

[54] *SS,* 28.

[55] Ibid.

For Chauvet this degradation of truth to causes, and at the limit to an ultimate cause, is simply a matter of self-assertion. It is "symptomatic of a visceral *anthropocentrism*: the need to begin with the certitude of the self, with the presence of the self to the self, by which everything else in the world is ultimately to be measured."[56] The gravamen of Chauvet's complaint is this:

> From the notion of being-as-substance as present permanence to the notion of the subject-substance as permanent presence, it is the same logic at work, a logic of the Same unfolding itself: a utilitarian logic which, because of fear of all difference, of what is by its nature permanently open, and finally of death, reduces being to its own rationality and, unknowingly, makes of it the glue that bonds a closed totality.[57]

This "logic of the Same" reduces the otherness of being to the rationality of the subject-substance who becomes the foundation of all being, which Chauvet, applying his understanding of Heidegger, proposes as the single logic of all metaphysical thinking—"that is why every metaphysics is, at its base and when building on this base, itself the Foundation that gives an account of the base, explains it, and finally asks it to explain itself."[58] The only way out of the logic of the same is by coming to terms with the place of language in human understanding.

2.1. Language and the Mediation of Being

After offering his interpretation of Heidegger's account of the logic of Western metaphysics, Chauvet argues that the metaphysical tradition promotes the dichotomy between being and language as a result of an inherently dualistic worldview extending back to Plato. A rupture was opened between the two by Plato's view that "the things of this world are now no more than shadows cast by the 'ideal' realities represented by thought and

---

[56] Ibid.

[57] Ibid.

[58] Ibid., 29. Chauvet is citing a French translation of Heidegger's *Identität und Differenz: "Daher ist alle Metaphysik im Grunde vom Grund aus das Gründen, das vom Grund die Rechenschaft gibt, ihm Rede steht und ihn schließlich zur Rede stellt" (Identität und Differenz* [Pfullinggen: Neske, 1957], 55). In English, see Martin Heidegger, *Identity and Difference*, trans. Joan Stambaugh (Chicago: University of Chicago Press, 2002).

objectified by language."[59] Language is no longer "the very place where the world happens," but a mere instrument used for objectifying thought.[60] Despite variations in the metaphysical traditions, Chauvet agrees with Heidegger that "one can discern a common way of representing being as '*something facing human beings which stands by itself*' in relation to humans' thinking and speaking."[61] Language has been reduced to a tool, an instrument for objectifying mental contents; it is conventional, arbitrary, ultimately a result of the fall and therefore not "natural" to the human being.[62]

Chauvet identifies this reduction of language to the status of an instrument in Thomas's theory of knowledge. As we will see, Chauvet's summary reveals a misreading that Lonergan spent much of his career seeking to correct.

> One could briefly summarize Thomas' theory as follows. (1) The object imprints its image (2a) in the senses by its sensible "impressed species" (*species impressa*)—the particularity of the thing—and (2b) in the mind through its intelligible impressed species—the universal aspect of the thing. Through the abstractive powers of the active intellect, the mind constructs (3) the concept, which is the mental representation of the thing, or the presence of the thing itself in the mind by way of its mental representation, and which is called the "interior word" (*verbum cordis* or *mentis*). The concept is then transmitted to the outside by (4) the exterior word in a discourse which is a judgment.[63]

Chauvet further simplifies his summary, arguing that for Thomas "there are only three truly distinct elements: the thing, the moment of intellectual activity (the formation of the concept) and the moment of judgment."[64] The key to Thomas's realism is that the object is naturally present in the mind through its mental representation. According to Chauvet, "Thomas' 'realism,' as is immediately evident, takes its point of departure from the conviction that the real is an object, an objective to *be reached*."[65] We will return to this

---

[59] *SS*, 29. For this interpretation of Heidegger, Chauvet relies on Jean Beaufret, *Dialogue avec Heidegger* (Paris: Minuit, 1973).

[60] *SS*, 29.

[61] Ibid., 30.

[62] Ibid.

[63] Ibid., 32., citing *De Veritate*, q. 4, a. 1–2, and *De Potentia*, q. 8, a. 1.

[64] Ibid.

[65] Ibid.

interpretation below, but I want to underline here how Chauvet interprets the relation between humans and being for Thomas as a confrontation between subject and object mediated by the *"instrumental intermediary"* of language.[66] In other words, Chauvet imposes the problem of bridging subject and object on Thomas, suggesting that the solution is the instrumentalization of language, as a consequence of which "language has ceased to be what it was at the dawn of pre-Socratic thinking; the *meeting place where* being and humankind mutually stepped forward toward one another."[67] Chauvet identifies that "meeting place" in the realm of symbolic mediation.

Before developing his symbolic approach, Chauvet examines the alternatives of analogical predication and negative theology. He readily admits that we cannot get by without analogy in theology, but, citing Serge Breton, he regards such analogy as "an inevitably mediocre compromise."[68] While it is clear that Chauvet rejects explanatory theologies that speak in terms of cause and effect, he likewise criticizes the negative theology that recurs throughout the theological tradition: "Negative theology, even in its most sublime moments where it transcends, through negation, the notion of being as cause, nonetheless remains viscerally connected to a type of language that is irremediably causal and ontological."[69] The only way through between positive and negative onto-theologies, Chauvet argues, is the mediation of language, which situated theology in the complex world of the subject. This is the critical issue for Chauvet. Subjects participate in saying, or unsaying, anything about God. The foundational issue is not God but the ones who talk about God.

By implicating the theologian in the language game, Chauvet hopes to illustrate that Christian theology is not reducible to concepts outside of the subjects engaged in the game. Chauvet has no interest in purifying concepts or replacing one theological concept with another. Theologians can grasp nothing "without at the same time recognizing themselves to be grasped by it."[70] Therefore, Christian theology's critical aspect should open a passage, continually undertaken, "from the attitude of a slave toward a master imagined as all powerful, clothed in the traditional panoply of the attributes

---

[66] Ibid., 32–33.
[67] Ibid., 33.
[68] Ibid., 40, citing Serge Breton, *Écriture et révélation* (Paris: Cerf, 1979), 160.
[69] *SS*, 42.
[70] Ibid., 43.

of *esse*, to the attitude of a child toward a God represented far differently because this God is seen always in the shadow of the cross, and thus to the attitude of a brother or sister toward others."[71]

The shift is twofold. As it regards the image of the subject, there is a turn away from imagining the self as a calculating subject discovering the universal and necessary and deploying the metaphysical language of causality to explain the relations between them, toward the self as always already speaking and being spoken, and so to letting oneself be spoken into being as Christian in the sacraments. As it regards the operative image of God, there is a shift away from a concept of God as *causa sui*, or being itself, or necessary being, or a master manipulating human slaves through causes, toward an image of a God in the shadow of the cross as loving self-giving.

Chauvet contrasts the metaphysical method of mastering concepts to his theory of the symbolic by evoking the *manna* of Exodus. The symbolic, according to Chauvet, reveals the order of grace more fully than the Thomist notion of causality because it is the order of "non-value . . . the way of the never-finished reversible exchange in which every subject comes to be."[72] For Chauvet grace is without limits and therefore not to be represented or defined in the manner of a value. Contrary to the Western tradition's emphasis on logic, Chauvet's appropriation of Heidegger opens up a space for play in thinking theologically out of "the ontic-ontological difference."[73] Only through difference is grace able to emerge in its fullness as a question, a non-value, that is, as a symbol. Hence he appeals to *manna* as a sheer gratuitousness that speaks the question "what is this?" or "man-hu?"[74] The symbolic explodes the "logic of the Same," which is based on an aggressive forcing of identity, because it is wholly other and wholly gift. Grace cannot be thought within the metaphysics of presence. Rather, grace is "of an entirely different order."[75]

2.2. Overcoming Onto-Theology?

Chauvet intends to overcome onto-theology by turning to the symbolic, with its openness and embrace of difference. But he wonders whether we

[71] Ibid.
[72] Ibid., 44.
[73] Ibid.
[74] Ibid., 45.
[75] Ibid.

can simply decree the replacement of one method with another. He asks, "Are we able to think in any way other than the metaphysical?"[76]

He responds to these questions by outlining his proposal for overcoming metaphysics. Any attempt to reconfigure metaphysics cannot simply be an inversion of tradition, or merely a new set of terms that nonetheless remains within the tradition of Western metaphysical thinking, which would amount to pitching a new tent on the same ground. Rather, Chauvet envisions a complete *"change of terrain*—if it is true, as we will maintain, that the question here becomes inseparable from the *mode* of questioning, and the latter in its turn is constituted *by the questioning subject itself*: 'It is the way which sets everything on its way, and it sets everything on its way inasmuch as it is a speaking way.'"[77] Thus the questioning subject, as speaking and being spoken, is the terrain he selects as the starting point for the symbolic, not the subject in an abstract sense but as one already spoken into being by a particular historical context.

On this terrain metaphysics is an event in the history of Being. In the Heideggerian vein, Chauvet argues that the event (Heidegger's *Ereignis*) of metaphysics is the result of Being's revealing itself in this late stage in the history of Western philosophy as that which was forgotten and controlled by the calculating dominance of metaphysical thinking. Heidegger clarifies this destiny of Being: "The *Ge-stell* is in no way the result of human contrivance; on the contrary it is only the final stage of the history of metaphysics, that is, of the destiny of Being."[78] The retreat of Being in the face of technological

---

[76] Ibid.

[77] Ibid., 47, citing Heidegger, *Acheminement vers la parole* (Paris: Gallimard, 1976), 183, 187, a French translation of *Unterwegs zur Sprache* (On the Way to Language); see Martin Heidegger, *Basic Writings*, ed. David Farrell Krell (San Francisco: Harper, 1977, 1993), 393–426.

[78] *SS*, 48, citing Heidegger, *Le séminaire de Zähringen*, in *Questions* 4, trans. Jean Beaufret (Paris: Gallimard, 1976), 326. Heidegger uses *Ge-stell* to refer to the technological "enframing" of the world that shapes our horizon. The world is "enframed" as a "standing reserve" available for deployment. And yet the reduction of the world in this way, at the same time that it represents an extreme danger for humanity, carries with it the possibility of a "saving power" insofar as it brings about the possibility of questioningly pondering technology understood without reference to truth. Such questioning is facilitated by art, which challenges technology's reduction of everything to the standing-reserve. See Martin Heidegger, "The Question Concerning Technology," *Basic Writings*, 308–41, especially 325ff. See also Rüdiger Safranski, *Martin Heidegger: Between Good*

advance at the same time reveals itself as the forgotten question of modernity. Therefore, in order to overcome metaphysics one need not invent a new system; rather, the goal is to return to the forgotten origin of all metaphysical constructions, to Being itself.

a. Metaphysics as Event

For Heidegger, as for Chauvet, one cannot simply escape metaphysics. Overcoming metaphysics from this perspective means thinking the very thing classical metaphysics excludes, i.e., Being.[79] Any reflection on Being as event, however, is bound to confront metaphysics. Chauvet wants to insist that for the sake of a sacramental theology it is better not to prop up some new metaphysical system but, rather, to maintain the ontological difference neglected by the forgetfulness of Being. While the origins of metaphysics lie in the original play of *Dasein* and *Sein*, metaphysics eventually reduces Being to its own representations of Being. Being itself is forgotten. Only the representations remain, and "the dance of advance and retreat which being carries out, its movement of presence in absence, has been reduced to the presence of an available foundation."[80] The key to overcoming metaphysics is to undertake a return to the original playfulness. For Chauvet, overcoming metaphysics is therefore a matter of conversion: "This is a test of conversion: Can we consent to leave the solid, reassuring ground of our represented foundation and the stable, fixed point in order [to] let ourselves go toward this demanding *letting-be* in which we find ourselves out of our depth?"[81]

---

and Evil (Cambridge, MA: Harvard University Press, 1999), 399: "The *Gestell* is something man-made, but we have lost our freedom with regard to it. The *Gestell* has become our 'destiny.' What is so dangerous about this is that life in the *Gestell* threatens to become one-dimensional, lacking alternatives, and that the memory of a different kind of world encounter and world sojourn is expunged."

[79] *SS*, 50.

[80] Ibid.

[81] Ibid., 51. In his critical assessment of *Symbol and Sacrament*, Vincent Miller seizes on Chauvet's use of *Gelassenheit* (translated here as "letting-be"): "For Eckhart, *Gelassenheit* functions between a human soul and a loving God. Thus, an uncritical letting-be is a quite appropriate posture for the human to take. With Heidegger and Chauvet, however, the context includes the added dimension of the human symbol world. In order for *Gelassenheit* to function here, one would have to assume that the symbolic mediation in human culture is as unsullied as God's mystical presence in the soul. This is clearly not the case." See Vincent J. Miller, "An Abyss at the Heart of Mediation: Louis-Marie

Chauvet's appropriation of Heidegger and his critique of the metaphysical tradition culminates in this demand for conversion, or "letting-be" in theology that leads away from the firm foundations of scholastic metaphysics and into the mystery of Being. However, Chauvet recognizes the indebtedness to metaphysics such a critique must have. Again he quotes Heidegger: "The essence of metaphysics is something other than metaphysics itself. A thinking which pursues the truth about Being does not rest content with metaphysics; still, it does not *oppose* metaphysics."[82] Chauvet recognizes that the root of metaphysics, the foundation, is not something out there to be discovered, some particular concept or privileged view. Instead, with Heidegger, he proposes that the essence of metaphysics is everywhere and lies within us.[83] Therefore living authentically with metaphysics is not a matter of questing for universal and necessary causes; rather, it is to participate in the event that is Being by "letting-be" in the playfulness of being.

In light of the event of Being, the history of philosophy reveals that Being is not only concealed by a particular tradition's forgetfulness of Being, but also that Being's withdrawal is characteristic of its essence. The essence of Being is discovered as absence. The very forgetfulness of Being reveals something about being to those who wish to reflect on it, i.e., that any attempt to think about being will ensure Being's retreat and concealment. Thinking means thinking about the forgetfulness of Being. Therefore, "there is no other method for thinkers to overcome this forgetfulness than to 'settle themselves and stand within it.'"[84] Chauvet concludes that metaphysics is really the business of thinking itself.

Chauvet's Fundamental Theology of Sacramentality," *Horizons* 24, no. 2 (September 1, 1997): 230–47, at 240. Miller suggests a more critically grounded understanding of the symbol can be found in the works of Paul Ricoeur and Jürgen Habermas. While Miller focuses his criticisms on Chauvet's use of *Gelassenheit* in regard to the sacraments, his use of the term as a fundamental posture for thought is also inadequate. There is a critical apparatus in human thinking that goes beyond the passivity of letting-be, from thinking to knowing, which we will explore in depth with Lonergan's help. On the other hand, Chauvet is right to call our attention to the need for openness as the primary posture toward the real, especially as a way of overcoming conceptual systems that attempt to fit experience into preexisting concepts and categories.

[82] Ibid.
[83] Ibid.
[84] Ibid., 52.

b. Difference and Questioning: A Philosophical Method

In describing metaphysics as the very business of thought, Chauvet enacts a philosophical method by which one can never go beyond metaphysics or "overcome" metaphysics; indeed, one need not "oppose" metaphysics at all. What the philosopher must do in this case is question all metaphysical systems, undertake a return to that original difference, the infinity that has been masked by the putative certainty of metaphysics. A hermeneutical philosophy implicates the subject in the metaphysical tradition. The constant interplay between questioning and answering and questioning again highlights the difference between thinking and being, between presence and absence. The "rediscovery" of the difference revealed by the play of presence and absence, of the event that uncovers and the arrival that covers, enables a critical hermeneutics and philosophy.[85]

Hermeneutical philosophy requires conversion. Because we are unable to "jump outside" the metaphysical tradition, the tradition in which we live, we must instead learn to reverse the direction of our questioning, informed as it is by our traditions, and allow ourselves to be questioned by Being. Since the hermeneutic turn executed by Heidegger, the self-critical element is at the center of philosophy. Chauvet describes self-criticism, or the critique of one's tradition, simply as "learning to 'let go.'"[86] However, the ease with which this might ultimately be accomplished does not detract from the fact that it is also "the most difficult because it requires us to unmask the false evidence on which rests the eidetic representations of being, the first of which is the almost ineradicable habit of representing Being as 'something facing humans which stands by itself.'"[87] Philosophy consists in uncovering the forgotten presuppositions of metaphysics.[88]

However, the only way to unmask the presuppositions of metaphysics, without at the same time repeating the mistakes of metaphysics by cobbling together an alternative foundation, is to let go of the possibility of ever arriving at an ultimate foundation.[89] The only possibility remaining for philosophers, according to Chauvet is to "orient themselves in a new

[85] Ibid., 51–52.
[86] Ibid., 53.
[87] Ibid.
[88] Ibid.
[89] Ibid.

direction . . . starting from the uncomfortable *non-place* of a permanent questioning, which both corresponds to and guarantees being."[90] Permanent questioning entails "an unachievable task, a task whose very essence is its incompleteness."[91] Chauvet captures an important insight from contemporary philosophy that has significant ramifications for theology: all knowing is conditional precisely because finite subjects are always implicated in the process. Human beings do not exist vis-à-vis being as an object but are always already implicated in being. Any metaphysics grounded in an epistemology of knowledge by confrontation is overcome in this hermeneutical approach. Whether metaphysics itself is thereby overcome is a further question.

c. Beyond Language as Instrument: Speaking Being

One of the key consequences of Chauvet's reconfiguration of being outside of a subject-object relationship is that it acknowledges the role of language as more than a mere instrument. Instead, "language is 'the house of being, in which humans live and thereby ex-sist.'"[92] Echoing Heidegger, Chauvet sees the instrumentalization of language as a key reversal in the history of philosophy that has led humans to think of themselves as the masters of language. Consequently, humans attempt to control the world around them through language understood as a means not only of communication but also of coercion: "It is by one movement that humans, putting themselves at the center of the universe, imagine they dominate the world because they are the point of reference and see themselves as the masters of language: the explicative reduction of the world and the instrumental reduction of language go hand in hand."[93] If this is the case, everything needs rethinking. We need to rediscover language as "the house of Being in which man ex-sists by dwelling, in that he belongs to the truth of Being, guarding it."[94]

Rediscovering language as the horizon within which human beings live leads to a new understanding of the role of language in the communication

---

[90] Ibid.

[91] Ibid.

[92] Ibid., 55. See Heidegger, *Lettre sur l'humanisme, Questions* 3 (Paris: Gallimard, 1980), 106. English translation in Martin Heidegger, *Basic Writings*, 213–66, at 237.

[93] Ibid.

[94] Heidegger, "Letter on Humanism," *Basic Writings*, 237.

of meaning: "Language is neither primarily nor fundamentally a convenient tool of information nor is it a distributor of carefully regulated titles. . . . It is summons—*vocation.*"[95] This evocative character of language is discovered primarily in poetry. The poem is a summons into being. Chauvet asks: "Which of the two presences is the higher, the more real: that which spreads itself out before our eyes, or that which is summoned?"[96] Language makes our human world.

While Chauvet recognizes that language has an instrumental "pole," he emphasizes that the instrumental aspect of language is joined to a more fundamental pole, belonging to a different level of being. He argues: "At this ontological level, language is of an order completely different from that of the useful instrument that rhetoric exploited so well as a means of manipulation and power."[97] This level of language constitutes the horizon of being in which humans move. Human beings do not deploy language as a tool; rather, we are already spoken into being by language and never prior to language. Poetry reveals the ontological fullness of language because poetry creates a world and calls to humans, asking them to become poets who allow themselves to be spoken by language, by first becoming listeners: "Thus is brought about, within language itself, the coming-to-presence of what is summoned."[98]

d. *Presence as Absence, Presence as Trace*

Chauvet contrasts this coming-to-presence with what he calls the "simple factuality of 'what lies before our eyes.'"[99] Rather than a "frozen metaphysical presence of a subsisting entity," *coming-to-presence* is a presence "whose very essence is the 'coming,' the advent, and which is *thus essentially marked by the stroke of absence.*"[100] Here, Chauvet returns to the center of his critique of onto-theology, i.e., that the permanent presence of being in traditional metaphysics erases the trace of difference that reveals the basic absence at the heart of the real. Chauvet recognizes that presence is always marked by absence, is always "presence-as-trace; trace of a passing always-already

---

[95] *SS*, 56.
[96] Ibid. See Heidegger, *Acheminement vers le parole*, 22–23.
[97] *SS*, 56.
[98] Ibid., 58.
[99] Ibid.
[100] Ibid.

past; trace thus of something absent. But still trace, that is, the sign of a happening which calls us to be attentive to something new still to come."[101] The notion of "presence-as-trace" calls us to attend to the absence that is forgotten by traditional metaphysics. The poet resists this closure by constantly engaging the trace and the absence of transparent meaning "in a gracious attitude of letting be the gratuitousness of being and of letting oneself be spoken by it."[102]

2.3. Theology as Hermeneutical

Chauvet's challenge to theologians in light of Heidegger's hermeneutical philosophy is to *become* theologians by enacting theology, for "theologians are not outside their work; rather, they make spectacles of themselves, they ex-pose themselves, they take risks, since they are required by their profession not to demonstrate anything by a calculating knowledge but to *give witness to that in which they know themselves to be already held.*"[103] Therefore theology cannot be "reduced to a science that seeks to explain everything" or be used to justify the world by responding to the question "why?"

Chauvet employs Paul Ricoeur's hermeneutics as a method for thinking theologically. A hermeneutical theology, emerging out of a confrontation of worlds in the reading of texts, poses its questions about God in history. Such a theology does not have recourse to blank metaphysical concepts like "nature" or "person." Rather, the question "who is God?" becomes concrete, "takes flesh for us not by descending from the theologies of the hypostatic union but rather by rising from the languages of the New Testament witnesses, which are historically and culturally situated."[104] Chauvet recalls Heidegger's reading of the Pauline declaration in 1 Corinthians 1:23 that the cross is folly to the Greeks and a stumbling block to the Jews to indicate the direction of a hermeneutical theology that goes beyond the wisdom of the world for its methods. The shift to a Greek conceptuality is, for Chauvet, an inevitable compromise and an attempt to reclothe the denuded and crucified God of the passion. He cautions that "if theology cannot express the message of

---

[101] Ibid.

[102] Ibid., 60.

[103] Ibid., 65. There are resonances between Chauvet's claims here and Lonergan's functional specialty "Foundations," as we will see in chap. 4 below.

[104] Ibid., 69.

the cross, it must nevertheless begin its thinking with that message," which "disenthralls it from itself."[105] This involves a "permanent work of *mourning*" for the theologian who consents to the "presence of the absence" of God in the shadow of the cross.[106]

Consent to the presence of the absence of God involves theologians from the start in the symbolic sphere rather than in the realm of clear and distinct ideas. Thus Chauvet discerns a homology between his theological method and the therapeutic philosophy of Heidegger: "The path of theological thought on a crucified God keeps us in an attitude of 'folly' that is homologous to the path of philosophical thought on Being, although there is no passage from one to the other."[107] He expounds on his meaning, noting "It is a 'folly' because we must accept the death of the illusion *everything in us desperately wants to believe, that is, the illusion that we can somehow pull ourselves out of the necessary mediation of symbols*."[108] The desire to escape symbolic mediation is manifest in our frequent recourse to talk about the real as something that is self-evident.[109]

2.4. Summary of Chauvet's Method

Chauvet's critique of the onto-theological presuppositions of scholastic metaphysics touches on three key problems confronting any contemporary theology of the sacraments: first, the inadequacy of causality to express the symbolic mediation of the divine-human encounter in the sacraments; second, the always-already mediated character of human knowing and therefore the centrality of language as "world" rather than instrument; third, the inadequacy of thinking of the divine as permanent presence rather than the self-effacing God of the cross. The net result of confronting these questions is a methodological orientation that thinks theologically out of the difference preserved by a conversion to the presence of the absence of God. Following this articulation of his methodological orientation, Chauvet uses the remainder of his treatise to reflect on the sacraments, primarily the eucharistic liturgy, where he puts his method into practice.

[105] Ibid., 73.
[106] Ibid., 74.
[107] Ibid., 82.
[108] Ibid.
[109] Ibid.

3. A Test: Chauvet's Eucharistic Theology

Before we access Chauvet's methodology, it will help to understand how he applies it in articulating a theology of the Eucharist. First, Chauvet considers the sacrificial aspect of the Eucharist as "anti-sacrifice." Second, the presence of Christ in the Eucharist is conceived not as substance, but as "ad-esse."

3.1. The Anti-sacrificial Character of Christian Liturgical Sacrifice[110]

While he rejects the classical understanding of eucharistic sacrifice, Chauvet recognizes that he is constrained by the language of the Eucharistic Prayer, which he attempts to reinterpret in terms of his theory of symbolic exchange. First, he employs the metaphor of the "Easter tear," because the rending of the temple curtain in the Synoptic accounts of the death of Christ has significant consequences in relation to cultic action.[111] Thus "the Holy of Holies is thereafter empty; the temple of the presence of God is now the body of the Risen One (John) or the community of the faithful (Paul)."[112] Second, Chauvet applies both Pauline theology and the theology of the priesthood in the letter to the Hebrews to expand his claim: "It is thus the entire Jewish system which through its symbol, the Temple, is rendered obsolete as a means of access to God: the Holy of Holies is empty. Christians have no other Temple than the glorified body of Jesus, no other altar than his cross, no other priest and sacrifice than his very person: *Christ is their only possible liturgy.*"[113] This establishes the Christian cult on a very new and different terrain.

A major consequence of Chauvet's reading is a move away from propitiatory or expiatory sacrifice to symbolic exchange. The former modes of offering belong to a cult in which sacrifice mediates the divine presence through the activity of the priestly caste. Christians, according to Pauline theology, no longer require the mediation of the divine presence "through the performance of good works, ritual or moral, or through the intermediary of

---

[110] Chauvet employs the notion of "anti-sacrifice" as a third term that extricates him from the polarity of "either sacrifice or non-sacrifice" in thinking about the eucharistic liturgy. He criticizes the thesis of René Girard for heading too far in the direction of the latter.

[111] *SS*, 248.

[112] Ibid., 248–49.

[113] Ibid., 250.

a priestly caste," because "Jesus has finally sealed, in his Pasch, especially in its culmination, the gift of the Spirit."[114] Salvation as gift "radically subverts the existing system: it attacks it decisively at its very root."[115] What, then, is Christian sacrifice?

Chauvet focuses his attention on the thanksgiving offering, *todah*, or offering of the first fruits in Deuteronomy 26 as the appropriate model for understanding Christian sacrifice as in some way "anti-sacrificial." Yet he is not unaware of a danger in attempting to move away too quickly from the notion of sacrifice that for centuries has shaped Christian liturgical practices, especially in the West. He notes that in criticizing the notion of liturgical sacrifice that was accepted up to the Second Vatican Council "we must be on our guard against judging it according to a more recent cultural sensibility . . . and against too hastily denigrating what we have only recently—and perhaps equally uncritically—eulogized."[116] And so Chauvet asks us to understand Christ's work as indeed a sacrifice, but in terms of an existential rather than a ritual modality. This enables him to interpret the sacrifice of Christ as *kenosis*, thus bringing a central sacrificial idea to bear, but not on the terrain of ritual sacrifice. The language of sacrifice retained in the eucharistic prayer takes on new meaning in light of this interpretation.

The *kenosis* of Christ is understood as "the *consent to his condition as Son-in-humanity and as Brother of humanity.*"[117] The Son's kenotic self-giving is a reversal of Adam's sin, which Chauvet interprets according to a master-slave dialectic, in which humankind lives "its relation with God according to a pattern of force and competition, a pattern whose typical representation is the *slave* trying to seize for him or herself the omnipotence of the *master* and to take the master's place."[118] Christ "consents to taste humanity to its extreme limit, death experienced in the silence of a God who would not even intervene to spare the Just One this death"[119] The Son's

---

[114] Ibid., 252. Chauvet's caricature of the temple cult may not be adequate to the Jewish understanding of law and covenant. The prophets, after all, remained Jews.

[115] Ibid.

[116] Ibid., 291.

[117] Ibid., 301.

[118] Ibid., 299. Chauvet uses Hegel's master-slave dialectic as elaborated by Jean Hyppolite. See *Genesis and Structure of Hegel's* Phenomenology of Spirit, trans. Samuel Cherniak (Chicago: Northwestern University Press, 1979).

[119] *SS*, 301.

consent is the exemplar of "letting-be" of "de-mastery," a self-sacrifice of his divine authority in filial trust in the Father.

Chauvet develops the notion of filial trust in order to clarify the place of the expiatory dimension within an anti-sacrificial understanding of eucharistic sacrifice, arguing that "it would be wrong to imagine that the Christian 'anti-sacrificial' viewpoint could assume the sacrifice of communion to the exclusion of the sacrifice of redemption."[120] The line of anti-sacrificial demarcation is not meant to separate expiation and communion but to distinguish "a servile attitude and a filial attitude with regard to the entire sacrificial order."[121] This allows Chauvet to accept the sacrificial language of the liturgy while transposing it into a new modality.[122] The transition from the servile attitude, which is indicative of thinking of the divine-human relation in terms of the master-slave dialectic, to the filial attitude allows us to understand sacrifice as a pedagogy for learning "to acknowledge ourselves as *from others and for others* by recognizing ourselves to be *from God and for God.*"[123] The filial identity of the church as a community of sisters and brothers of Christ, daughters and sons of the Father, makes of it a "eucharistic people" whose task is to give flesh here and now to the crucified God by exercising true freedom in loving God and neighbor, which is the "true sacrifice" of the Eucharist as "anti-sacrifice."[124]

3.2. The Eucharistic Presence as Ad-esse

In his interpretation of eucharistic presence Chauvet argues that transubstantiation is "not an absolute and thus it is theoretically possible to express the specificity of Christ's presence in the Eucharist in a different manner."[125]

---

[120] Ibid., 310.

[121] Ibid., 311.

[122] Chauvet notes that the necessary demythologization of sacrifice "cannot be carried to a complete jettisoning of the myth without foundering, like Bultmann, on the new myth of a faith without a mythic residue" (*SS*, 302). This requires regarding as legitimate the "ineradicable" language of sacrifice in Christian liturgy, but taking care lest it slide into a servile connotation.

[123] Ibid., 314.

[124] Ibid., 315.

[125] Ibid., 383; see also 382–89. Whether Chauvet is correct in his assessment of the dogmatic use of the term as one, if the most fitting (*aptissime*), among other ways of conceiving the eucharistic transformation is a matter of dispute. Herbert McCabe agrees with

Chauvet focuses his interpretation of Thomas's theology of transubstantiation on the problem of an ultra-realism raised by magisterial opposition to Berengar's symbolic approach to the sacrament. Because Thomas understands substance in relation to intellect and not the senses, according to Chauvet, his treatment of the eucharistic change avoids gross physicalism. But Chauvet's problem with Thomas's understanding of transubstantiation is what he sees as a failure to account for the human destination of the consecrated gifts. This failure has two results: "First [the Eucharist] 'contains' Christ himself 'absolutely,' whereas the other sacraments have efficacy only *in ordine ad aliud*, that is, relative to their application to the subject. From this comes the second difference: its first effect (*res et sacramentum*) is *in ipsa materia* ('in the matter itself'), whereas in baptism the effect is *in suscipiente* ('in the one who receives it')."[126] Chauvet finds this mode of explanation "dangerous," and instead offers an understanding of eucharistic presence that takes the destination of the gifts as "constitutive" of its mode of being as *ad-esse*.[127]

First, the presence of Christ is located in the entirety of the eucharistic celebration, so that the eucharistic presence is a "*crystallization*" of Christ's presence in the congregation and the Scriptures. This allows the manifold "presences" of Christ in the liturgy to inform our understanding of the Eucharist.[128] The one who "comes to presence" in the Eucharist is "already present" in the body of the church and the body of the Scriptures, so that from "beginning to end the architectural dynamic of the vast *sacramentum* which the whole of the celebration forms forces one to realize the relational '*for*' belongs to the very concept of the eucharistic 'presence.'"[129]

Chauvet's interpretation in *God Still Matters*, ed. Brian Davies (New York: Continuum, 2002), 115. Stephen Brock argues to the contrary that transubstantiation alone expresses the whole conversion; see his "St. Thomas and Eucharistic Conversion," *The Thomist* 38 (1974): 734–46. Both Matthew Levering and Reinhard Hütter have echoed Brock on this point. See Levering, *Sacrifice and Community*, 117ff.; and Hütter, "Transubstantiation Revisited: *Sacra Doctrina*, Dogma, and Metaphysics," 21–79, in *Ressourcement Thomism: Sacred Doctrine, the Sacraments, and the Moral Life; Essays in Honor of Romanus Cessario, O.P.*, ed. Reinhard Hütter and Matthew Levering (Washington, DC: CUA Press, 2010).

[126] *SS*, 387–88. See *ST* III, q. 73, a. 1, ad. 3.

[127] *SS*, 389.

[128] Both *Sacrosanctum Concilium* and *Mysterium Fidei* refer to the multiple presences of Christ in the liturgy.

[129] *SS*, 391.

Second, in addition to the multiple presences of Christ that "appear" in the liturgy and constitute already the eucharistic presence as a "for," Chauvet directs our attention to the whole of the Eucharistic Prayer, which presents the memorial and eschatological aspects of Christ's eucharistic presence. Here, he finds an indication of the absence at the heart of what is too easily taken to be an already accomplished, full presence in the Eucharist. There is a distance between the cross of Golgotha and the parousia. The eschatological distance "crosses out its very truth of presence with the stroke of absence and prohibits us from conceiving it as a 'full' presence in the Gnostic manner."[130]

Third, Chauvet exegetes the "for" in the institution narrative as revealing the presence as an *ad-esse*. The acts of taking, eating, and drinking are constitutive of the salvation offered by Christ (John 6:53-57). It is the eating that brings the presence to its fulfillment as "being for."

Fourth, Chauvet explores the biblical symbolism of bread and wine as food, not simply food in the sense of sustenance but as gifts of the earth and revealers of our radical dependence on daily gifts, and at the same time as bringers of joy and feasting. He points out that the scholastics did not take into account the richness of the biblical imagery surrounding bread and wine, because they only treat them as the ontological substrate for the emergence of the body and blood of Christ.[131] Chauvet wants to emphasize that the very being of bread makes it suitable for incorporation into the human body. As the "work of human hands," bread is not reducible to its chemical compounds but is already a social reality. As a socially constituted reality bread is a symbol of sharing. Bread offered to God is the highest recognition of God as God, as the one who gives the gift of bread and indeed of all life. Chauvet proposes: "Bread is never so much bread as in the gesture of thankful oblation where it gathers within itself heaven and earth, believers who 'hold fellowship' in sharing it, and the giver whom they

---

[130] Ibid.

[131] A particularly striking example of this kind of thinking can be seen in Thomas's argument that bread and wine are not in fact artifacts but natural realities. See Christopher M. Brown, "Artifacts, Substances, and Transubstantiation: Solving a Puzzle for Aquinas' Views," *The Thomist* 71 (2007): 89–112. This is critical for Thomas because artifacts do have substance and therefore cannot undergo transubstantiation.

acknowledge to be God: in this way a new communion of life is established between themselves and God."[132] All bread is already symbolic.[133]

The traditional claim that the bread is no longer bread after the consecration is based on a metaphysical notion of substance. Chauvet argues instead that authentically to proclaim the bread as the body of Christ "requires that one emphasize all the more [that] it is indeed still bread, but now essential bread, bread which is never so much bread as in this mystery."[134] He interprets John 6 according to this symbolic understanding of the eucharistic bread as "true bread": "the *artos alethinos* where the truth of bread, always forgotten (*a-letheia*), is revealed."[135] Because this bread is a word, it nourishes human beings in their humanity as language-bodies. As bread "par excellence," this bread is the bread of life. Consequently, Chauvet understands the phrase "truly, really and substantially" employed by the Council of Trent "in an *altogether different way* from that of classic onto-theology."[136]

In light of his concern to integrate the subject into the very being of the bread as *ad-esse*, Chauvet defends his position against those who would criticize it as subjectivist.[137] In the symbolic order presence is always experienced as absence, thereby preserving the real from any subjectivist reduction. The sacraments resist such a reduction on account of their concrete exteriority; no sacrament does so more than the eucharistic body that, because of its exteriority and anteriority, resists our desire to dominate the real with the "logic of the Same." Indeed, the Eucharist conceals at the same time as it discloses. And this is crucial to Chauvet's understanding: the presence of Christ is always an absence. Christ's eucharistic presence must be "marked by an absence for the 'icon' of the Eucharist . . . to preserve through its

---

[132] *SS*, 398.

[133] Ibid.

[134] Ibid., 400.

[135] Ibid.

[136] Ibid.

[137] From the context it is probable that Chauvet is responding to issues raised by Jean-Luc Marion, *God without Being* (Chicago: University of Chicago Press, 1991), which was published some years earlier in the French original, *Dieu Sans Être* (Paris: Fayard, 1982), particularly since Chauvet employs the categories of "idol" and "icon" in subsequent pages in the same way they are employed by Marion, and depends on the same work by Christoph Schönborn (*L'icône du Christ. Fondements théologiques élaborés entre le Ier et le IIe Conciles de Nicée [325–787]* [Fribourg: Éditions Universitaires, 1976]) from which Marion draws his categories (p. 403).

own material consistency and spatial exteriority, against which the faith stumbles, Christ's absolute 'difference.'"[138] The ritual breaking of the bread is *the* mark of absence.[139]

The mark of absence in the Eucharist does not make an encounter with the crucified Lord unavailable; instead, it invites an *existential* sharing in the body of the Lord rather than a reduction of it to a present object. The absence, constitutive of a presence inasmuch as it is not conceived according to the permanent presence of metaphysics but is experienced as coming-into-presence, also reveals the absence with which every presence is negated.[140] Thus the Eucharist is the *"paradigmatic figure of this presence-of-the-absence of God."*[141] It invites us into the symbolic labor of becoming believers. The mode of that absence in broken bread opposes the image of the risen Christ as a closed or contained reality who is a permanent presence. The breaking of the bread manifests the ultimate reality of bread as a "being for" that unites the church in a communion between members and with Christ as brothers and sisters in sharing eucharistic communion. But this communion is not self-worship; rather, those joined in communion are joined in being open to the concrete historical mediations of the symbolic Other, in relation to others—especially "those others whom people have reduced to less than nothing through an economic system which crushes the poorest and a cultural system which makes them scapegoats."[142] Chauvet's emphasis on ethics in the culmination of his treatment of the Eucharist highlights his concern throughout *Symbol and Sacrament* to break open Christian sacramental practice. Far from being a closed grace delivery system, the sacraments are invocations of a new way of being in the world. The ethical is the site of the verification of sacramental grace, such that any thinking of sacramental causality in an onto-theological mode is put to the test in the historical life of the believer. There is still causality here, as we will discuss

---

[138] *SS*, 403–4.

[139] See Louis-Marie Chauvet, "The Broken Bread as Theological Figure of Eucharistic Presence," 236–64, in *Sacramental Presence in a Postmodern Context*, ed. Lieven Boeve and Lambert Leijssen (Leuven: Peeters, 2001).

[140] *SS*, 404.

[141] Ibid., 405.

[142] Ibid., 407.

presently, but it is conceived according to Chauvet's understanding of the sacrament as "revealer" and "operator" of grace in history.[143]

4. Assessing Chauvet's Method

While Chauvet's criticisms of metaphysics and his subsequent elaboration of a theory of the symbol raise important questions for future sacramental theology, he has overlooked some critical matters in his elaboration of theological method. Fundamentally, he commits what we might call an oversight of insight. Why is this important? Chauvet's failure to attend to the role of insight and understanding in human thinking and knowing undermines his constructive project. His attempt to wrest the sacraments from a metaphysical scheme of cause and effect otherwise remains captive to the logic of causality, if not the language, because of a failure to deal adequately with the acts of understanding underlying Thomas's theory of causality. Allow me to explain.

At the conclusion of *Symbol and Sacrament,* Chauvet describes the sacraments as "operators" and "events" of grace. Raymond Moloney asks in his review of the work: "Is this not efficient causality under another name?"[144] Moloney also highlights Chauvet's reference to the efficacy of the symbol in the context of his discussion of the performative dimension of language acts in the theory of J. L. Austin.[145] Indeed, Chauvet is aware that his project will simply reinscribe causality in the sacraments if he does not successfully get beyond classical onto-theology. Sacraments can only be described as "operators" in a symbolic view of the world. Because the symbolic "transcends the dualistic scheme of nature and grace,"[146] it conceives the relation between God and humankind as openness to the other. Sacraments are "operators" and "revealers" of this relationship where both divine and human are rendered open to each other. As a "being for," the Eucharist is the self-offering of the humanity of God that reveals the self-emptying God of the cross.

---

[143] The terms "revealer" and "operator" emerge in the context of a discussion of the sacraments as "effective symbolic expressions" (pp. 425–45).

[144] Raymond Moloney, review, "*Symbol and Sacrament,*" *Milltown Studies* 38 (Autumn 1996): 148.

[145] See *SS,* 130.

[146] Ibid., 544. Chauvet's claim that his position transcends dualistic thinking is complicated by his depiction of the mode of being open as an encounter between human and divine persons in an opposed relation, even if an open one.

Chauvet therefore concludes his treatise by revealing the pastoral purpose of his vast undertaking. He writes:

> Our *fundamental difficulty* lies, not in the affirmation of "sacramental grace" as such, but in what this presupposes, specifically, the humanity of the divine God revealed in the scandal of the cross, a scandal which is irreducible to any justifying "reason" and continues to work upon us when we dare to "envisage" the disfigured ones of this world as the image of our crucified Lord and thereby to transfigure our tragic history into a salvific history.[147]

While I quite agree with Chauvet's identification of the disfigured ones of this world with the image of the crucified Lord, I am not as clear how the cross effects a transformation of the tragic history of humanity into a salvific history without communicating some meaning that can be shared and borne into history by the church. Further, how does the Eucharist participate in that transformed history, if not as a kind of cause? If Chauvet has admitted that his fundamental difficulty is not with sacramental grace as such, can we fruitfully understand sacramental grace in terms other than instrumental causality? To conclude the present chapter let me briefly respond to Chauvet's reading of sacramental causality and his interpretation of the cross before undertaking a more systematic inquiry into these problems in eucharistic theology with Lonergan.

4.1. Causality in Thomas Aquinas

Bernard Blankenhorn's trenchant analysis of *Symbol and Sacrament* seizes on Chauvet's misinterpretation of Thomistic causality under the genus of "production/ augmentation."[148] Although Chauvet explored the transition in Thomas from dispositive causality in the *Commentary on the Sentences* to efficient instrumental causality in the *Summa Theologiae*, he missed the meaning of this shift. Chauvet understood that Thomas's change to an Aristotelian-Averroist model of efficient causality is meant to avoid reducing the sacrament to a sign of some future grace, as one would have in dispositive causality. Thomas recognized that the fathers consistently

---

[147] Ibid., 538.
[148] Bernard Blankenhorn, "Instrumental Causality in the Sacraments," Nova et Vetera 4, no. 2 (2006): 255–94. See p. 10.

taught that the sacraments are not only signs but also causes of grace.[149] Blankenhorn clarifies that the shift in question is not a result of preferring one theoretical model over another. Indeed, Blankenhorn shows that both disposing and perfecting causality occur in Avicenna. Thomas's change of mind was motivated by the church fathers, who used the language of efficient causality. Furthermore, Thomas is not simply baptizing philosophical language by employing a notion like causality. Instead, Thomas's thought on instrumental causality "*begins* with a fairly strict Aristotelian approach and proceeds to an original philosophy."[150]

Blankenhorn pinpoints the shift in Thomas at a clarification of sacramental grace in the *De Veritate*, where Thomas explains that grace is not a created thing but a transformation of the form of a subject.[151] Because grace is not created in the sense applied to subsistent beings, but cocreated in a subject, Chauvet's criticisms of scholastic onto-theology for reducing grace to a thing would be misplaced, at least in relation to Thomas. Blankenhorn clarifies: "Grace is neither a thing nor a being, but a way of being. Grace is a 'that by which,' not a 'that which.'"[152] In fact, had Chauvet understood Thomas correctly on precisely this point he might have used this understanding of grace in his elaboration of a sacramental way of being or existential orientation.

Ultimately the shift in the language from disposing causality to perfecting instrumental causality in Thomas's theology of the sacraments is based on an improved understanding of the analogical relations between supernature and nature, primary and secondary causality, and principal and instrumental causality. One should not assume a dualism in these distinctions, as Chauvet seems to.[153] In Thomas any dualism is dissolved by the

---

[149] *ST* III, q. 62, a. 1, cited in *Symbol and Sacrament*, 16.

[150] Blankenhorn, "Instrumental Causality in the Sacraments," 267. Lonergan makes much the same point in his *Grace and Freedom*, to which we will turn in chap. 5.

[151] *Quaestiones Disputatae de Veritate*, a. 27, q. 3, ad 9: "Nam creari proprie est rei subsistentis, cuius est proprie esse et fieri: formae autem non subsistentes, sive substantiales sive accidentales, non proprie creantur, sed concreantur: sicut nec esse habent per se, sed in alio: et quamvis non habeant materiam ex qua, quae sit pars eorum, habent tamen materiam in qua, a qua dependent, et per cuius mutationem in esse educuntur; ut sic eorum fieri sit proprie subiecta eorum transmutari." See Blankenhorn, "Instrumental Causality in the Sacraments," 269 n. 50.

[152] Ibid., 270.

[153] See n. 146 above.

recognition of massive divine involvement in what is natural, secondary, and instrumental, especially in the Incarnation. "A powerful consequence of the hypostatic union is that by his human nature, Christ instrumentally operates that which is proper to God alone!"[154] Christ, a divine person with a human nature, communicates supernatural life humanly, a communication that continues in the sacraments.

In Chauvet's initial critique of sacramental causality putatively conceived according to onto-theological metaphysics, the idea of production or augmentation is seen as inadequate for talking about the relations between persons, because the beloved is not a product but a subject in process.[155] This is, of course, true. But what Chauvet fails to see here is that the relation between divine lover and human beloved is a relation across two ontological orders, supernature and nature. Both as created and as recipients of the divine self-communication, human beings *are* radically dependent on divine love for their being.[156] The beloved in this case are made beloved by God, not as completed projects *per se*, but as infinitely lovable in the eyes of the creator/lover. Chauvet is right to point out that the beloved is a subject, not a product. But he fails to note that a "beloved subject" is something different from just any "subject"; the "beloved subject" is complete in its lovableness as a beloved. There is nothing I can do to make myself infinitely lovable in the eyes of the one who loves me. My becoming as infinitely beloved is a matter of seeing myself as my lover sees me, as infinitely lovable. It is a process, to be sure, but one headed toward a vision of me that is not my own, in this case a divine vision that is already complete eschatologically.

That loving vision of God is fully expressed in Christ's passion and resurrection, from which the sacraments derive their power. But Chauvet's theology of the cross incorporates his critique of metaphysics in a way that is both startling and eventually unsatisfying. Relying heavily on Jürgen Moltmann's *The Crucified God*, Chauvet holds that the passion is constitu-

---

[154] Blankenhorn, "Instrumental Causality in the Sacraments," 278.

[155] See *SS*, 22–26, "The Reduction of the Symbolic Scheme to the Technical Scheme." Chauvet offers a lengthy refutation of what he believes is the productionist scheme in Plato's *Philebus*.

[156] Chauvet would help his case by clarifying his understanding of creation. His decision to focus solely on Heidegger's human being as a being-in-the-world leaves the question of creation aside and with it some fundamental positions on the divine-human relation. See Blankenhorn, "Instrumental Causality in the Sacraments," 280–81.

tive of God's Trinity.[157] Its redemptive function is to reveal this aspect of God as a self-effacing kenotic deity, not the god of our conceptual idolatries or political manipulations. Thus, in suffering at the hands of our idolatry in the passion, Christ exposes our idolatry inasmuch as we have crucified the true God in the name of "God." Chauvet asks, "How can we thereafter speak of God on the basis of the cross without being ourselves implicated down to the very marrow of our desire?"[158] Our complicity in the suffering of Christ is rooted in our desire to confine what is *other* within our own categories. The inescapable result of Chauvet's analysis is that all metaphysical thinking is implicated in the sufferings of Christ because the human "rage" to know crushes what is other, reducing it to sameness. The desire to know is thereby rendered sinful. Ultimately this interpretation reproves those, especially in the Christian tradition, who experience their desire to know as a questing after the hidden God in much the same way one searches out the heart of a beloved, not in order to possess it but in order *to give oneself* to the beloved more fully.[159]

4.2. Thinking against Knowing: A Performative Contradiction

In fact, Chauvet's interpretation of the passion reveals a performative contradiction in which he is involved from the start. As human we do not simply think, we desire to know and in fact do know things. We make judgments. Indeed, Chauvet makes a series of judgments throughout *Symbol and Sacrament*, even while embracing the humility necessary to let God be God. Nevertheless, the correspondence, or homology, between Chauvet's theological method and Heidegger's philosophical method is called into question by this performative contradiction. Heidegger's philosophical method prescinds from the fact that God has revealed God's self. Whether or not Heidegger's method is ultimately useful for theological inquiry is of less concern in the present work than the degree to which Chauvet's method limps under the weight of Heideggerian presuppositions that he reads into

---

[157] *SS*, 502.

[158] Ibid., 501.

[159] The connection between the desire to know and the desire for God as it emerges in Western Christianity is explored in Jean Leclerc, *The Love of Learning and the Desire for God: A Study of Monastic Culture*, 3rd ed., trans. Catherine Misrahi (New York: Fordham University Press, 1982).

the Christian tradition, as for example in his theology of the passion. This is not to deny that Chauvet's project is worthwhile, especially in its therapeutic dimension. But if a deconstruction of the onto-theological presuppositions of Western metaphysics does help to counteract some real deficiencies in decadent scholasticism, and the kind of sacramental theology and liturgical practices it promoted, it does so in this case by simply caricaturing the achievement of Thomas Aquinas.

In the end Chauvet's work exhibits the all-too-frequent failure of postmodern reflection to come adequately to terms with its own claims. Chauvet makes a number of truth claims, indeed some very important ones, despite consistently rejecting the possibility of "knowing" in favor of a method of permanent questioning or "thinking." This is because he fails to attend fully to his own performance as a thinker/knower. He may even be willing, in fidelity to his method, to dispense with most of the philosophical foundations of *Symbol and Sacrament*. I will argue that Lonergan offers a way out of this contradiction by attending to human performance. Nevertheless, Chauvet builds on three critical insights from his thinking that are critical for any contemporary sacramental theology: (1) human knowledge of reality is contingent and always embedded in worlds mediated by and constituted by meaning; (2) theology is necessarily hermeneutical, involving the theologian in a circle (or spiral) of questions, answers, and further questions; it is not to be a closed system; and, most crucially, (3) the presence of the divine in history is a presence *as* absence, a truth revealed paradigmatically on the cross, and the key to a eucharistic eschatology.

Chapter Two

Toward Critical Realism
Bernard Lonergan's Cognitional Theory

If I indicated a problem with Chauvet's method at the end of the previous chapter, nevertheless his effort to rethink the sacramental along Heideggerian lines has been instructive. Indeed, one cannot but be concerned that the traditional formulations of sacramental causality and eucharistic presence have been prone to misinterpretation and distortion, sometimes with tragic pastoral consequences such as a lack of participation by the laity. But Chauvet seems to be ensnared. On one side he eliminates the possibility that Thomist theological method might be relevant for contemporary questions. On the other side stands Heidegger's hermeneutical phenomenology. Chauvet opts for the latter and uses it to interpret eucharistic doctrines outside the strictures of metaphysical notions like causality and substance, but with some problematic results. I have shown in the introduction, however, that Lonergan was also concerned that categories like the instrumental causality of the sacraments were too narrow and needed to be "broadened out," so that Lonergan seems to agree with Chauvet's motives, if not perhaps with his conclusions. Although Lonergan never undertook the broadening out he envisioned, his works provide a number of ideas for moving in that direction. Elucidating those ideas will be the task of the present chapter; applying them will be the task of subsequent chapters.

Granting that Chauvet has framed the postmodern problematic confronting contemporary sacramental theology, I have suggested how his presentation of the "Western metaphysical tradition" lacks detail. Therefore, if Lonergan is to be a resource for filling in what is missing in Chauvet's attempt we have to attend to the specific problems at the root of his postmodern critique, indicate the relevance of Lonergan's thought for facing postmodern challenges, and sketch in Lonergan's critique of the Western tradition, particularly in regard to human subjectivity. Subsequently we will explore Lonergan's magnum opus, *Insight: A Study of Human Understanding*, at length in order to explain the full range of its implications. Lonergan invites the reader of *Insight* to a personal decisive act, and so his method is pedagogical. We must follow that method here so that Lonergan's metaphysics will not be misunderstood from the start. Certainly brevity would be preferable, but in order to meet the postmodern critique of metaphysics, the case for a critical metaphysics must be made carefully. Without careful attention to his cognitional theory and epistemology in this and the following chapter, Lonergan's metaphysics will not be understood. With this caveat in mind, we turn to a consideration of Lonergan's "postmodern" concerns.

1. Lonergan and Postmodern Philosophy

While Lonergan's name is rarely mentioned in postmodern bibliographies, he shares key insights with postmodern thought as well as crucial differences.[1] Frederick Lawrence has proposed the term "integral postmodern" to describe the Canadian Jesuit's method.[2] Lawrence argues that "Christian philosophy and theology today have something important to learn from postmodernism, and . . . Lonergan can help us to learn it."[3] One of the central lessons of the postmodern critique is the priority of the ethical, or concern for the other, as constitutive of philosophical reflection.[4]

---

[1] See Paul Kidder, "The Lonergan-Heidegger Difference," *Philosophy & Theology* 15, no. 2 (2003): 273–98.

[2] Frederick G. Lawrence, "Lonergan, The Integral Postmodern?," *Method: Journal of Lonergan Studies* 18 (2000): 95–122, at 95.

[3] Ibid.

[4] Ibid. See also Lawrence, "The Fragility of Consciousness: Lonergan and the Postmodern Concern for the Other," 173–211, in *Communication and Lonergan: Common Ground for Forging the New Age*, ed. Thomas J. Farrell and Paul A. Soukup (Rowan and Littlefield, 1993); also in *Theological Studies* 54 (1993): 55–94. Chauvet exhibits this concern throughout *Symbol and Sacrament*, particularly in the elaboration of his theory of symbolic gift exchange. Indeed, one might read Chauvet's entire project as one of reconnecting the sacramental and the ethical.

Lonergan spent little time on moral theology, but the driving concern throughout his career was a transformation of the world historical situation. One of his earliest student works, "*Panton Anakephalaiosis*," explored the restoration of all things in Christ through a meditation on the eschatological missions of the Trinity.[5] Lonergan was bothered by moral theology's and the magisterium's commonsense precepts, whose flaws he grasped in relation to a world in the throes of economic catastrophe. Therefore during the Great Depression Lonergan turned his attention to economics. As Lawrence notes, "Lonergan was challenged by Pope Pius XI's encyclical on social order, *Quadragesimo Anno*. He began to think seriously about how Catholic social teaching could go beyond issuing 'vague moral imperatives' to ground precepts for social justice in concrete economic and social reality."[6] Lonergan's thought emerged out of concrete concern for the other, and that motivated him to go beyond abstractions and vague moral precepts as he tried to understand the issues involved in transforming history.

1.1. Lonergan's "Postmodern" Critique

That Lonergan never abandoned the concrete concerns that led him to study economics may establish his *bona fides* as regards the postmodern primacy of the practical order, yet his thought is still considered by many theologians as abstract, scholastic gnoseology or onto-theology.[7] Theologians who think that theology should be concerned with the practical and the pastoral tend to read Lonergan as a theoretician or methodologist. The postmodern philosopher might be seriously skeptical about Lonergan's emphasis on cognitional theory and his apparent ignorance of *différance*, never suspecting that, as Lawrence notes elsewhere, Lonergan shares

---

[5] See Bernard Lonergan, "*Panton Anakephalaiosis*," *Method: Journal of Lonergan Studies* 9, no. 2 (October 1991): 139–72.

[6] Lawrence, "Lonergan, the Integral Postmodern?," 108. See Bernard Lonergan, *For a New Political Economy,* CWBL 21, ed. Philip J. McShane (Toronto: University of Toronto Press, 1998, 2005); Lonergan, *Macroeconomic Dynamics: An Essay in Circulation Analysis,* CWBL 15, ed. Patrick H. Byrne, Frederick G. Lawrence, and Charles C. Hefling, Jr. (Toronto: University of Toronto Press, 1999).

[7] Some read Lonergan as endorsing Hegelian reduction to system, thus offering a total explanation of reality in the form of onto-theology. Others read his relation to Hegel as a kind of eversion, or turning Hegel inside out. See Mark Morelli, "Going beyond Idealism: Lonergan's Relation to Hegel," *Lonergan Workshop* 20 (2008): 305–36.

Heidegger's "opposition to the error of locating the criteria of knowledge and choice in the realm of *Vorhandenheit* in the sense of a manipulable, intersubjectively measurable immediacy of sense."[8] Indeed, for Lonergan, what he terms the "already-out-there-now-real" identifies being or the real with what is present to the senses; to counter this assumption Lonergan's "project of self-appropriation promotes the already consciously immanent and operative but not objectively known criteria for the world mediated and constituted by meaning to full explicitness."[9] The criteria for the real are not found in *a priori* categories or by intuiting essences, and "since those criteria turn out to be the inbuilt dynamisms of the endlessly questioning and questing human subject as subject, their fuller explication does not and indeed never can render them present and intersubjectively controllable."[10] The fuller explication of the criteria of the real is the responsibility of each individual, not a ready-made schema or set of categories to be found in a book and overlaid on top of experience.

Lawrence connects Lonergan's project to Heidegger's hermeneutical phenomenology. The proper targets of Heidegger's critique were identified by his student, Hans Georg Gadamer: namely, "'the nominalist prejudgment' and the horizon of *Vorhandenheit*."[11] These two presuppositions about human knowing generate distorted epistemological assumptions throughout the history of philosophy. Lawrence provides a taxonomy of these assumptions, whose impact in eucharistic theology may be immediately apparent to the reader:

> (a) *Abstract Deductivism*: an overweening concern for the logical model of subsumption or syllogistic reasoning together with an exaggerated estimate of the need for apodicticity or the requirements of universality and absolute necessity.

---

[8] Frederick Lawrence, "Gadamer and Lonergan: A Dialectical Comparison," *International Philosophical Quarterly* 20 (1980): 25–47, at 41.

[9] Ibid.

[10] Ibid.

[11] Frederick Lawrence, "Language as Horizon?," 13–34, in *The Beginning and the Beyond: Papers from the Gadamer and Voegelin Conferences*, supplementary issue of *Lonergan Workshop* 4, ed. Frederick Lawrence (Atlanta: Scholars Press, 1984), at 17. Kant assumes the "nominalist prejudgment" and the "horizon of *Vorhandenheit*" that Heidegger tries to overcome.

(b) *Conceptualism*: a preoccupation with the universality and necessity proper to concepts, words, terms, or names which often accompanies the assumption that concepts arise unconsciously, for example, the Scotist view that knowledge is primarily intuition, producing a perfect replica of a universal *a parte rei*, in order to be intuited intellectually as regards their mutual compatibility or commensurability, or applied or fit onto the world out there in some sense.

(c) *Perceptualism*: the conviction that knowing *tout court* basically either is or has to be like taking a look at what is already-out-there-now.

(d) *Reification of consciousness*: the literal application of spatial metaphors to the process of knowing based on the conviction that consciousness is a container of some sort.[12]

These assumptions about human knowing contribute to exactly the kind of metaphysical thinking Chauvet rightly critiques but only specifies by highlighting the "family resemblances" of the Western metaphysical tradition in a rather global and extrinsic way.[13] Lawrence argues further that these distortions combine in the modern orientation toward knowing and being, characteristic of Descartes,[14] but even more of Bacon,[15] Locke,[16] and Hume.[17] Because of these assumptions about knowing, the epistemological question becomes one of certitude and consequently leads to materialist or empiricist solutions. Rather than attending to the operations of consciousness, the questioner imagines knowing as surmounting a "primordial split" between subjects and objects, i.e., "How can subjectivity dwelling within itself (*res cogitans*, and the like) be sure it gets out to, and brings back in,

---

[12] Lawrence, "Language as Horizon?," 18.

[13] This leads to Chauvet's misreading of Thomas on *intelligere*. His summary of Thomist cognitional theory completely overlooks the role of insight into phantasm in understanding.

[14] See René Descartes, *Discourse on Method and Meditations on First Philosophy*, trans. Donald A. Cress (Indianapolis: Hackett Publishing, 1998).

[15] See Francis Bacon, *The New Organon*, ed. Lisa Jardine and Michael Silverthorne (Cambridge: Cambridge University Press, 2000).

[16] See John Locke, *An Essay Concerning Human Understanding*, ed. Kenneth P. Winkler, 2 vols. (Indianapolis: Hackett Publishing, 1996).

[17] See David Hume, *An Enquiry Concerning Human Understanding: A Critical Edition*, ed. Tom L. Beauchamp (Oxford: Clarendon Press, 2000).

what is really existing out there (*res extensa*, and the like)?"[18] The question is, in other words, how can we be *certain* of our knowledge of things out there? It is no surprise, then, that on the one side modernity is forced into the empiricism of Bacon, Locke, Hume, et al., and on the other side into Immanuel Kant's immanentist withdrawal from things-in-themselves and ultimately Hegel's absolute idealism.

When the epistemological question is reframed in terms of the subject-object split, knowing is imagined as having to solve the problem of the bridge: getting my self-contained consciousness out there to the objects of perception in order to bring them back into my consciousness, at least as an impoverished replica, for the abstraction of their essences. Heidegger's critique of the horizon of *Vorhandenheit* attacks this assumption. Thinking of things as present-to-hand involves us in an attempt to control them for the sake of knowledge according to the logical ideal of science, which involves violating the integrity of the thing as a whole by making it manipulable. This is the target of Chauvet's characterization of science in *Symbol and Sacrament* as a rage to know.[19] But this pseudoscientific way of thinking is really just what Lonergan calls "picture thinking."[20]

Lonergan unpacks this epigrammatic phrase in a 1968 lecture titled "The Subject," a summary diagnosis of contemporary philosophical problems through a genealogy of the modern subject.[21] In the lecture he uncovers three ways of misunderstanding the human subject that lead to the turn

---

[18] Lawrence, "Language as Horizon," 18.

[19] Louis-Marie Chauvet, *Symbol and Sacrament: A Sacramental Reinterpretation of Christian Existence* [= *SS*], trans. Patrick Madigan and Madeleine Beaumont (Collegeville, MN: Liturgical Press, 1995), 54. Heidegger's reflection on "broken tools" highlights the shift in *Dasein* from the horizon of *Zuhandenheit*, or the ready-to-hand (the forerunner of his notion of the "fourfold"), to the horizon of *Vorhandenheit*, which defines the essence of a thing according to its constituent parts. The original unity of *Dasein* with its tools (which includes every "thing," not just hammers and hardware) is shattered in the horizon of *Vorhandenheit*. This shift inspires the words cited by Chauvet in *Symbol and Sacrament*, 395: "Scientific knowledge had already destroyed things insofar as they are things, long before the atom bomb explosion." See Martin Heidegger, *What Is a Thing?*, ed. Eugene Gendlin, trans. William Baynard Barton and Vera Deutsch (Chicago: Henry Regnery, 1970).

[20] Cf. *SS*, 47.

[21] See Bernard Lonergan, "The Subject," 69–86, in *Second Collection*, ed. William F. J. Ryan and Bernard J. Tyrrell (Toronto: University of Toronto Press, 1974).

to the existential subject and eventually open the way for the emergence of the alienated postmodern subject. The first misunderstanding is rooted in the neglect of the subject in the neoscholastic reaction to modernity, which "so emphasize[d] objective truth as to disregard or undermine the very conditions of its emergence and existence."[22] This unbalanced concern for objectivity is closely connected with the problems in Catholic theology discussed in the introduction: "If at the present time among Catholics there is discerned a widespread alienation from the dogmas of faith, this is not unconnected with a previous one-sidedness that so insisted on the objectivity of truth as to leave subjects and their needs out of the account."[23] Subjects are ruled out of the equation of knowing because objectivity is just a matter of correctly seeing what is out there. If knowing deals with what is obviously perceivable, then any need for an interpreter of sense data becomes merely subjective. Lonergan suggests that this neglect of the role of the subject in knowing is rooted in a short-circuited and dogmatic emphasis on metaphysics, yielding a dogmatic realism that frequently gives way to skepticism.

The second misunderstanding Lonergan mentions is the "truncated subject," which is implicated in an overlooking of insight that leads to conceptualism.[24] If one holds that knowledge is basically sense perception, and concepts are unconsciously generated representations not grounded in understanding, then knowing is a matter of being certain that concepts represent accurately, or that concepts are compatible with each other, or that inferences are drawn rigorously. All these presuppositions oriented toward certainty constitute what is meant by conceptualism. Knowing, then, is a matter of "acknowledging what is certain and disregarding what is controverted."[25] Certitude becomes a matter of what is *conceptually* self-evident. Concepts impress themselves on intellect, thus reducing the intellect's role to that of a conceptual mirror. The task of the subject here is to look at the concepts and then compare them with the things that are out there.[26] For Lonergan this conceptualism has three basic defects: the first is

---

[22] Ibid., 71.
[23] Ibid.
[24] Ibid., 73.
[25] Ibid., 74.
[26] Ibid. See also *Insight*, 430.

"anti-historical immobilism."[27] Because concepts are abstract, "they stand outside the spatio-temporal world of change," and so conceptualism cannot account for the development of concepts or the minds that form them.[28] The second defect is excessive abstractness. Conceptualism abstracts universals from the particular, and so "it overlooks the concrete mode of understanding that grasps intelligibility in the sensible itself."[29] The third defect has to do with the fact that conceptualism is confined to abstract universal concepts. It follows that the conceptualist regards "being" as "implicit in every positive concept and . . . thus the most abstract of all abstractions," a concept that is "least in connotation and greatest in denotation."[30]

Third, if the neglected or truncated subject is focused on objects, whether sensory or conceptual, then the misunderstanding Lonergan calls the "immanentist subject" grows from a desire to critically ground the objectivity of knowing. Insofar as picture thinking reduces knowing to looking and so employs a notion of objectivity that is merely a matter of "seeing all that is there to be seen and nothing that is not there,"[31] the turn to the immanent subject, although it does not reject the notion that knowing is looking, thus maintaining the picture thinking of the neglected and truncated subjects, acknowledges that the contents of sense perception as subsumed under categories attain objective knowledge of appearances (phenomena) alone, while the underlying thing-in-itself (noumenon) is only apprehended subjectively. Here, Lonergan singles out the Kantian argument. By funneling objectivity through sensitive intuition of phenomena alone, Kant reduces the knowable world to the phenomenal world, so that our judgments and reasoning only regard phenomena, never the things themselves, thus opening the door to Hegel's absolute idealism and eventually inspiring Husserl's desire to get back to the things themselves.

In the mid-nineteenth century the anti-Hegelianism of Søren Kierkegaard's focus of philosophical reflection falls on the "existential subject" in its concrete historicity. For Kierkegaard the subject is not simply a knower, or a disembodied objective mind, but fundamentally a human, one who must make

---

[27] Lonergan, "The Subject," 74.

[28] Ibid.

[29] Ibid., 75.

[30] Ibid. The formulation of being as the concept that is least in connotation and greatest in denotation is from John Duns Scotus. See also Lonergan, *Insight*, 392.

[31] Lonergan, "The Subject," 77.

decisions to act in history. Human decisions and actions, more than simply changing the world, transform the subject. Our decisions and deeds make us who we are.[32] A decadent metaphysical account of the soul hypostasizes intellect and will and fails to advert to the substance (itself misconceived) that knows and chooses, let alone the dynamic structure of its conscious operations.[33] According to Lonergan's account of the shift from subject as substance that prescinds from consciousness to the conscious subject, we become subjects gradually. The metaphysics of substance cannot take this dynamism in human subjectivity into account.[34] Lonergan's point here is that the existential subject evolves by means of the levels of consciousness concretely distinguishable in human performance. Briefly, I am a certain substance whether I am sleeping or waking, but I am not a subject as much in a deep and dreamless sleep as in my waking life.

The shift to the existential subject in the late nineteenth and early twentieth centuries is not without its difficulties, manifest in the notion of alienation, which became a key philosophical category beginning with Jean-Jacques Rousseau, and famously in Karl Marx's analysis of the relationship between labor and capital. It describes the existential subject's experience of being able to become itself freely and with dignity in a world that has settled into an absurd routine that degrades the human being into nothing more than a meaningless producer and consumer. Lonergan identifies this alienation in the subject whose desire for the good is derailed into doubting the goodness of the universe and feeling alien in an indifferent universe.[35] Such alienation is expressed in various philosophies of the absurd that proclaim the death of "God." In a statement that brings out the contrast between his work and certain postmodern trends in theology, Lonergan cautions:

> [T]hat absurdity and that death have their roots in a new neglect of
> the subject, a new truncation, a new immanentism. In the name of

[32] Ibid., 79.

[33] Ibid., 79–80.

[34] Chauvet recognizes the same problem in his criticism of the "productionist scheme of representation" characteristic of Western metaphysics. See *SS*, 21–43.

[35] There is an echo here of the account of "hope against hope" or "asking God for God" that is so central to the post-Holocaust theology of Johann Baptist Metz. See Johann Baptist Metz, *A Passion for God: The Mystical-Political Dimension of Christianity*, trans. and ed. J. Matthew Ashley (Mahwah, NJ: Paulist Press, 1997).

phenomenology, of existential self-understanding, of human encounter, of salvation history, there are those that resentfully and disdainfully brush aside the old questions of cognitional theory, epistemology and metaphysics. I have no doubt, I never did doubt, that the old answers were defective. But to reject the question as well is to refuse to know what one is doing when one is knowing; is to refuse to know why doing that is knowing; it is to refuse to set up a basic semantics by concluding what one knows when one does it.[36]

To overcome the alienation of the contemporary subject Lonergan demands that we pay close attention to the questions of cognitional theory, epistemology, and metaphysics, but in a way that does not ignore the facts of human suffering and the frequent absurdity that distorts the human community. This was Lonergan's goal in *Insight*.

2. Lonergan's Invitation to Postmodern Subjects: Understanding Understanding

In the preface to *Insight* Lonergan's description of the problem of human living together defines his project in terms of the concrete transformation of history.[37] Here we find the connections between his project and the ethical concerns of continental philosophy that motivated the *"Destruktion"* of metaphysics as first philosophy. Lonergan offers a clear-eyed assessment of a culture in the grip of decline and a rationale for beginning at the beginning, with human understanding, in order to transform the historical situation. So he asks bluntly, "What practical good can come from this book?"[38]

The answer is that a study of cognitional theory, especially the role of insight in understanding, regards all the activities of intelligence, not only theory, but practice as well. Normally we think before we act. From that base one is also able to develop a theory of history that identifies vectors of progress and decline in courses of action that either build on previous insights or blunder about in a flight from understanding. That flight is often sustained by the pressure to provide commonsense solutions with short-term benefits.

---

[36] Lonergan, "The Subject," 86.

[37] See Richard M. Liddy, *Transforming Light: Intellectual Conversion in the Early Lonergan* (Collegeville, MN: Liturgical Press, 1993), 84–90.

[38] Lonergan, *Insight*, 7.

Theoretical understanding therefore comes to be regarded as irrelevant to daily living, and, Lonergan writes, "Human activity settles down to a decadent routine, and initiative becomes the privilege of violence."[39] The delicate work of overcoming decline asks that we learn "to distinguish sharply between progress and decline, learn to encourage progress without putting a premium on decline, learn to remove the tumor of the flight from understanding without destroying the organs of intelligence."[40] The challenge of historical transformation Lonergan confronts in *Insight* continues in our own time. So does a bias against theory. And yet, "no problem is at once more delicate and more profound, more practical and perhaps more pressing. How, indeed, is a mind to become conscious of its own bias when that bias springs from a communal flight from understanding and is supported by the whole texture of a civilization?"[41]

Clearly, Lonergan is no heir of the Enlightenment myths of progress, but neither is he a victim of the radical pessimism that lurks in the background of some continental thought. His goal is social transformation, even the restoration of all things in Christ, and his means is attending to the humble, everyday experience of insight. By attending to the experience of insight he hopes to discover not a metaphysical system but the concrete conditions for the possibility of cultural transformation that emerge in an investigation of the recurrent structure of human knowing. Lonergan divides his text into three sections. First, he explicates his cognitional theory. Second, he confronts epistemological questions regarding objectivity. Finally, he employs the foregoing analyses to elaborate a methodically and empirically grounded metaphysics of proportionate being and a heuristic structure for theological concerns and existential ethics. Again, while we could begin with a consideration of metaphysics, we want to take Chauvet's criticisms seriously by following Lonergan's example and beginning with the concrete conditions for the emergence of a critical-realist metaphysics derived from a cognitional theory and an epistemology.

2.1. Lonergan's Cognitional Theory

Unlike his scholastic forebears, Lonergan does not begin with metaphysics. Frederick Crowe reports that Lonergan discovered through his contact

---

[39] Ibid., 8.
[40] Ibid.
[41] Ibid., 8–9.

with Plato and Augustine, Aristotle and Thomas that the universal concepts that dominated later scholasticism were almost beside the point.[42] He found that each of these philosophers emphasized *intelligere*, or understanding, *not* universal concepts like "being." Concepts depend on understanding; otherwise they are just mystification or empty talk. The key is to get to the act of understanding from which concepts get their meaning. Therefore Lonergan investigated the meaning of *intelligere* for Thomas.[43] He writes, "In working out his concept of verbum Aquinas was engaged not merely in fitting an original Augustinian creation into an Aristotelian framework but also attempting, however remotely and implicitly, to fuse together what to us may seem so disparate: a phenomenology of the subject with a psychology of the soul."[44] Thomas's phenomenology of the subject derives from Augustine's inquiry into his own desire to know God in his early Cassiciacum dialogues on knowing.[45] In his explorations of *intelligere* in Thomas, Lonergan discovered the elements of an account of knowing that was verifiable in experience and that embraced the human subject in all its concrete complexity. The challenge for Lonergan was to find out if the language of Thomist faculty psychology that explained intellect and will in terms of the potencies of the soul was performatively and empirically grounded in what Lonergan thematizes as intentionality analysis.[46]

---

[42] See Frederick E. Crowe, "Editor's Introduction," xii–xvi, in Bernard Lonergan, *Verbum: Word and Idea in Aquinas*, CWBL 2, ed. Frederick E. Crowe and Robert M. Doran (Toronto: University of Toronto Press, 1997).

[43] Ibid., xv. Chauvet's summary of Thomas's theory of knowing, which omits the act of understanding by identifying the inner word with the concept, thereby interpreting him as a conceptualist, which he was not, rests on a failure to account for *intelligere*. Consequently, his interpretation of Thomas on sacramental causality and eucharistic presence is conceptualist in the manner of baroque scholasticism. I agree with Chauvet that we can move beyond Thomas's metaphysics in order to offer a fruitful understanding of the doctrines to contemporary Christians. But moving beyond requires a transposition rather than a deconstruction. In order to transpose, we must first understand what has come before.

[44] Lonergan, *Verbum*, 3.

[45] See especially Augustine's dialogue with his son Adeodatus, "*De Magistro* (The Teacher)," 69–101, in *Augustine: Earlier Writings*, ed. John H. S. Burleigh (Philadelphia: Westminster Press, 1953).

[46] See Bernard Lonergan, "Insight Revisited," 263–78, in his *Second Collection*, ed. William J. F. Ryan and Bernard J. Tyrrell (Toronto: University of Toronto Press, 1996).

Lonergan's long apprenticeship to Thomas laid the groundwork for his magnum opus, *Insight*. He had already shown in the *Verbum* articles of the 1940s that for Thomas "cognitional theory is expressed in metaphysical terms and established by metaphysical principles."[47] In the intervening centuries a massive paradigm shift had occurred in philosophy and the sciences so that their basic terms and relations are now independent of metaphysical terms. The shift toward statistical verification in the sciences and the turn to the subject in philosophy demand that one begin with a consideration of psychological facts rather than universal and necessary causes;[48] therefore in *Insight* "metaphysics is expressed in cognitional terms and established by cognitional principles."[49] But Lonergan avers, "If Aquinas had things right side up—and that is difficult to deny—then I have turned everything upside down."[50] The shift is methodological. It is related to a distinction made regularly by Aristotle and Thomas between what is "first for us" (*priora quoad nos*) and what is "first in itself" (*priora quoad se*). To take metaphysical terms and relations as a starting point is to explain things in relation to themselves (*priora quoad se*), and Thomas, following Aristotelian science as understanding things according to their universal and necessary causes or first principles, used this method. To begin with cognitional theory, however, is to start from what is first in relation to us (*priora quoad nos*) in order to identify a verifiable account of human knowing grounded in the concrete experience of the knowing subject. Lonergan does this by attending to the human experience of acts of understanding.

In order to clarify the difference between what is first for us and what is first in itself, consider an example from Aristotle's *Posterior Analytics*. From our position on earth we can observe the phases of the moon.[51] The phases are what we notice; they are first *for us*. From our observations of the lunar phases we are able to conclude that the moon is a sphere. On the other hand,

---

[47] Bernard Lonergan, "Insight: Preface to a Discussion," 142–52, in his *Collection*, CWBL 4, ed. Frederick E. Crowe and Robert M. Doran (Toronto: University of Toronto Press, 1993), at 142.

[48] Lonergan analyzes much of this historical shift in the first half of *Insight*, especially chap. 4, "The Complementarity of Classical and Statistical Investigations."

[49] Lonergan, "Insight: Preface to a Discussion," 142.

[50] Ibid.

[51] See Bernard Lonergan, "Theology and Understanding," 114–32, in *Collection*, CWBL 4, at 119–20. Cf. Lonergan, *Insight*, 272.

the moon *is* a sphere, and its sphericity, what is first *in itself*, explains why there are phases. To use the scholastic language, the phases of the moon are the *causa cognoscendi*, the cause of our coming to know that the moon is a sphere. The sphericity of the moon is the *causa essendi*, the cause of there being phases. If one begins with metaphysics one reflects on the *priora quoad se*, or what is first in itself, things as they relate to each other, in terms of causes, the *causa essendi*. But if one begins with the *priora quoad nos*, or what is first for us, things as they appear to us, one moves from experience to understanding in order to discover the intelligibility (causes) of things. If the former attempts to define the particular by means of a universal, the latter begins by grasping the intelligible in the singular and, pivoting on itself, expresses this intelligibility in a universal definition that holds *omni et soli* (i.e., for every instance of that kind and only of that kind).[52] Why is this distinction important?

Distinguishing the order of questions is essential to understanding what metaphysical terms like "substance" mean. Simply put, substances are not first for us. We do not experience or observe substances; we observe the particular concrete data of things, or accidents. This is significant in relation to Lonergan's criticism of the "basic counterposition" of naïve realism that assumes knowing is like looking. Our sense experience, our seeing, pertains only to things as they relate to our *sensorium*, such as the rising and setting of the sun, and therefore to what Lonergan calls the first "level of consciousness." The privileged look or intuition that would grant access all at once to an essence or a substance hidden somewhere underneath the surface appearances cannot be verified, and it renders sense experience illusory. Instead of searching for a privileged look or an intuition that would allow us to know reality in a single glance, Lonergan invites us to pay attention to our inner experience of the data of consciousness when we are asking and answering questions for understanding and questions for reflection. Only then can we discover the dynamic structure of human knowing that begins with experiencing of data, moves through understanding and defining to

---

[52] These two ways of knowing are related to two ways of ordering the answers to theological questions. The *ordo inventionis*, or way of discovery, begins with what is first for us and moves gradually from data to resolve further questions by understanding through analysis until it attains their first principles. The *ordo doctrinae* begins with what is first in itself as expressed in defined premises or doctrines.

weighing the evidence that allows us to judge truth from falsehood and so reality from illusion.

Lonergan sums up his project in *Insight* with a slogan: "*Thoroughly understand what it is to understand, and not only will you understand the broad lines of all there is to be understood but also you will possess a fixed base, an invariant pattern, opening upon all further developments of understanding.*"[53] *Insight* invites the reader to come to a decision by attending to his or her own experiences of questioning and insight in order to understand understanding—what Lonergan calls "self-appropriation."[54] The book leads the reader through a series of experiments in which the conscious events of questioning and insight might be experienced, reflected on, and appropriated. Our concern here is conveying the results of that attention, reflection, and appropriation in answering the questions "what am I doing when I am knowing?" the answer to which is a cognitional theory that provokes the question "why is doing that knowing?" or the epistemological question. Only after answering these preliminary cognitional theoretical and epistemological questions can we understand Lonergan's metaphysics.

a. The Desire to Know: Questioning as Foundational

Whatever else Lonergan has to say relies on the basic affirmation that human beings both desire to know and *de facto* often do know. To reject this premise would be to reject Lonergan's ideas arbitrarily. Further, to reject the desire to know necessarily involves a performative contradiction insofar as the negation of the desire to know would have required engaging the desire implicit in the question, "Do we really desire to know?" But performative contradiction is not necessarily the most persuasive evidence. If one attends to the behavior of toddlers, however, one cannot but notice that they ask "why?" They want to know, and their ability to question is seemingly unlimited.

---

[53] Lonergan, *Insight*, 22. Talk of "fixed bases" or "invariant patterns" will raise the hackles of those committed to the anti-foundationalist approach of postmodernism, but Lonergan is very clear elsewhere that the invariant pattern is not "a set of rules to be followed meticulously by a dolt" (Lonergan, *Method in Theology* [New York: Herder & Herder, 1972], xi) and therefore not an abstract foundation; rather, it is a heuristic structure that just happens to be (i.e., contingently) verifiable in experience.

[54] See Lonergan, *Insight*, 13: "more than all else the aim of the book is to issue an invitation to a personal, decisive act."

Not only do human beings have a desire to know, then, as our experience of toddlers reveals, our capacity for questioning is potentially infinite. The fact that answers to questions give rise to ever-further questions reveals that our desire to know is *unrestricted*. Human intending is infinite. The desire to know is an unrestricted desire, even if our actual knowing is restricted. Lonergan explains that this "primordial drive, then, is the pure question. It is prior to any insights, any concepts, any words; for insights, concepts, words have to do with answers, and before we look for answers we want them; such wanting is the pure question."[55] The pure desire to know is "an intellectual desire, an eros of the mind," and "[w]ithout it there would arise no questioning, no inquiry, no wonder."[56] The postmodern suggestion that we linger on the activities of questioning and thinking helps to correct a tendency in modern philosophy to ask questions about objectivity and certitude too hastily. To dwell instead on the fact of human questioning not only reveals our native and spontaneous desire to know but may also indicate that the first question is not "how do we know?" but "what are we doing when we know?"

In other words, questions intend answers. Thinking is not aimless musing but the beginning of a process that heads toward answering "what? how? why?" by understanding, because "*no one just wonders. We wonder about something.*"[57] Our questions intend answers, but the answers are not reached by mere experience or perception; they emerge as the term of the processes of experiencing, understanding, and judging. Our intending unfolds on three distinct levels linked by questions. Experiences of the data lead to the question "what is it?" The question moves us to further investigation of and attention to the data until we experience an insight into some intelligible pattern. Subsequently we seek to express what was learned in the insight by formulating a guess or articulating a hypothesis or a definition on the level of understanding.

But our definition is only a guess or hypothesis. We want to know if we have understood correctly, so we inquire, "is it so?" To answer that question requires marshaling and weighing the evidence until a reflective insight reveals that the conditions that would have to be fulfilled have in fact been fulfilled, or that sufficient warrant has been established to verify the definition.

[55] Ibid., 34.
[56] Ibid., 97.
[57] Ibid., 34.

From such a reflective insight comes a judgment in which the definition is affirmed. Such, briefly, is Lonergan's cognitional theory. It is not a set of prescriptive steps to be followed but a description of what we do every day when we ask questions and try to answer them correctly. The process unfolds so frequently and spontaneously that it is easily overlooked, as much in philosophy as in our daily living.[58]

Whether Lonergan's description is accurate can only be verified by each individual inasmuch as one attends to one's own asking and answering questions. Lonergan proposes in *Insight* that such attending to one's self in the process of knowing is a matter of "self-appropriation." Self-appropriation both leads to a verifiable account of human knowing and ultimately grounds the explication of the integral heuristic structure of proportionate being, or metaphysics, implicit in the operations of rational self-consciousness. But first let us clarify how Lonergan arrives at his conclusion.

b. The Experience of Insight

In the first half of *Insight* Lonergan leads the reader through a series of exercises meant to elicit the occurrence of insight within one's own inner awareness. Even if we are familiar with the experience of the tension and frustration brought on by our questions, we may be less familiar with the occurrence of insight. Insights come as a release of the tension of inquiry. It is the often subtle, sometimes dramatic relief we feel at having figured it out. It is perhaps less notable because it is less worrisome than the often anxious questioning that precedes it. Indeed, Lonergan often remarked that insights are a dime a dozen.[59] But there are dramatic instances, for example, Archimedes crying "Eureka!" as he ran naked through the streets of Syracuse.[60] Often, however, insight is the subtler recognition of a student in the classroom, a researcher in the lab, or a mechanic in the garage that routinely goes unnoticed and therefore unappropriated.

---

[58] Lonergan often laments the fact that philosophers and scientists fail to attend to themselves in the process of asking and answering questions. Among the notable exceptions are Augustine and Descartes, though the latter's procedure was distorted by asking how we know with certitude. See *Insight*, 414.

[59] Audio available at http://www.bernardlonergan.com/archiveitem.php?id=124.

[60] See Lonergan, *Insight*, 27–32.

Insight is the pivot between the images evoked by sense data and the concepts that, based on understanding, refine the data into a hunch or perhaps even a definition. Insights depend on both an experience of data, either of sense or of imagination, and a desire to know enacted by questions. If either of these is lacking, insights will not occur, as, for example, in a deep and dreamless sleep, or, as we will see, in cases of bias. Data are only *merely* sensed when we are just staring, but regularly data are assembled into images and patterns or phantasms. For the radical empiricist, knowing is reduced to these acts of sensing, especially seeing. But, if we attend to our own acts of seeing we will readily admit that at times we are reduced to gaping, eyes open but "seeing" nothing, or our seeing might simply be mistaken. And even seriously attentive looking is not the totality of knowing; rather, it stimulates questions that seeing alone cannot answer. Sensing provokes a series of questions. We inquire of our sense experience, "What is it?" We try out answers in cooperation with our memory and imagination as we try to figure things out.

Here, we find the core of what Lonergan learned about understanding from Thomas Aquinas and Aristotle: *insight into phantasm*. In fact, the frontispiece of *Insight* is a quotation from Aristotle: "τά μέν οὖν εἴδη τὸ νοητικὸν ἐν τοῖς φαντάσμασι νοεῖ."[61] Properly speaking, insights occur when we try to answer questions about data represented in the mind as images or phantasms. Whatever is ultimately understood is understood as an intelligible pattern through the medium of an image, either sensed or imagined. While discussing the topic of insight into phantasm in his early work on *verbum* in Thomas, Lonergan uses a lengthy footnote to distinguish between the teaching of Thomas and Aristotle and the typical Scotist or Platonist positions on knowing.[62] For Scotus, concepts come first, so that understanding is a matter of discovering the relationship between concepts, without any explanation of the origin of concepts.[63] Therefore knowing the

---

[61] Lonergan translates the Greek, at *Insight*, 699: "forms are grasped by mind in images."

[62] See Lonergan, *Verbum*, 39 n. 126.

[63] There is no small amount of confusion between the positions of Scotus and Aquinas, especially their respective views on the existence of particulars. Many have accused Aquinas of being primarily concerned with abstract universals and, by way of contrast, attribute concern with the particular to Scotus's notion of *haecceitas*. This is a misinterpretation of Aquinas, as Lonergan has amply demonstrated in *Verbum*. See also

actual existence of a thing is a matter of confrontation with an object "out there," which one tries to match with the concepts "in here," in one's mind. But for Thomas and for Lonergan insight into phantasm is the event without which concepts remain utterly meaningless formulae, platitudes, or clichés. Lonergan emphasizes that insight into phantasm is a concrete experience and therefore a verifiable act of human understanding. Concepts are generated by the intellect in response to the experience of insight.[64]

The fact that understanding emerges in response to questions about data also confirms that understanding depends on data and is therefore a concrete encounter with reality, not a vague intuition. Understanding does not occur in a vacuum but in contact with the myriad data we experience through the senses. Insights into phantasm pivot between the concrete sensible data and the abstract conceptualization or definition of the intelligibility one has grasped in images. From the experience of the data one only moves to understanding through questioning "what is it?" In insight we grasp only a possible answer to that question. Archimedes had to perform the necessary experiments in order to verify that his insight into the principle of the displacement of water was correct. Insight gets the ball rolling.

For example, imagine a cartwheel.[65] Various images emerge, perhaps of a rough-hewn hay wagon, or a royal carriage, or a lone wheel propped against the side of a barn. But the image may provoke the question "what is it?" or *quid sit?* How are the parts related? What enables a cartwheel to do what it does? The answer, of course, is that it is round. But what is roundness? Roundness is characteristic of things that are circular. And what makes a cartwheel circular? Here, we employ our image of the wheel again in order to see how the parts relate to each other and perhaps get the insight that the

---

James Reichmann, "Scotus and Haecceitas, Aquinas and Esse: A Comparative Study," *American Catholic Philosophical Quarterly* 80 (2006): 63–75.

[64] Scotus places the formation of concepts outside of consciousness. The question, then, is whether concepts have real being. Scotus thought they did. After all, one cannot think of nothing. Thinking at all means thinking about something. That something is being. But being itself remains mysterious, the most abstract of concepts. Therefore, the concept of being can be predicated univocally of God and created reality. See Denys Turner, *Faith, Reason, and the Existence of God* (New York: Cambridge University Press, 2004), 125–48.

[65] Lonergan employs the example of a cartwheel to illustrate the experience of insight; see *Insight*, 31–34.

spokes on the cartwheel appear to be the same length. That the spokes have something to do with what makes a cartwheel round is an insight that heads in the right direction, but, as Lonergan notes, the imagined spokes cannot be the only measure, for at least two reasons: (1) they may be sunk into the hub at different depths, and (2) the rim may be somewhat flat between two of the spokes. Indeed, an octagon will not do the work of a cartwheel, and a spoke sunk into the hub too deeply, even if it measured the same as the others, would cause the rim to flex and keep the wheel from rolling smoothly. Further investigation is required to confirm our hypothesis.

In order to overcome these challenges to our insight that the spokes make the wheel round, we abstract from the data of the cartwheel. Reduce the hub to a point and the spokes and rim to lines. We imagine the more refined data of points and lines such as we might draw with a pencil. These imagined points and lines, offering a simplified phantasm, might reveal that the distance from the center to any point along the arc must be the same in order for it to roll smoothly. Now we can hypothesize that what makes the wheel round is that the distance between the center of the hub and the rim is always equal. Having experienced an insight into the intelligibility of the cartwheel, i.e., that its parts are related in a way that allows it to move a load easily, we go further in refining our understanding by refining the phantasm and abstracting from the image the basic elements of a circle we can sketch. An even further refinement of the intelligibility of a circle requires that we go beyond imagined dots and lines and move into the realm of geometry, where our points become locations mapped out on a coordinate system, and lines refer to relations between coordinate points in the realm of purely conceptual definition.

We abstract from the image in order to discover the intelligibility of a circle because we are not concerned with the variety of other data that make up the image, for example, the species of wood or the kind of metal from which the rim is made, its color, the fact that it is sitting on a dirt road or a grassy field, whether it is dawn or noontime. Even the imagined pencil drawing must eventually be set aside. All of these data are part of what Lonergan refers to in *Insight* as empirical residue.[66] These data, especially the "hereness" and "nowness" of our encounter with the material or imagined wheel,

---

[66] See ibid., 50–56; 538–43. Contrast Lonergan's position here with Heidegger's emphasis on temporal extroversion. This distinction will be clarified in our discussion of Lonergan's notion of "things."

are not directly relevant to understanding the intelligibility of a circle and judging that one has understood correctly. The empirically residual data do, however, offer the particular instance of an intelligibility to be known. Only subsequently are concepts like points, lines, and curves employed in order to refine the image of the circle into a definition: a series of coplanar points equidistant from a center, which expresses the intelligibility of our cartwheel.

Now if we believe we have understood what makes the cartwheel round, the further question is a question for judgment: "is it so?" or "have I understood correctly?" This further question, corresponding to the Latin *an sit?* brings us beyond the level of understanding by a call for reflective understanding that seeks to verify whether we have understood correctly. In brief, a judgment in the affirmative indicates that we know that our possibly relevant answer is actually relevant, so that we have knowledge of a virtually unconditioned fact. Judgment assesses the sufficiency or insufficiency of the evidence for affirming that we have understood correctly.

However, before moving to the level of judgment we must first attend to the complexity of our experience, because in fact our questions are conditioned by our experiences and shaped by our involvements in the world mediated by meaning. This raises a further question about our knowing. Do we really go through our lives seeking intelligibilities, as we have just proposed with regard to the cartwheel?[67] Do we in fact ask "what is it?" as Lonergan suggests we do? And if we do, do we do it regularly? Aren't we often reduced to mere gaping, even habitual gaping? But Lonergan was naïve neither about the complexity of human psychology nor about the prospect of actual human knowing. Here, we must consider some additional aspects of human experience that will help us establish a sufficiently critical, verifiable account of human knowing. If the preceding analysis argues that we *may* know things, we must now give an account of the concrete circumstances in which we actually know things by attending to the subject as subject.

c. *What Is Consciousness? The Subject as Subject*

According to Lonergan the structure of human knowing unfolds on three distinct levels: experiencing, understanding, and judging. Passage from one level to another is promoted by questions that reveal the dynamism of the

---

[67] For the moment we will prescind from Heidegger's problematic of *Vorhandenheit*. It will return in our consideration of Lonergan's notion of the "thing."

human desire to know. The questions "what is it?" and "is it so?" are operators that move our conscious intentionality from one level to the next. The
formally dynamic structure of human knowing is a self-assembling unity
that, unlike a biological process such as metabolism, occurs "consciously,
intelligently, rationally."[68] In order for the process to begin, one must be
conscious. Human knowing begins in experiencing sensible data through
acts of hearing, tasting, touching, smelling, and seeing. Human experience,
however, is mediated by human consciousness, which assembles data and
the images that give rise to insights. What do we mean here by consciousness? Lonergan uses the term in a unique but simple way.[69]

Consciousness for Lonergan is not an elevated state to be achieved or
an abstraction of mind; rather, it is simply being aware. Therefore being
conscious is the opposite of being unconscious, as when someone is literally knocked out. Lonergan notes that to be conscious we must at least be
present to ourselves so that we are present to the world, e.g., feeling hot or
cold, hearing noises, seeing light, dark, and color. When we are in a deep
and dreamless sleep we are minimally conscious, and the world goes on
without us. We are still human, but more like a substance: a compound of
physical, chemical, biological, and psychological processes sustaining the
specific organism we call human. But the degree of consciousness increases
when we begin to dream. For example, Lonergan cites the "dreams of the
night"[70] in which bodily disturbances, perhaps an arm gone numb, draw

[68] Bernard Lonergan, "Cognitional Structure," 205–21 in his *Collection*, CWBL 4, at
207. Each adverb relates to the respective levels of conscious intending.

[69] Consciousness is considered differently, depending on whether one is engaging
scientists or philosophers. See Antonio Damasio, *The Feeling of What Happens: Body
and Emotion in the Making of Consciousness* (New York: Harcourt, 2000); Damasio,
Descartes' Error: Emotion, Reason, and the Human Brain (New York: Penguin, 1994,
2005). See also the works of Peter Carruthers, *Consciousness: Essays from a Higher-Order
Perspective* (Oxford and New York: Oxford University Press, 2005); Carruthers, *Language,
Thought and Consciousness: An Essay in Philosophical Psychology* (Cambridge and
New York: Cambridge University Press, 1998); Carruthers, *Phenomenal Consciousness:
A Naturalistic Theory* (Cambridge and New York: Cambridge University Press, 2003).
For a survey of recent scholarship, see William Seager, *Theories of Consciousness: An
Introduction and Assessment* (London and New York: Routledge, 1999).

[70] Bernard Lonergan, "Self-Transcendence: Intellectual, Moral, Religious," 313–31, in
his *Philosophical and Theological Papers, 1965–1980*, CWBL 17, ed. Robert C. Croken
and Robert M. Doran (Toronto: University of Toronto Press, 2004), at 316.

us out of deep sleep with images and half-conscious questions. We might dreamily wonder "have I lost my arm?" Again, in the dreams of the morning, while emerging into wakeful consciousness, we experience images under the influence of desires and fears reflected in obscure symbols concerning the world we will encounter when we awaken.[71] In that liminal state between sleeping and waking our senses may be activated by data but the mind lags behind, incorporating sensed data into the world of the dream, so that for a moment perhaps the sound of the alarm clock is inserted into the dream's plot or accompanies its images like a musical score.

Upon awakening we are met by a flood of sensible data. There is the alarm clock, the piercing light of dawn, or the dark of winter mornings. We smell the familiar odors of home, we feel kinks in the neck or the warmth of the bed. However, "sensations, feelings, movements are confined to that narrow strip of space-time occupied by immediate experience . . . beyond that there is a vastly larger world."[72] As subjects we move beyond the world of immediacy (which for the infant may constitute an entire horizon, but for the adult emerging from sleep usually lasts but an instant), and we enter a world mediated by meanings and motivated by values.[73] It is the world we find in our daily morning rituals, in the foods we eat and the clothes we wear, but also in the complex social arrangements that shape our experience of family, community, religion. Put simply, consciousness is the intentionality normally at work in the waking life of the human subject. More specifically, consciousness is "an awareness immanent in cognitional acts."[74] It is the self-presence of the subject to himself or herself in the acts of experiencing, understanding, and judging.

The notion of conscious self-presence is easily misinterpreted. Lonergan cautions that "consciousness is not to be thought of as some sort of inward look. People are apt to think of knowing by imagining a man taking a look at something, and further, they are apt to think of consciousness by imagining themselves looking into themselves."[75] The problem with this common image of introspection is that it presumes an ocular metaphor, or picture thinking, in which knowing occurs by confrontation with some object that

[71] Ibid.
[72] Ibid., 317.
[73] Cf. Lonergan, *Method*, 28, 76–77, and 89.
[74] Lonergan, *Insight*, 344.
[75] Ibid.

occupies our gaze. When this metaphor is employed to describe introspection, the subject is reduced to just one more object at which to look. Even an inward look is looking at something.[76] Lonergan clarifies his position: "I have been attempting to describe the subject's presence to himself. But the reader, if he tries to find himself as subject, to reach back and, as it were, uncover his subjectivity cannot succeed. Any such effort is introspecting, attending to the subject, and what is found is not the subject as subject, but only the subject as object; it is the subject as subject that does the finding."[77] Lonergan wants to attend to an awareness immanent in acts of sensing, understanding, formulating, reflecting, judging, and deliberating. It is a presence to self that is experienced in sensing. We do not simply see; rather we see colors, shapes, and patterns; we look for something. So also, we know the difference between simply gazing and cooperating with sight in assembling data. Conscious self-presence is not a deliberate activity in addition to sensing[78] but the awareness that accompanies the act of sensing, which "not only intends an object but also reveals an intending subject."[79] We discover ourselves as subjects in the operations we perform. In a deep and dreamless sleep we are barely aware of ourselves; we are more substance than subject, but in all the operations of our waking life we are simultaneously present to ourselves and to the world of our experience.[80]

The subject *as* subject, as present to itself and its world, i.e., as conscious, is often forgotten in modern philosophy with its desire to discover the universal foundations of objectivity, beginning with Descartes' method of universal doubt. Postmodern thinkers frequently argue that the modern subject appears to be a disembodied intellect unencumbered by its historicity, unaware that experience is mediated through a body and culture.[81]

---

[76] See also Lonergan, *Method*, 8: "There is the word, introspection, which is misleading inasmuch as it suggests an inward inspection. Inward inspection is just a myth. Its origin lies in the mistaken analogy that all cognitional events are to be conceived on the analogy of ocular vision."

[77] Lonergan, "Cognitional Structure," 210. Chauvet's criticism of the presence of the self to the self identifies this problem but does not redress it by attending to the subject as subject, that is, as present to self in the experience of what is other.

[78] See Lonergan, *Insight*, 345.

[79] Lonergan, *Method*, 15.

[80] See Lonergan, "Self-Transcendence," 316.

[81] A central aspect of Chauvet's treatment of thinking in *Symbol and Sacrament* regards the modes of embodiment that shape human subjects. See *SS*, 149–52.

But this is only true of the subject as the primary object of modern epistemology. Lonergan is well aware of this problem in his exploration of human consciousness, as we noted above with regard to his analysis of modern distortions of the subject. He recognizes that human experience is mediated and complex, that human consciousness is polymorphic and, indeed, nothing like a mirror.

2.2. The Polymorphism of Human Consciousness

Human beings operate in contexts that attract their attention in various directions. "Polymorphism" refers to this orientation or patterning of human experience. In *Insight*, Lonergan claims that "the polymorphism of human consciousness is the one and only key to philosophy."[82] Lonergan's recognition of this polymorphism aligns with postmodern concerns about the embodied character of human knowing and acting and the cultural mediation of experience. He explains:

> No doubt, we are all familiar with acts of seeing, hearing, touching, tasting, smelling. Still, such acts never occur in isolation both from one another and from all other events. On the contrary, they have a bodily basis; they are functionally related to bodily movements; and they occur in some dynamic context that somehow unifies a manifold of sensed contents and of acts of sensing.[83]

To see, one must open one's eyes, turn one's head, etc., in order to observe certain data. All the senses require a coordination of bodily movements and bodily integrity in order to function. For example, we know the challenge of smelling and tasting when suffering from sinus congestion. We might know or be able to imagine the challenges hearing loss presents to our ability to hear not simply sounds but meaningful speech. Thus, for Lonergan, the body and its integrity are central to knowing.[84]

---

[82] Lonergan, *Insight*, 452. See Gerard Walmsley, *Lonergan on Philosophic Pluralism: The Polymorphism of Consciousness as the Key to Philosophy* (Toronto: University of Toronto Press, 2008).

[83] Lonergan, *Insight*, 205.

[84] It should be noted here that it is not only the perfectly healthy who can know things. Indeed, there are innumerable examples of individuals who overcome significant bodily ailments or disabilities to reach high levels of expertise. We might think of Helen Keller

In addition to adverting to the role of the body in the process of human knowing, Lonergan speaks about the problems of human psychology in the mediation of experience. He explains: "Both the sensations and the bodily movements are subject to an organizing control. Besides the systematic links between senses and sense organs, there is, immanent in experience, a factor variously named conation, interest, attention, purpose."[85] There is, then, a purpose or direction in our sensing and in our questioning. Lonergan discusses issues regarding the directing of our experience by employing the notion of patterns. We find ourselves in various patterns of experience depending on the dominant direction of our attention at a given moment: for example, Thales stumbling into a well because his attention is focused on the stars.[86] The image of the stumbling, or "absent-minded" intellectual highlights the fact that human experience is a compound of competing interests. Being human is not simply keeping one's head down in order to get safely from point A to point B; we are also drawn to the stars, to wonder. Nor is that the whole of human being. If we did not eat and drink, the mind would cease to function completely. Human experience is concrete and complicated. Our polymorphic consciousness inhabits different patterns of experience.

2.3. Patterns of Experience: The Subjective Field of Common Sense

Our experience varies depending on the kinds of questions that direct our attention, but we are not pure intellects. The goal of the scientist may be disinterested inquiry into the relevant data, but scientists are only human and they, too, shift from disinterested analysis of data to making broad pronouncements on human nature in a rather unscientific way. Nor is the laboratory isolated from the larger range of human experiences. Human experience is neither restricted to asking and answering questions in the laboratory nor capable of being subordinated without remainder to the rigors of scientific and mathematical precision. When they leave the lab, scientists are men and women of common sense. This is because science and common sense are variously concerned with the same data or concerned with different ranges of data. In order to get at the complexity of human

---

or Stephen Hawking. The point here is that the bodily basis of sensing requires that we attend to the body in any adequate reflection on human knowing.

[85] Lonergan, *Insight*, 205.

[86] Plato, *Theaetetus*, 174a.

experience Lonergan shifts his inquiry in *Insight* from the many mathematical and scientific examples of human knowing he employs in the first part in order to examine human knowing as it pertains to common sense, to the world mediated by meanings and values, the world of our daily living.

The world of common sense is the dominant horizon of things as they appear to us. "Where the scientist seeks the relations of things to one another, common sense is concerned with the relations of things to us."[87] The results of commonsense investigations are not mathematical proofs or scientific laws but the developments of a culture and especially of a politics. Human experience is shaped by communities, but communities are historical, therefore, "not only does the self-correcting process of learning unfold within the private consciousness of the individual; for by speech, and still more by example, there is effected a sustained communication that at once disseminates and tests and improves every advance, to make the achievement of each successive generation the starting point of the next."[88] We take the stage *in medias res*. Consequently, Lonergan suggests, "Not only are men born with a native drive to inquire and understand; they are born in a community that possesses a common fund of tested answers."[89] Human knowing occurs within these culturally mediated ranges of previously answered questions or assumptions about the world that shape the kinds of questions that occur in any individual consciousness at any time and place. What emerges as a question for one culture need not emerge in another. The common sense of one culture may not be at all common to another. Indeed, it may even be considered nonsense.

Lonergan took common sense and its cultural entanglements seriously by adverting to the polymorphism of consciousness. His investigation of human understanding therefore moves out of the laboratory's mode of detached inquiry and into the culturally mediated world of common sense in order to ground his cognitional theory in psychological and historical facticity familiar to everyone. The vast majority of human experience unfolds in the world of common sense. Where the scientist looks for universally valid laws, common sense is concerned with the concrete and the particular. Common sense relates things to our experience. After all, we do not experience gravity as a formula; we feel its pull. Lonergan clarifies further that

---

[87] Ibid., 204.
[88] Ibid., 198.
[89] Ibid.

there is "a subtle ambiguity in the apparently evident statement that common sense relates things to us. For who are we? Do we not change? Is not the acquisition of common sense itself a change in us?"[90] Consequently, in order to understand human understanding we have to attend closely to the concrete historical subject in his or her development through time—what Lonergan calls the "subjective field."[91] Human intelligence is not a pristine mirror or transparent lens through which reality is intuited; it is easily distracted, frequently obtuse, and prone to biases. Distinguishing among various patterns of experience establishes a sufficiently critical account of human knowing and is prior to epistemological questions about objectivity.

a. The Biological Pattern of Experience

The biological pattern is that part of human experience that we share with other animals. The pattern is called biological to indicate that these sequences converge on the basic animal drives toward consuming food and reproducing, what we normally mean by "self-preservation." The biological pattern is driven by immanent vital processes that are preconscious or nonconscious, but become conscious when their functioning is disturbed.[92] For example, with the pang of hunger consciousness begins to assemble the data relevant to the acquisition of food. Nonconscious processes like digestion and metabolism switch into the conscious need for sustenance. The biological pattern is extroverted and manifests the confrontational element in consciousness, for stimulus demands movement—the fleeing prey pulls the hungry predator along. However, Lonergan notes that in the purely biological pattern consciousness is part-time work. An empty stomach growls for food and heightens consciousness of hunger, but when we have had our fill we drift off to sleep. The appetitive and reproductive desires of animality impact our human experiencing, for we are animals, but the biological pattern is not the whole of human living.

b. The Aesthetic Pattern of Experience

The aesthetic pattern of experience is observable in the transformation of the biological purposiveness of the hunt into the play of the young.

---

[90] Ibid., 204.
[91] Ibid.
[92] See ibid., 206–7.

Play is a kind of liberation, the joy of experience no longer confined to the demands of biological purposiveness. For conscious living "is itself a joy that reveals its spontaneous authenticity in the untiring play of children, in the strenuous games of youth, in the exhilaration of sunlit morning air, in the sweep of a broad perspective, in the swing of a melody."[93] If kittens and pups frolic and chase, humans transform play into art. Free from the demands of the biological pattern, the human being takes in the view, smells a blossom, feels the wind, or revels in the sparkle of light on the surface of a river, all without any ulterior motive of safety or sustenance. The artistry of the aesthetic pattern is a twofold freedom. On the one hand, it liberates the imagination from the ends demanded by the biological pattern. On the other hand, it frees the intelligence from the rigors of the laboratory or the practicality of common sense. The insights of the artist in the aesthetic pattern find their expression in symbols.

Through symbols the artist invites others to share an experience of liberation. Art is not only an objectification of the purely experiential pattern of living but a "reenactment of the artist's inspiration and intention."[94] The art critic attempts to interpret the symbols by appeal to canons of color and form, pitch and tempo, rhyme and meter, but the symbol's obscurity and its meaning may escape the critic's grasp. The obscurity of symbols invites participation rather than objectification and analysis. For example, a Mark Rothko canvas will not dazzle the eye but may evoke a range of feelings, from terror to joy. Rothko wanted to draw the viewer into the work of art itself and confront the viewer with himself or herself.[95] Perhaps more ger-

---

[93] Ibid., 207.

[94] Ibid., 208.

[95] See especially the Rothko Chapel in Houston, Texas; images available at www .rothkochapel.org. Sheldon Nodelman describes the chapel's effect: "The work seems to afford no point of imaginative entry; instead the frustrated viewer is thrown back upon himself or herself. . . . The rejection of recognizable images and of the customary avenues of psychological engagement is accompanied for the viewer by a troubling sense of exposure." *The Rothko Chapel Paintings: Origins, Structure, Meaning* (Austin: University of Texas Press, 1997), 297–98. Rothko shared something of Lonergan's insight into the aesthetic pattern and the role of the artist in the creation of symbols. He was famously critical of the mutually destructive relationship of professional artists and critics that robs the work of art of its symbolic obscurity by reducing art to categories like formalist, colorist, and abstract expressivist. See James E. B. Breslin, *Mark Rothko: A Biography* (Chicago: University of Chicago Press, 1998).

mane to our inquiry is the example of the Christian icon. If the obscurity of the symbolic is what prevents its being explained (away) by the critic, the icon, like the best of contemporary art, resists. The level of abstraction in Eastern Christian iconography can strike the Western critic schooled in the canons of renaissance realism as cartoonish. Icons are restricted to a two-dimensional plane; the perspective is off, the light and shadow are confused. Indeed, it is not uncommon for Western art historians to suggest that Byzantine iconography is merely a phase on the path toward realism. The icon represents a technical problem in the canonical art-historical narrative of the evolution of technique. This interpretation is not even false; it simply misses the point, as would analyzing eucharistic bread according to the techniques of Parisian baguette baking. The composition and style of the iconographic tradition is not for the purpose of portraiture, but to convey meaning, and those meanings evoke feelings, hopefully the desire to pray or worship; in fact, the abstraction *preserves* the symbolic element that invites the viewer to encounter the person depicted in the image, not the image itself.

It is significant that Lonergan recalls us to this basic experience of the symbolic in art, and to the role of the symbol in human meaning. It is prior to critical objectification because it is an invitation to participation. He notes that the very obscurity of art is its most generic meaning because it corresponds to the pure question, the "deep-set wonder" which is the source and ground of human questioning.[96] He writes: "As an expression of the subject, art would show forth that wonder in its elemental sweep. Again, as a twofold liberation of sense and intelligence, art would exhibit the reality of the primary object for that wonder."[97] What, we may ask, is that primary object? At the risk of getting ahead of ourselves, we may say that it is being in its totality. But before we can arrive at a notion of being we must complete our analysis of the polymorphism of human consciousness.

c. The Intellectual Pattern of Experience

Aesthetic liberation prepares and opens the way for the intellectual pattern of experience. The displacement away from the biological pattern

---

[96] Lonergan, *Insight*, 208.
[97] Ibid.

enacted by the free play of images in the creative exploration of aesthetic experience becomes a "ready tool for the spirit of inquiry."[98] The intellectual pattern of experience needs aesthetic liberation and the free creation of images in order to generate phantasms that enable insights. But in the intellectual pattern the images come under the control of the desire to know, the spirit of inquiry. The scientist need not be an artist, but the scientist employs images in order to gain an insight into the relationships between data. The overriding concern of the intellectual pattern is understanding. Therefore in the intellectual pattern the subject forgets biological concerns and refines the free flow of images in order to move beyond the symbolic obscurity of aesthetic liberation to acquire an explanatory understanding of the thing in question. For example, in the biological pattern a bison offers sustenance, and consciousness is ordered toward capturing it; in the aesthetic pattern it is a thing of beauty and strength to be represented in symbols, even celebrated in myths and rituals as a source of life for the community. But in the intellectual pattern the bison is a zoologically defined species bearing particular genetic markers. In this pattern questions are ordered toward understanding, so that what is irrelevant to explanatory understanding is set aside and what is germane leaps forward. But the intellectual pattern is neither a pure state nor a permanent achievement. Again, even scientists leave the lab and exist in a far larger world. That larger world is dominated by the drama of human living.

d. The Dramatic Pattern of Experience

The dramatic pattern is ordinary human living, which is not dominated by biological purposiveness, artistic play, or intellectual rigor. In the dramatic pattern questions are ordered toward dealing with others and getting things done.[99] The three previous patterns are sublated into the everyday drama of human living. Try as we might, we cannot escape our animality, so the biological pattern remains, but our biological striving is subsumed and transformed in the aesthetic pattern—sustenance becomes cuisine, clothing becomes fashion, shelter becomes interior design, sex becomes romance. The aesthetic pattern generates a range of images of the self that become

[98] Ibid., 209.
[99] Ibid., 210.

incarnate in the drama of living. Lonergan notes that not only is "man capable of aesthetic liberation and artistic creativity, but his first work of art is his own living."[100] Because the human being is a social animal its living is not isolated, and its artistry is never wholly original. The dramatic pattern refers us to the fact that human living is "limited by biological exigence, inspired by example and emulation, confirmed by admiration and approval, sustained by respect and affection."[101] By following the example of others and seeking (often preconsciously) their approval, we become part of a culture. Cultures are shaped by the approval and reprobation that limit the range of innovation except among the courageous, the prophets. The unfolding drama draws the individual through the plasticity of childhood and the experimentation of adolescence to the formation of adult personality that results from our deliberation and decisions.[102] And yet we are not perfectly free because "our past behavior determines our present habitual attitudes; nor is there any appreciable effect from our present good resolutions upon our future spontaneity."[103] The drama of human living does not follow a script, but it is radically conditioned by family, religion, culture, and the approval and reprobation that issue from these institutions.

e. Dramatic Bias and Scotosis

We do not merely fulfill roles, acquiring the motivations and emotions to successfully build a character. Rather, all our conscious intending is already informed by feelings and desires mediated by a culture. Abstractions like "soul" and "human nature" often omit this fact of human historicity. If the goal of knowing is knowledge of what actually is the case in its particularity, then that knowing must occur in the concrete, and the concrete dramatic subject is exceedingly complex. While Lonergan argues that human intellect exhibits an unrestricted desire to know, this does not occur with the necessity of a mere abstraction. Lonergan is fully aware of the fact of the flight from understanding.

Recognizing that this is the case, Lonergan probes the dramatic subject and discovers the dynamic interplay of psychic and neural demands in the

---

[100] Ibid.
[101] Ibid., 211.
[102] Ibid., 212.
[103] Ibid.

formation of the images that in turn create the psychic conditions for the possibility of insight. But the flow of questions and images that emerges from the interplay of the psychic censor and neural demands is prone to disruption and disturbance, particularly by the phenomenon of dramatic bias. The wonder of youth expressed in the incessant questioning of the toddler does not necessarily endure, because in addition to the desire to know, expressed in human questions, we also find the flight from understanding. The full ramifications of dramatic bias reveal that without rigorous attention to psychological fact, philosophy would be reduced to irrelevant rationalism. Lonergan traces the problem of dramatic bias this way:

> To exclude an insight is also to exclude the further questions that would arise from it, and the complementary insights that would carry it towards a rounded and balanced viewpoint. To lack that fuller view results in behavior that generates misunderstanding both in ourselves and in others. To suffer such incomprehension favors a withdrawal from the outer drama of human living into the inner drama of fantasy. This introversion, which overcomes the extroversion native to the biological pattern of experience, generates a differentiation of the persona that appears before others and the more intimate ego that in the daydream is at once the main actor and the sole spectator. Finally, the incomprehension, isolation, and duality rob the development of one's common sense of some part, greater or less, of the corrections and the assurance that result from learning accurately the tested insights of others and from submitting one's own insights to the criticism based on others' experience and development.[104]

Lonergan calls this aberration of understanding a *scotosis* and the resulting blind spot a *scotoma*.[105] We may be familiar with the solipsism of the adolescent who finds no point in learning and nothing to be learned from others. This might be a mere developmental curiosity were it not for the fact that so many people throughout their lives revert to this adolescent posture toward the world. Dramatic bias impedes the dynamism of our conscious intending with a preemptive refusal of possible understanding or the paranoid world of conspiracy.

---

[104] Ibid., 214–15.
[105] Ibid., 215.

Dramatic bias is not merely a momentary lapse in what is otherwise a life ordered toward increasing understanding. It indicates a habitual orientation that not only resists questioning but rationalizes its refusal to ask questions. Questions prompt the imagination to consider the possibilities and to form images into which we might gain some insight, but the preemptive assessment that there is nothing to understand stifles the questions, leading to scotosis. Further, insight occurs in relation to images or phantasms. The liberation of the aesthetic pattern enables the free creation of images in an intellect released from biological ends, but these images are obscure. In inquiring, the intellectual pattern refines the image, focusing only on those aspects that pertain to the question at hand, as we noted in the example of the cartwheel. Questions stimulate the formation of images. The emergence, or failure of emergence, of images conditions the possibility of insight and therefore of knowing. Scotosis, therefore, cuts the process off at the root. And when, in the total range of eventualities, contrary insights emerge, scotosis refuses the further questions or brushes aside the contrary insight in an "emotional reaction of distaste, pride, dread, horror, revulsion."[106] Scotosis reinforces itself through a rationalization of its refusal to question by declaring the meaninglessness of experience.[107]

From this account of the "subjective field" of common sense vis-à-vis the various patterns of experience that account for the polymorphism of human consciousness, Lonergan proceeds to consider the "objective field" of the commonsense world and expands his exploration of the biases that lead to disorders in the objective situation that, in terms of probability, he calls cycles of decline. Biases, both our own and those of others, distort situations to such a degree that they cast a pall of unreality over our capacity to understand and judge reality in order to decide and act.

2.4. Culture and Bias: The Objective Field

The objective field of common sense refers to the reality in which we live as human beings. It is not, as postmodern theorists have clarified, a state of

---

[106] Ibid.

[107] Lonergan expands at this point to treat the psychological problems of repression and inhibition in human performance. These issues are explored further in Robert M. Doran, *Subject and Psyche: Ricoeur, Jung and the Search for Foundations* (Lanham, MD: University Press of America, 1977); Doran, *Psychic Conversion and Theological Foundations* (Milwaukee: Marquette University Press, 2006); see also Doran, "Psychic Conversion," *The Thomist* 41 (April 1977): 200–236.

pure nature. The development of the objective field is a process that involves changes not only in the objective situation but in subjects as well. Just as an individual incorporates the commonsense insights of the culture into which he or she is educated, so also cultures change, new insights and courses of action emerge, and with them new possibilities for the subject. To clarify the changing situation into which human subjects emerge, Lonergan undertakes a brief explanation of human historical development according to his notion of emergent probability.[108] However, unlike the physical universe, the human world is not merely moved but moves itself under the influence of good ideas and the failures of the past. History is marked by both progress and decline, each of which increases the probability of further progress or decline. In addition, the movements of progress and decline are mixed. A technologically advanced society may exhibit great progress and decline at once: it may be able to prolong human life but know not to what end; it might treat bodily disease with great success even while generating a variety of psychic disorders; it might open lines of rapid communication across the globe, at the same time inciting economic competition and rivalry. All human cultures exhibit the dialectic of progress and decline. For Lonergan the source of decline is a human bias that originates in a shift away from the spontaneous intersubjectivity that lies at the base of community and society and toward the solipsism that breaks the bonds of community.

There is the *individual bias* of the egoist who, though his intellect is operative, restricts his line of questioning to match his own concerns. He is not wholly ignorant of the further questions that would bring his self-centered choosing under scrutiny, but he rationalizes his behavior due to the immediacy of practical concerns. While the egoist may distort the role of spontaneous intersubjectivity in a quest for some advantage over others, groups can manipulate such intersubjectivity in order to privilege their members over those of other groups. *Group bias* distorts intersubjective spontaneities by restricting their range to the interests of the members of the group. As groups compete for advantages within the social order, the order itself becomes distorted. Classes emerge as one group's economic ad-

---

[108] Lonergan's theory of emergent probability accounts for the emergence and survival of different schemes of recurrence that allow for the development of increasingly complex life forms in biological evolution, but it also illuminates the evolution and breakdowns of human history as well as individual biographies.

vantage leads to the others' disadvantage. But "just as the individual egoist puts further questions up to a point, but desists before reaching conclusions incompatible with his egoism, so also the group is prone to have a blind spot for the insights that reveal its well-being to be excessive or its usefulness at an end."[109] Over time this arrangement becomes normative, until "deep feelings of frustration, resentment, bitterness, and hatred" issue in calls for revolution.[110] A new group can take control, yet the distortion in the social fabric remains. Political power becomes merely a tool for implementing biased versions of reality. The distortions of both individual and group bias are further exacerbated by the pervasive influence of *general bias*.

General bias rests on a belief in the omnicompetence of common sense. While common sense can be a specialized and often sophisticated mode of understanding things in relation to us, it is prone to overstating its claims and consequently abetting decline. Common sense tends to seek practical solutions to current problems without concern for the long-term ramifications. It wants results. Consequently, detailed theoretical analysis of potentially harmful courses of action is dismissed as impractical. Likewise, science is frequently ridiculed because it often contradicts the obvious evidence of common sense. But the general bias of common sense has vast implications because its broad influence reinforces a longer cycle of decline. Lonergan describes general bias in terms of what he calls the social surd. It is akin to what is now commonly called *structural* sin.[111] Reinforcing the consequences of the longer cycle of decline, Lonergan notes, are the distorted social situations and the complicity of religion and philosophy in decline: "Culture retreats into an ivory tower. Religion becomes an inward affair of the heart. Philosophy glitters like a gem with endless facets and no practical

---

[109] Lonergan, *Insight*, 248.

[110] Ibid., 249.

[111] The idea of social or structural sin is emphasized by theologies of liberation and political theologies. See, for example, Gustavo Gutiérrez, *A Theology of Liberation: History, Politics, Salvation*, trans. Caridad Inda and John Eagleson (Maryknoll, NY: Orbis Books, 1988), 103; Jose Ignacio Gonzalez Faus, "Sin," 536–39, in *Mysterium Liberationis: Fundamental Concepts of Liberation Theology*, ed. Ignacio Ellacuría and Jon Sobrino (Maryknoll, NY: Orbis Books, 1993); Dorothee Soelle, *Political Theology*, trans. John Shelley (Philadelphia: Fortress Press, 1974), 83ff. The terminology is included in the regular *magisterium* of the Catholic Church in the encyclicals of John Paul II, *Solicitudo Rei Socialis* (37) and *Evangelium Vitae* (59).

purpose."[112] The relegation of detached and disinterested inquiry to the status of a relic spells the collapse of a culture.

By its restriction of thought to the realm of the practical, general bias creates new forms of culture, religion, and philosophy. But the new form "is not apriorist, wishful thinking. It is empirical, scientific, realistic. It takes its stand on things as they are. In brief, its many excellences cover its single defect. For its rejection of the normative significance of detached and disinterested intelligence makes it radically uncritical."[113] Lonergan's concern is that a great deal of contemporary philosophy, theology, and social science has failed to account sufficiently for the human being. Lonergan traces the historical transformations shaped by general bias:

> The wars of religion provided the evidence that man has to live not by revelation but by reason. The disagreement of reason's representatives made it clear that, while each must follow the dictates of reason as he sees them, he also must practice the virtue of tolerance to the equally reasonable views and actions of others. The helplessness of tolerance to provide coherent solutions to social problems called forth the totalitarian, who takes the narrow and complacent practicality of common sense and elevates it to the role of a complete and exclusive viewpoint. On the totalitarian view every type of intellectual independence, whether personal, cultural, scientific, philosophic, or religious, has no better basis than nonconscious myth. The time has come for the conscious myth that will secure man's total subordination to the requirements of reality. Reality is the economic development, the military equipment, and the political dominance of the all-inclusive state. Its ends justify all means. . . . The succession of less comprehensive viewpoints has been a succession of adaptations of theory to practice. In the limit, practice becomes a theoretically unified whole, and theory is reduced to the status of a myth that lingers on to represent the frustrated aspirations of detached and disinterested intelligence.[114]

At the center of Lonergan's project is nothing less than a struggle against the totalitarian nightmare of the longer cycle of decline. The theoretical orientation of detached and disinterested intelligence is the only check

---

[112] Lonergan, *Insight*, 254.
[113] Ibid., 255.
[114] Ibid., 256–57.

against the totalizing machinations of commonsense practicality. But what does this mean for cognitional theory?

Lonergan's point is that the context within which human beings negotiate the innate desire to know is a complex dialectic of both individual and social variables, including distinct patterns of experience and biases. The cultural current often runs against the free play of disinterested and detached inquiry, yet only such inquiry is sufficiently critical to unmask the biases that lie at the base of the distorted social situation. As this survey of the subjective and objective fields of common sense shows, Lonergan's cognitional theory does not fail to acknowledge the complexity and facticity of the subject. Therefore his account of history as grounding his philosophy does not shrink from the complexities either of human psychic performance or the culturally mediated worlds in which knowing occurs. Fully aware of the culturally and linguistically mediated horizon emphasized by postmodern thought, Lonergan offers a realistic assessment of the situation while remaining convinced that, despite all the complexity of human experience, people do in fact have experiences of understanding and judgment, so that if one is attentive to one's conscious operations one can identify the components of a generalized empirical method. Exploring the subjective and objective fields of common sense highlights the dialectic that affects a generalized empirical method's tense experience of the exigencies of the pure desire to know in the face of the concrete circumstances, both individual and social, within which that desire unfolds.

2.5. Summary

This survey of the fundamentals of Lonergan's cognitional theory began from a consideration of the desire common to human beings to know, as manifested in the native wonder that asks questions about things: "What is it? Why does this happen? What does it mean?" and so on. He identifies the experience of insight that reveals the advent of understanding at least a portion of the intelligibility in the data of experience. Insights enable us to formulate our understanding in definitions and concepts that in turn call forth the critical awareness that asks, "Is it so?" Reflective insights reveal either the sufficiency or insufficiency of the evidence and drive us to affirm or deny the correctness of our understanding in judgments. Otherwise the lack of evidence for affirmative judgment sends us back to inquiry, to discover another possibly relevant intelligibility in the data of experience.

Crucially, knowing does not occur in a vacuum. Human intelligence moves in a variety of patterns that bring different phenomena into our focal awareness in different ways. The fact that we move in different patterns as we engage the world around us reveals the polymorphism of human consciousness. Knowing is not a single, obvious, incorrigible intuition but a process that moves from the "blooming, buzzing confusion" of the infant's world of immediacy into a world that is already linguistically and culturally constructed—a world mediated by meaning. The larger world mediated by meaning, what we normally mean by the "real world," is not of our own making. It is a concrete historical reality that our desire to know encounters. It already includes any number of ready-made answers that constitute the common sense of the culture. Consequently, if we are to know anything beyond the conventions of our culture, if we are to face the Socratic question whether the opinions of our culture actually explain the truth of things, and to move with John Henry Cardinal Newman *ex umbris et imaginibus in veritatem*,[115] then we have to understand correctly what it means to understand in order to be sufficiently critical, and in order to attain the real as real beyond cultural convention.[116] Our consideration of the polymorphism of human consciousness and the biases that attend the objective field of common sense reveals both the dialectic of the dramatic subject and the dialectic of community that affect the conditions for the possibility of human knowing. Again, in a clear-eyed and critical account Lonergan explains both the experience of the desire to know and the failure of knowing for a number of reasons, whether psychological or cultural. Whatever the obstacles, in fact we do know things by having insights, formulating them in definitions, testing them, and judging that we have understood correctly.

3. Things and Bodies:
Terminological Disputes and the Objects of Knowing

I have not yet explained what Lonergan means by "things." We have discussed "things in themselves" and "things for us," but what are these

---

[115] See "Cognitional Structure," 219.

[116] This is not to suggest that the experience of the real can be had outside of the world mediated by meaning into which we are thrust. There is no neutral position from which we can know the real. The postmodern thinker's desire to remind us of this fact is strong medicine. Nevertheless, Lonergan hopes to convey that generalized empirical method represents a transcultural base on which a shared understanding can be had without first defining and agreeing on abstract, logical premises.

things? "Thing" refers to a unity, identity, whole in data that is grasped by attending to concreteness and totality, not by abstraction.[117] Lonergan uses the example of a dog to illustrate his meaning: "To say that Fido is black or that he is a nuisance is to conceive both a unity in a totality of aspects and some aspect out of the totality, and then to attribute the latter to the former."[118] Fido is a thing, whether black, a nuisance, thirty pounds, five years old, a Schnauzer, or housebroken. Each of these data pertains to the thing called Fido.

Lonergan explains that sensible things are "extended in space, permanent in time, and yet subject to change."[119] When we are dealing with things, spatially distinct data that pertain to the same unity may change from moment to moment. Lonergan clarifies his meaning by explaining attribution. Explanatory or theoretical or even descriptive (commonsense) understanding abstracts an intelligibility that it formulates in universal terms from experiential or explanatory "conjugates."[120] The problem with abstracting in this way is that our predication frequently reduces the subject to the predicate by means of the copula in such a way that we easily forget that what is predicated is only a single aspect of a multifaceted whole. The thing is the unity that bears all the related characteristics, what Lonergan calls either experiential or explanatory conjugates.[121]

---

[117] See Lonergan, Insight, 270–71. Recall that Heidegger's critique of the horizon of *Vorhandenheit* was partially aimed at the failure to consider things in their wholeness, hence his later elaboration of the "fourfold" as an attempt to think things in all their dimensions: human, historic, cosmic, and divine. Lonergan's notion of the thing takes this original wholeness in things seriously without making science a villain.

[118] Lonergan, *Insight*, 272.

[119] Ibid., 271.

[120] Lonergan uses the term "conjugates" where scholastic language uses "accidents" or "properties." "Conjugates" expresses more clearly to the contemporary reader that these data inhere in a particular way in things; they are not mere ephemera or phenomena, as the connotations of "accidents" and "properties" may suggest. See the discussion of the elements of metaphysics below, 113–17.

[121] Earlier in *Insight* Lonergan established a distinction between experiential conjugates and explanatory conjugates. He explains: "Experiential conjugates are correlatives whose meaning is expressed, at least in the last analysis by appealing to the content of some human experience" (p. 102). Experiential conjugates relate to the senses; they are first for us. Explanatory conjugates relate things to each other. They are "correlatives defined implicitly by empirically established correlations, functions, laws, theories, systems" (p. 103). So temperature as felt is an experiential conjugate. Temperature as defined is an explanatory conjugate. Both refer to data, and both pertain to things. Something

Lonergan contrasts his notion of a thing with what we normally think of when we imagine knowing as taking a look; this he calls a "body." By "body" Lonergan means primarily "a focal point of extroverted biological anticipation and attention."[122] By including the term "biological" here he refers us back to the biological pattern of experience in which our experiencing is oriented toward what satisfies a need or desire. He offers an explanatory definition that elaborates on the analogy with the biological pattern. A body is an *already-out-there-now-real.*

> "Already" refers to the orientation and dynamic anticipation of bio-
> logical consciousness; such consciousness does not create but finds
> its environment; it finds it as already constituted, already offering op-
> portunities, already issuing challenges. "Out" refers to the extroversion
> of a consciousness that is aware, not of its own ground, but of objects
> distinct from itself. "There" and "now" indicate the spatial and temporal
> determinations of extroverted consciousness. "Real," finally, is a sub-
> division within the field of the "already out there now."[123]

In other words, the contrast between "thing" and "body" highlights the fact that "not a few men mean by 'thing' or 'body,' not simply an intelligible unity grasped in data as individual, but also an already out there now real which is as accessible to human animals as to kittens."[124]

---

feels warm or cold or maintains a certain temperature, but there is not just warm and cold or degrees Fahrenheit; conjugates inhere in things.

[122] Ibid., 279. Lonergan's terminology here may be a bit jarring to the reader informed by the positive connotations of "embodiment" and the negative connotations of "reification" as these terms are often used in contemporary, especially postmodern, discourse. In our discussion of the elements of metaphysics below, the meaning of these terms will come into greater relief so that the ambiguity is sorted out through the use of more explanatory terms.

[123] Ibid., 276–77.

[124] Ibid., 277. Lonergan adduces some historical examples of thinking of the real in terms of the "already out there now real" to clarify his meaning: "When Galileo pronounced secondary qualities to be merely subjective, he meant that they were not 'already out there now real.' When the decadent Aristotelians and, generally, people that tend to rely on good common sense insist that secondary qualities obviously are objective, they mean that they are 'already out there now real.' When Descartes maintained that material substance must be identical with spatial extension, his material substance was the 'already out there now real.' When Kant argued that primary and secondary qualities

Because of our heavy reliance on the senses we are prone to accept a notion of the real as an object of extroverted biological anticipation. Put more simply, we are prone to picture thinking. The ocular metaphor for knowing is the basic counterposition Lonergan overcomes by elaborating a cognitional theory in accord with the facts of human knowing. His position is that the real emerges through a process of questioning that unfolds on the levels of experiencing and understanding and is known in a judgment.[125]

Picture thinking reduces reality to the level of sense experience. Because questions do not figure into the genesis of this way of knowing, it is not only unquestioned but unquestionable. There is no moment in the process when one might ask "how did you come to this conclusion?" because there has been no process. One simply looks, and what one sees is known.[126] For Lonergan, however, experience is merely the first step in knowing reality, supplying the data about which we ask questions. Answering the question is what constitutes knowing. This approach to knowing is both self-critical and open to criticism. One can ask about it: "what questions did you ask?" in order to determine whether additional relevant questions or data were taken into account by the hypothesis. The point is to draw a critical distinction, because often enough we move between picture thinking and knowledge by verification without adverting to it. In philosophy, failing to advert to the experience of knowing that moves through experiencing and understanding to judgment has the result that many philosophers think about knowing in terms of an ocular metaphor.

Distinguishing the two types of knowing allows Lonergan to embrace the paradigm shift of modern science. Thinking of knowing in terms of looking cannot account either for the verified correlations that pertain to a thing or for the diverse specializations of science that seek intelligible and verified correlations in different data. There has emerged a succession of scientific viewpoints wherein the higher viewpoints explain the lower but not vice versa. Lonergan's account of classical, statistical, genetic, and dialectical methods in the empirical sciences can heuristically explain the

---

are merely phenomenal, he meant that for him the reality of the 'already out there now real' was mere appearance" (p. 277).

[125] Ibid.

[126] This applies whether the objects of one's gaze are "things themselves," phenomena, or concepts.

divisions among the sciences in their synthetic and hierarchical orderings: thus the "laws of physics hold for subatomic elements; the laws of physics and chemistry hold for chemical elements and compounds; the laws of physics, chemistry, and biology hold for plants; the laws of physics, chemistry, biology, and sensitive psychology hold for animals; the laws of physics, chemistry, biology, sensitive psychology, and rational psychology hold for men."[127] Each of the fields has its own sets of laws that, though they continue to function in the other disciplines, cannot offer a fully explanatory account of each successive higher ordering of things.

For example, one could follow a mechanist or determinist position in arguing that human psychology can be reduced to electro-chemical events in the brain but not be able to explain the confluence of particular electro-chemical events into regular patterns that unfold in accordance with certain stimuli. A mechanist can show that experiences of fear cause a particular area of the brain to "light up" or glands to secrete a particular hormone but be unable to explain why one person reacts fearfully to a particular stimulus while another finds the same stimulus innocuous, because that is the task of the psychologist. The sensitive psychologist then can predict a dog's reaction by associating the ringing of a bell with food but would be utterly surprised if the dog objected, "why do you keep ringing that bell, when you have no food?!" A rational psychologist deals with how human animals ask and answer questions and how they know things. As regards the distinction between chemistry and biology, if a chemist can explain why certain reactions take place but be unable to explain, using the same methodology, why a particular chemical reaction recurs regularly within a particular type of cell, it is because that is the task of the cell biologist, who is called on to explain cell behavior.

However, the higher orders do not interfere with the functioning of the lower orders. Oxygen does not cease to be oxygen when inhaled into the lungs of an animal. The oxygen molecule is still very much oxygen, and without it the animal would suffocate. But the oxygen molecule as inhaled into the lungs becomes part of a highly organized and delicate system that

---

[127] Ibid., 280–81. Lonergan's distinction between sensitive and rational psychology relates to his distinctions of both the biological and intellectual patterns of experience as well as the distinctions between things and bodies. Rational psychology pertains only to human beings because only human beings know things in the sense defined by Lonergan.

is no longer explainable in terms of the chemistry that was capable of defining the oxygen molecule. The higher-order thing can sublate lower orders of being into a higher, perhaps larger, synthetic system. The lower-order thing is not destroyed when it is inserted into a higher order of intelligibility or a higher genus. That lower-order things can be found in the higher might lead to the objection that the higher is really only an aggregate of its lower-order constituents. But there are "no things within things."[128] Thinking in terms of images might well lead one to the opposite conclusion, but in Lonergan's understanding of "things" the totality of the data can only pertain to one thing. Why?

The distinction between things and bodies helps to clarify why. Frequently people's use of the word "things" to refer to what are really bodies, or the *already-out-there-now-real*, suggests that looking at a thing (rather than understanding a unity, identity, whole) is to see an agglomeration of bodies. Recall Fido. He has various characteristics that, put together in a particular fashion, make him to be *this* dog, a particular breed of the genus canine. When we look at him or imagine him we see parts—fur, teeth, ears, tail, eyes, nose, paws—and if we could look inside we would see muscles, bones, blood vessels, bacteria, cells, chemicals. These each appear to be things, which remain themselves even when functioning together as Fido. Before they are put together according to a particular pattern they are just more-or-less-complex parts. We can imagine them separately, so we might think of the dog as something composed of other things. But fur, teeth, ears, muscles, cells, etc., taken separately are not a dog. A specific relationship of the parts to each other must obtain in order for there to be a dog; otherwise we might have any number of mammals composed of similar parts. The parts participate in the larger unity that is Fido. They are still parts, but they are not a dog. Lonergan's point here has dramatic consequences for how we begin to think through eucharistic doctrines, a point to which we will turn below.[129] For the moment it will be helpful to summarize our inquiry into Lonergan's methodology up to this point.

[128] Ibid., 283.

[129] Certain interpretations of eucharistic doctrines fall into treating eucharistic presence as a "body" in Lonergan's sense. The confusion is played out over the meaning of the word "substance." For example, Karl Rahner argues that since the scholastic meaning of substance is obscured by the more popular understanding "one can only regard a morsel of bread as an agglomeration of substances and we do not know in which elementary

4. Summary

In the preceding sections we have discovered the unrestricted desire to know that is the origin of human questioning: the wonder that draws us into the world to understand, judge it correctly, make decisions about it, and take action. We explored the experience of insight that partially fulfills our desire to know. We explained the shift from insight to definition and showed how intelligence unfolds in operations of understanding, conceptual definition, and judging the sufficiency or insufficiency of the evidence to verify our proposed understanding. But the question arose as to whether our knowing really works as the simple example of a circle would have us believe. We examined the polymorphism of human consciousness through an analysis of patterns of experience and also investigated the historicity of the subject, demonstrating the complexity of the psychological and cultural mediation of human experience. Subsequently we showed how two distinct views of knowledge correlate with the distinction between "body" as an *already-out-there-now-real* and Lonergan's notion of a "thing" as a unity, identity, whole.

For Lonergan human knowing is a process that begins with questions, pivots on insight into phantasm, proposes definitions, and inquires into the sufficiency of the evidence. It is a cognitional theory that is verifiable in experience. In addition, Lonergan's elaboration of the subjective and objective fields of common sense recognizes that human knowing can be fraught with difficulty. Not only does the subjective field operate in a variety of patterns within which humans experience their world, but the objective social reality is distorted by dramatic, individual, group, and general biases that are reinforced by cultural decline. If one might get the impression that

---

particles the notion of substance is verified." This is because "the substance of bread as envisaged by St. Thomas and the Fathers of the Council—envisaged, not defined—does not exist" (Karl Rahner, "The Presence of Christ in the Sacrament of the Lord's Supper," 287–311, in his *Theological Investigations IV*, trans. Kevin Smyth (Baltimore: Helicon, 1966), at 307–8). Rahner is employing an image of substance as a "body" such that bread can be called an agglomeration of substances. Properly speaking, substances are unities, not agglomerations, let alone agglomerations of other substances. Rahner can deny the notion of substance employed by Thomas and Trent only because he falls into thinking of the real as a metaphysical essence grasped by intuition. For Rahner what is intuited is the symbolic presence of Christ in the Eucharist. By "symbol" Rahner does not mean "not-real" but precisely a *Realsymbol*. The problem lies in whether such a reality can be affirmed to exist. More on that later.

Lonergan is a modern rationalist, his assessment of psychological and historical fact shows the critical edge of his thinking. His critique of the *already-out-there-now-real* has led people to wonder whether he is an idealist, but his notion of "things" returns to the concrete. The further question that needs answering is the epistemological question: why is doing that knowing? Is what Lonergan has had to say about human knowing true? These questions lead us to the matters of judgment and objectivity and serve as a transition to Lonergan's exploration of metaphysics.

Chapter Three

Knowing and Being
Lonergan's Critically Grounded Metaphysics

In the preceding chapter we provided a basic outline of Lonergan's theory of cognition and indicated his emphasis on the facticity of human knowing. We are knowers, but in a context replete with obstacles to knowing. Our intending is infinite but our knowing is finite. While the previous chapter focused primarily on conscious operations, this one will relate the activities of intelligence to intelligible reality. We begin by considering Lonergan's account of reflective understanding as the level where knowing takes place. Then we turn to what is known. Having established that we do in fact know reality, we will offer a presentation of critical-realist metaphysics in terms of its methods and elements. Finally, we will examine causality.

1. Lonergan's Epistemology: Performative Verification

We have posed the question about knowing: What are we doing when we are knowing? We have described knowing as a process that begins with wonder and is directed by questions. That process unfolds on the levels of experiencing, understanding, and judging, which are connected by questions. The simplest way to answer the question whether what Lonergan has had to say about knowing is true is to ask it for ourselves. By asking, we are moving to the level of judgment in order to test Lonergan's hypothesis: regarding this cognitional theory, is it so? The question itself reveals that, once intelligence is satisfied by insight and formulation, knowing heads toward the third level, that of reasonableness, the level of assessing the evidence and of judgment. There is, as Lonergan puts it, an ulterior motive in conceiving and defining, or forming hypotheses.[1] These activities of thinking call forth the question for knowing: "Is it so?" We really want to know whether we have understood correctly. "Can I affirm that what I understand is true, or is it back to the drawing board?" Our answer takes the form of a judgment.

1.1. *Reflective Understanding and Judgment*

But the answer comes as a result of reflective understanding, which returns to the hypothesis and scrutinizes it in order to verify the sufficiency of the evidence for a judgment in the affirmative. If the evidence is lacking, a return to examining the data more closely and raising further questions for understanding is in order. Our knowledge of reality comes in the form of a judgment, but judgment "is the last act in the series that begins from presentations and advances through understanding and formulation ultimately to reach reflection and affirmation or denial."[2] As the last act in the series, judgment brings understanding to its term. Judgments are concerned with the real. Though we are not immune to the self-delusion of dramatic bias and the inherited, biased delusions of a distorted culture, the goal of detached and disinterested inquiry remains knowledge of the real.[3] By affirming what we have understood initially through the burst of insight and then formally in the process of defining, we claim to know reality, but only in an incremental way. A single judgment does not necessarily yield a total explanation.

A single judgment is a full increment in knowing that calls forth additional questions about what remains to be known. The incremental unfolding of our knowing reveals that pretending to total explanation does not square

---

[1] Bernard J. Lonergan, *Insight: A Study of Human Understanding*, ed. Frederick E. Crowe and Robert M. Doran (Toronto: University of Toronto Press, 1992), 298.

[2] Ibid., 301.

[3] See ibid., 293: "The attainment of the critical position means not merely that one distinguishes clearly between things and 'bodies' but also that one distinguishes between the different patterns of one's own experience and refuses to commit oneself intellectually unless one is operating within the intellectual pattern of experience." Frequently we are not so careful. As our exploration of the general bias of common sense shows, we frequently make judgments that have very little to do with reality because we are not operating in the intellectual pattern, with the result, for example, that one unseasonably cold day contradicts decades' worth of data in judging whether global warming is a verifiable phenomenon.

with the facts of human knowing: "For we can make but one judgment at a time, and one judgment cannot bring all we know into the full light of actual knowing."[4] Instead, Lonergan suggests that knowing is habitual or cumulative. What we know is not present to us all at once; even if it is with us somehow in memory, it remains in the background of tacit awareness.[5] Our task then is not to discover the whole by adding to what we imagine to be a vault of previous affirmations or a secure database of answers that we sometimes call experience; rather, Lonergan advocates "relentless devotion to the task of adding increments to a merely habitual knowledge."[6]

The further question about how judgment in fact occurs is answered by examining reflective understanding or insight into the virtually unconditioned. We can readily admit that people make judgments and commit themselves to any number of positions about reality, but what makes a judgment true? Lonergan returns to the experience of insight. In this case insight is experienced as a reflective act of understanding that leads to an affirmation or denial of the virtually unconditioned. Just as the experience of insight is something that occurs to one, so a judgment rests on a reflective insight in which the sufficiency of the evidence is apprehended by intelligence. What, precisely, is sufficient evidence?

Lonergan explains that the sufficient evidence for judging is the fulfillment of conditions expressed in the hypothesis or guess. Rather than supposing that judgments pertain to the universal and necessary, Lonergan is content to show the provisional character of judgment. Our knowledge is of something virtually unconditioned: a conditioned occurrence or reality whose conditions happen to be fulfilled. It is "virtually unconditioned" as opposed to "formally unconditioned." The formally unconditioned would

---

[4] Ibid., 303.

[5] Ibid. Imagine the utter confusion that would paradoxically result if everything you had ever learned were somehow simultaneously present. The idea is suggestive of the way Lonergan specifies both the divine and the experience of the beatific vision, i.e., knowledge of everything about everything.

[6] Ibid. Remembered judgments are certainly important, but not as a body of factoids in the memory bank that, like a computer, we can access with the appropriate input. Rather, there is built up "an organized set of complementary insights" (p. 311) that facilitate further insights. Cf. Augustine, *Confessions*, book 10, trans. Henry Chadwick (Oxford: Oxford University Press, 1998); also "*De Magistro* (The Teacher)," 69–101, in *Augustine: Earlier Writings*, ed. John H. S. Burleigh (Philadelphia: Westminster Press, 1953).

have no conditions whatever, because it grasps the whole in a single act.[7] The virtually unconditioned judgment involves three elements: "(1) a conditioned, (2) a link between the conditioned and its conditions, and (3) the fulfillment of the conditions."[8] The three elements of the virtually unconditioned judgment show the provisional character of judgment at the same time as they clarify the character of a reflective insight, which grasps both the conditions and the fulfillment of the conditions.

The next question is how we know whether an introspective or reflective insight is correct. Just as a direct insight into the data of sense or the data of consciousness awaits further clarification and definition in order to specify what was understood in the insight, so the reflective insight needs some further verification. Here, Lonergan introduces the notion of an "immanent law" in cognitional process, which reveals that a reflective insight is correct if there are no further pertinent questions.[9] Now, what is meant by "further pertinent questions"? Are these not simply *my* questions about a thing and therefore extremely limited for the reasons discussed in the previous chapter? Are not the pertinent further questions themselves conditioned by the context in which they are raised? Lonergan is well aware of this difficulty, and so he distinguishes between the mere absence of questions and the realization that no further pertinent questions apply.

Because of the polymorphism of human consciousness, the mere absence of questions may be attributable to a variety of circumstances. Lonergan notes the problem of rash judgment or refusal to ask further pertinent questions, on the one hand, and indecision or introducing further impertinent questions in order simply to put off judging, on the other.[10] How is a happy medium to be found? The polymorphism of human consciousness complicates the level of judging just as it does experiencing and understanding. Just as scotosis and bias inhibit the generation of images and insights, so rashness and timidity inhibit the affirmation of a virtually unconditioned. What is required is intellectual alertness, taking one's time, conversation,

---

[7] Lonergan identifies this formally unconditioned with God, which is the same as saying that God is "pure act" or is not in potency to some future act. This is because God is eternal and therefore has no before and after. This is significant for understanding secondary causality, as we will see below.

[8] Lonergan, *Insight*, 305.

[9] Ibid., 309.

[10] Ibid., 309–10.

and collaboration,[11] but also "good judgment" is built up through "the acquisition of an organized set of complementary insights," especially within a particular domain, so that "[w]e become familiar with concrete situations; we know what to expect; when the unexpected occurs, we can spot just what happened and why."[12] There is a habit of "good judgment" found among experts in a particular field. Equally important is the matter of temperament. Rashness and indecisiveness often go unnoticed by those who embody such characteristics: "The rash man continues to presume too quickly that he has nothing more to learn, and the indecisive man continues to suspect that deeper depths of shadowy possibilities threaten to invalidate what he knows quite well."[13] Temperament is a habitual orientation that requires careful scrutiny by every would-be knower, for judgment requires both the patience of detached and disinterested inquiry and a discernment of the relevant questions that restrict that inquiry and make judgment possible. Lonergan puts his cognitional theory into practice and tests his epistemology of the virtually unconditioned by asking simply, "am I a knower?"

1.2. Self-Affirmation of the Knower: Caught in the Act

As noted previously, Lonergan introduces *Insight* by urging the reader to a "personal, decisive act," and here he shows the full impact of that action. If what Lonergan has been saying about knowing is verifiable, it will find its basic fulfillment in anyone's judgment, "I am a knower," which he calls the "self-affirmation of the knower."[14] Lonergan breaks the affirmation into its component parts thus: "By the 'self' is meant a concrete and intelligible unity-identity-whole. By 'self-affirmation' is meant that the self both affirms and is affirmed. By 'self-affirmation of the knower' is meant that the self as affirmed is characterized by such occurrences as sensing, perceiving, imagining, inquiring, understanding, formulating, reflecting, grasping the unconditioned, and affirming."[15] For those who are suspicious of Descartes' *cogito ergo sum* this might appear to be a rerun of the misadventure of modern rationalism.[16] For Lonergan the problem with Cartesian

---

[11] Ibid., 310.

[12] Ibid., 311–12.

[13] Ibid., 312.

[14] Ibid., 343.

[15] Ibid.

[16] For a detailed analysis and critique of Descartes and the question of the metaphysical status of the subject, see Jean-Luc Marion's many studies, especially *Cartesian*

rationalism is not its attention to thinking but its pretense of necessity. He clarifies: "The affirmation to be made is a judgment of fact. It is not that I exist necessarily, but merely that in fact I do. It is not that I am of necessity a knower, but merely the fact that I am. It is not that an individual performing the listed acts really does know, but merely that I perform them and that by 'knowing' I mean no more than such performance."[17] Affirmation of the knower demands only that the knower affirms that he or she performs certain kinds of acts. The question is not "whether the knower knows himself, [but] solely whether he can perform the act of self-affirmation."[18] For Lonergan the meaning of "knower" is given in consciousness for anyone who pays attention to what he or she is doing when knowing.

Recall that consciousness is not an abstract category for Lonergan but an "awareness immanent in cognitional acts."[19] Cognitional acts, as we have seen, are of different kinds. Empirical consciousness is manifested in acts of sensing, perceiving, and imagining that pertain to the level of experience. Intelligent consciousness is characteristic of acts of inquiring, conceiving, and formulating that pertain to the level of understanding. Rational consciousness is characteristic of acts of reflecting, grasping the unconditioned, and judging that pertain to the level of judgment.[20] The emphasis is on the acts of consciousness rather than the contents of the acts. The contents depend on the particulars of a given experience into which we inquire, but the conscious acts that enable us to understand our experience are the universal human acts of intending we perform. By affirming that we ask and attempt to answer questions that pertain to the intelligent and rational levels of consciousness, we simply affirm that we know the difference between catching on and missing the point in relation to "what is it?" questions and "is it so?" questions. If I have experienced that difference I can also affirm that I am, in fact, a knower.

As a knower, I am like other objects of inquiry, a unity. Just as there are unities on the side of whatever objects happen to be known, because things

---

Questions: Method and Metaphysics, trans. Daniel Garber (Chicago: University of Chicago Press, 1999); Marion, *On Descartes' Metaphysical Prism: The Constitution and the Limits of Onto-theo-logy in Cartesian Thought*, trans. Jeffrey L. Kossky (Chicago: University of Chicago Press, 1999).

[17] Lonergan, *Insight*, 343.
[18] Ibid., 344.
[19] Ibid.
[20] Ibid., 346.

are properly understood as *unity-identity-wholes*, so consciousness reveals a unity.[21] There is a danger in talking about consciousness in terms of levels. It might be imagined that at one moment we could watch ourselves being intelligent as one thing, and at a different moment being rational as another thing. Normally, however, our experience of knowing is of the unity of consciousness. Until we begin to reflect on the questions that emerge in consciousness, our assumption of the ocular metaphor for knowledge may prevent us from thinking clearly about distinct acts in our knowing. The unity of consciousness is given in our experience. It is only when inquiring into it that we can begin properly to distinguish empirical, intelligent, and rational levels of activity. This analysis of consciousness does not make us *more* conscious, although we might describe it as a "heightening of consciousness,"[22] by which is meant paying closer attention to the data of consciousness in the sense of attending to its operations above and beyond its contents. Lonergan explicitly affirms consciousness as a given:

> Consciousness is given independently of its being formulated or affirmed. To formulate it does not make one more conscious, for the effect of formulation is to add to one's concepts. To affirm it does not make one more conscious, for the effect of affirmation is to add to one's judgments. Finally, as consciousness is not increased by affirming it, so it is not diminished by denying it, for the effect of denying it is to add to the list of one's judgments and not to subtract from the grounds on which judgments may be based.[23]

The givenness of consciousness is the condition for the possibility of any inquiry into the inner workings of thought and of self-affirmation.

---

[21] Ibid., 349.

[22] See Lonergan, "Existenz and Aggiornamento," 222–31 in *Collection*, CWBL 4, at 222, where he refers to the German idea of *Besinnung* or "becoming [reflectively] aware." See also Bernard J. Lonergan, *Method in Theology* (New York: Herder & Herder, 1972):

> So man is confronted with three basic questions: What am I doing when I am knowing? Why is doing that knowing? What do I know when I do it? With these questions one turns from the outer realms of common sense and theory to the appropriation of one's own interiority, one's subjectivity, one's operations, their structure, their norms, their potentialities. Such appropriation, in its technical expression, resembles theory. But in itself it is a heightening of intentional consciousness, an attending not merely to objects but also to the intending subject and his acts. (p. 83)

[23] Lonergan, *Insight*, 350.

Self-affirmation, then, is not a process of experiencing, formulating, and judging in the way we affirm the intelligibilities of things as *unity-identity-wholes*. Self-affirmation responds to the question for judgment, "am I a knower?" Already this is a question for judgment, to be either affirmed or denied. The "I" in question is the unity given in consciousness and partially fulfills the conditions for affirming that I am a knower, for I am conscious in asking the question. The answer is affirmative if I perform the conscious acts that are involved in knowing. So we ask further questions: Do I see, hear, taste, touch, and smell? Do I ask questions about my experience? Lonergan raises the further questions: "Do I try to understand, or is the distinction between intelligence and stupidity no more applicable to me than to a stone? Have I any experience of insight, or is the story of Archimedes as strange to me as the account of Plotinus's vision of the One? Do I conceive, think, consider, suppose, define, formulate, or is my talking like the talking of a parrot?"[24] If each individual has to answer these questions for herself or himself, the fact that the questions are asked, and the possibility of answering, "are themselves the sufficient reason for the affirmative answer."[25]

Again, it is *not necessary* that I know things or affirm myself as a knower in order to be human. It is simply the case that, as a rationally conscious being, I am a knower. Lonergan emphasizes the contingent character of consciousness: "I might not be, yet if I am, I am. I might be other than I am, yet in fact I am what I am."[26] There is a conditional necessity in Lonergan's formulation: it need not be the case that I am a knower, but in fact I am a knower. By affirming this I take responsibility for what I know, and for how I know things. Lonergan explains the normative nature of this affirmation:

> Am I a knower? The answer yes is coherent, for if I am a knower, I can know that fact. But the answer no is incoherent, for if I am not a knower, how could the question be raised and answered by me? No less, the hedging answer "I do not know" is incoherent. For if I know

[24] Ibid., 352.

[25] Ibid., 353.

[26] Ibid. Here, Lonergan echoes Newman's reasoning behind the illative sense: "I am what I am, or I am nothing. I cannot think, reflect or judge about my being, without starting from the very point which I aim at concluding." See John Henry Cardinal Newman, *An Essay in Aid of a Grammar of Assent* (Notre Dame, IN: University of Notre Dame Press, 1979, 2005), 272.

that I do not know, then I am a knower; and if I do not know that I do not know, then I should not answer.

Am I a knower? If I am not, then I know nothing. My only course is silence. My only course is not the excused and explained silence of the sceptic, but the complete silence of the animal that offers neither excuse nor explanation for its complacent absorption in merely sensitive routines. For if I know nothing, I do not know excuses for not knowing. If I know nothing, then I cannot know the explanation of my ignorance.[27]

Lonergan criticizes the skeptic for falling into contradiction by failing to advert to the fact that she or he is empirically, intelligently, and rationally conscious even in his or her skepticism. The spontaneous drive of human knowing involves the skeptic in this kind of conundrum. Intelligence is inescapable, even if one can use it irrationally. The desire to know erupts spontaneously in experience. It prompts us to wonder about phenomena and to ask, "what is it?" and to assemble phenomena into intelligible patterns. There is an inevitability about the spontaneous wonder of human questioning.[28] But questioning and direct insights aim toward knowing. Again, human wonder is oriented toward something. It seeks answers, wants them to be correct, and so moves toward judgment. The contingency of human knowledge cannot negate the fact of human knowing. Though we do not and cannot know everything about everything in a single judgment, we do know some things, and we can and do know that we are knowers.

The self-affirmation of the knower is a concrete judgment of fact that is contingent and yet serves as a foundation. For Lonergan there is no deeper or more secure foundation than this affirmation. To seek a deeper foundation "involves a vicious circle; for if one seeks such a foundation, one employs one's cognitional process; and the foundation to be reached will be no more secure than the inquiry utilized to reach it."[29]

---

[27] Lonergan, *Insight*, 353.

[28] Recall that Lonergan is not unaware of the problem of human historicity. His accounts of (1) the dramatic bias of the subject, (2) the individual and group biases that distort our knowing, and (3) the general bias of common sense in its pretension to omnicompetence explain the facticity of human questioning in all cultures. But his account of the self-affirmation of the knower shows that self-affirmation is an immanent law in human questioning.

[29] Lonergan, *Insight*, 356.

What is foundational for Lonergan is the *performance* of human know-ing, and the structure of this process is not open to any major revision, because any revision would necessarily involve one in investigation of new data, inquiry into its intelligibility, formulation of what is to be revised, and affirmation that a revision is in order. Simply, any revision would be another performance of what is already taken to be foundational.

The epistemology in *Insight* answers the question "why is doing that (experiencing, understanding, and judging) knowing?" It is based on the self-affirmation of the knower, recognizing the fact that "if any judgment of fact occurs, there must also be as well the occurrence of its conditions."[30] Lonergan explains that all judgments of fact involve the affirmation of some object while at the same time they implicate the subject that does the affirm-ing. Every judgment of fact entails a subject and an object, and the concrete *unity-identity-whole* that is the subject is also a thing. It is "defined by an internally related set of operations, and the relations may be experientially validated in the conscious and dynamic states (1) of inquiry leading from the given to insight, (2) of insight leading to formulation, (3) of reflection lead-ing from formulation to grasp of the unconditioned, and (4) of that grasp leading to affirmation or denial."[31] Therefore cognitional theory "reaches its thing-itself by understanding itself and affirming itself as concrete unity in a process that is conscious empirically, intelligently, and rationally."[32]

---

[30] Ibid., 362.

[31] Ibid.

[32] Ibid. At this point Lonergan distinguishes his position from Kantian analysis. While he avers that he has performed something similar to what Kant would call a transcen-dental deduction, he contends that his yields rather different results. Lonergan outlines five differences from Kantian analysis: (1) Kant inquired into the *a priori* conditions for knowing an object, while Lonergan begins with the possible occurrence of a judgment of fact. (2) Kant distinguished between the thing-for-us and the thing-itself, or phenomenon from noumenon, so that he could restrict our "access" to the thing itself by focusing solely on the phenomenal, but Lonergan proposes a thing as a *unity-identity-whole* that is given and that, when described, is a thing-for-us, and when explained is a thing-itself. (3) Kant's concern for universal and necessary judgments takes a back seat to Lonergan's emphasis on judgments of fact. (4) While Kant formulates the ground of judgment by proposing categories to be fulfilled, for Lonergan judgment is self-authenticating because once one grasps the virtually unconditioned one is compelled by reason to affirm or deny; judgment is not a matter of checking categorical boxes. (5) Kant's account of conscious-ness, while it adverts to the empirical level of consciousness and includes an *a priori* that accompanies all cognitional acts, fails to address the dynamic states of inquiring and

Lonergan's cognitional theory yields an epistemology by its very enactment. Although the self-affirmation of the knower is the fundamental enactment of the dynamic structure of human knowing in Lonergan's transition from cognitional theory to epistemology, any concrete judgment of fact performatively answers both the questions "what am I doing when I am knowing?" and "why is doing that knowing?"[33] What links the knower and the known is the very functioning of the wondering, questioning desire of human conscious intentionality. The performance of the subject moves toward concrete judgments of fact that reveal *both* knower *and* known, subject *and* object, or what Lonergan will call "being."

2. Being: A Difficult Notion

Lonergan admits that the notion of being is a "tricky topic."[34] He defines being heuristically as *the objective of the pure desire to know*.[35] Being is *not*, for Lonergan, a characteristic or quality all things have (an opinion rightly and thoroughly criticized by Heidegger and his followers). Being is both what is known as well as all that remains to be known and is therefore what is to be known by the totality of true judgments. Lonergan's definition of being is a second-order one, identifying only how the meaning of being is to be determined. Being is all-inclusive and universal, because apart from being there is nothing. Being is completely concrete, for "over and above the being of any thing, there is nothing more of that thing."[36] Being is the proper object of the intellect, for when we desire to know, we desire to know being. Being is anything and everything that is the objective of the pure desire to know. But Lonergan distinguishes between the "being" that includes

---

reflecting, lending an element of the mysterious to his categories and leaving an opening for the absolute idealists. For further elaboration of the differences between Kant and Lonergan, see Giovanni B. Sala, *Lonergan and Kant: Five Essays on Human Knowledge*, trans. Joseph Spoerl, ed. Robert M. Doran (Toronto: University of Toronto Press, 1994).

[33] When inquiry is into the data of sense, the resulting judgment is verifiable by a return to the data. There is an element of reversibility when dealing with sensible data, but inquiry into the data of consciousness is verified by the questions themselves. There is only one answer to the question "do I ask questions?" The self-affirmation of the knower presents the simplest illustration of Lonergan's epistemology.

[34] Lonergan, *Insight*, 372.

[35] Ibid. Emphasis added.

[36] Ibid., 375.

anything that is known or remains to be known and the "notion of being" that is the intention of the whole in the desire to know.

2.1. *Knowing and Being: Isomorphism in Lonergan*

The spontaneously operative "notion" of being *is* the pure desire to know. While being is defined as the totality of true judgments, the notion of being is prior to judging, for the notion of being "extends beyond the known."[37] The notion of being "must be the detached and unrestricted desire to know as operative in cognitional process."[38] Lonergan further elaborates the notion of being by contrasting it with the levels of consciousness: "Desiring to know is desiring to know being; but it is merely the desire and not yet the knowing. Thinking is thinking being; it is not thinking nothing; but thinking being is not yet knowing it. Judging is a complete increment in knowing; if correct, it is a knowing of being; but it is not yet knowing being, for that is attained only through the totality of correct judgments."[39] The notion of being is both beyond and prior to the operations of consciousness. As a notion it anticipates the totality of true judgments, for a notion emerges heuristically. The notion of being is the desire to know that moves toward being as what is known and whatever remains to be known.

Consequently, the notion of being underpins all cognitional contents because without "the pure desire to know, sensitive living would remain in its routine of perception and conation, instinct and habit, emotion and action."[40] The notion of being penetrates all cognitional contents as the "supreme heuristic notion" that prior to every content "is the notion of the to-be-known through that content."[41] The notion of being "constitutes all contents as cognitional" because being is the to-be-known, and knowing is knowing being.[42] But to know being is to make a judgment about a to-be-known. Lonergan emphasizes that experience is a "kaleidoscopic flow," and thinking is simply a second-level operation that aims toward an affirmation or denial of an object of thought. The reality of being only emerges on the

[37] Ibid., 372.
[38] Ibid., 378.
[39] Ibid.
[40] Ibid., 380.
[41] Ibid.
[42] Ibid., 381.

level of judgment, for our experience can be hallucinatory and our thinking can head off in any direction at the behest of distractions or biases. Judgment brings our experiencing and thinking to their fulfillment by affirming what is and denying what is not.

Lonergan goes on to distinguish sources of meaning, acts of meaning, terms of meaning, and the core of meaning. Sources of meaning are the data, images, and concepts of our experiencing and understanding, but also the grasp of the unconditioned and judgment. The fundamental source of meaning is the unrestricted desire to know. Lonergan identifies three acts of meaning: formal, full, and instrumental. The formal act of meaning corresponds to the second level of conscious intending. It is an act of thinking and conceiving, of formulating and defining. The full act of meaning, then, is a judgment. It brings thinking and conceiving to their term by affirming or denying what is thought or conceived. Lonergan explains that the instrumental act of meaning "is the implementation of a formal or a full act by use of words or symbols in a spoken, written, or merely imagined utterance."[43] Terms of meaning are what is meant either as understood (formal terms of meaning) or as affirmed (full terms of meaning). Finally, the core of meaning is the intention of being.

It is worth noting here a distinction between Lonergan's use of language and Chauvet's. Lonergan finds a latent empiricism in theories of language that regard instrumental acts of meaning. For example, Chauvet's concern for the performative aspect of language and his use of J. L. Austin's theory of language enable him to criticize what he takes to be the classical understanding of language, especially in Plato and Augustine, as an instrument. He wants to argue, with Heidegger, that language is not merely an instrument to communicate some previously understood aspect of being; language is the "house of being," the place where *Dasein* and *Sein* meet "at the heart of the real." Consequently, in Chauvet's theory of the symbol, language/symbols *make* human beings by mediating the self to the self. Thus the body is the archsymbol because fundamentally we are our bodies, and our bodies mediate experience as language. It follows, on Chauvet's account, that sacramental causality should employ the categories of linguistic analysis

---

[43] Ibid., 381.

rather than those of metaphysics.[44] The sacramental effect results from a particular kind of utterance or gesture. Chauvet argues: "The communication of grace is to be understood, not according to the 'metaphysical' scheme of cause and effect, but according to the symbolic scheme of communication through language, a communication supremely effective because it is through language that the subject comes forth in its relations to other subjects within a common 'world' of meaning."[45] Of course, Thomas Aquinas knew that the point was communication and so identified the *form* of the sacrament in the words spoken by the minister.[46]

For Lonergan an instrumental act of meaning "presupposes formal or full acts of meaning, inasmuch as one knows what one means; and it refers to formal or full acts of meaning, inasmuch as all meaning refers to a meant."[47] The key to communication is the sharing of formal and full acts of meaning (understandings and judgments) through instrumental acts of speaking, gesturing, writing, etc. The empiricist theory of meaning, however, "identifies the valid field of full terms of meaning (that is, the universe of being) with the range of sensible presentations."[48] Hence for the empiricist the instrumental acts themselves indicate a full term of meaning.

Chauvet's discussion of the symbolic efficacy of sacraments seems to be heading in this direction because he fails to account for the act of understanding that could comprehend the meaning communicated in instrumental acts. Indeed, his critique of the "instrumentalization" of language derives from the argument that nothing is first understood and then uttered—an outright denial of the existence of inner words, and therefore of formal and full acts of meaning, perhaps owing to his misreading of Aquinas on knowing. Because of his failure to account for the inner word, Chauvet's critique of the instrumentalization of language misses the mark. Language remains very much an instrument, only now it is wielded by the group rather than the individual. Language is now the instrument of culture, with a foundational status in that it shapes individuals by inscribing their bodies

[44] See Louis-Marie Chauvet, *Symbol and Sacrament: A Sacramental Reinterpretation of Christian Existence* [= *SS*], trans. Patrick Madigan and Madeleine Beaumont (Collegeville, MN: Liturgical Press, 1995), 130–33.

[45] Ibid., 139–40.

[46] See *ST* III, q. 78, a. 5.

[47] Lonergan, *Insight*, 383.

[48] Ibid.

with the meanings and values of the culture and, in the case of Christian culture, with the meanings and values of the church. What emerges is a kind of cultural determinism characteristic of a failure to identify the dialectic of community. But also it ignores the operations of the second and third levels of consciousness. Because Chauvet avoids the question of knowing, it remains a mystery how sacraments communicate anything except by a kind of empiricism of speech-acts. Chauvet is right to criticize the image of formal and full acts of meaning as tightly wrapped concepts delivered to others by instrumental acts of oral or written communication; however, what is communicated is not only possibly relevant concepts but also virtually unconditioned judgments. We will return to these matters in chapter 5 with a discussion of Lonergan's ontology of meaning. At this stage the important point is that being is known in acts of meaning.

As the core of meaning, the intention of being means what actually exists. Lonergan notes that in a true judgment "there is harmony between what is intended and what is meant."[49] In a false judgment, however, there is a conflict between the desire to know, or the intention of being, and what is meant in the judgment as a full term of meaning. A false judgment means that a possibly relevant meaning does not in fact exist. Does this mean that false judgments are meaningless? No, it means that false judgments are false because they mean a state of affairs that is not actually the case, for they run contrary to the intention of being. Similarly on the level of conception, or formal terms of meaning, a distinction is to be drawn between what can be considered or what can be thought, and what kind of thinking is superfluous because it is merely thinking. Lonergan uses the example of the unicorn and the horse. We can think of both, we can conceive the characteristics of each, we might even purport to know the essence of each, but again we are not merely satisfied with thinking. Thinking is on the way toward knowing, because knowing occurs fully only in judgment. The core of meaning, the intention of being, is the desire to know reaching toward its full term in true judgments. Unicorns are often imagined, but they are not frequently affirmed as virtually unconditioned because they cannot be verified by recourse to sensible data.[50]

---

[49] Ibid., 382.

[50] Chauvet, and others, might object at this point that this is precisely what is wrong with metaphysical accounts: they leave out the possible, the unseen, or the eschatological.

Lonergan's notion of being is open because it is oriented toward an unrestricted object. It is not a notion of some essence to be conceived or defined, except at a remove that admits only that being is whatever is to be known by correct acts of understanding. The notion of being is only determined by correct judgment, and it aims toward the totality of correct judgments.[51] To know being as determined in its totality we would need to know everything about everything, and clearly we do not. However, "the making of judgments is a determinate process, and one does not have to make all the judgments to grasp the nature of that process. It is this fact that makes cognitional theory a base of operations for the determination of the general structure of the concrete universe."[52] Identifying the process of arriving at true judgments about the universe of being has been the goal of inquiring into cognitional theory and the implementation of that theory in the self-affirmation of the knower. Discovering the process of knowing and the rational self-appropriation that begins in adverting to that process lays the groundwork for arriving at a notion of being that is open, concrete, and operative in human knowing.

For Lonergan, knowing and being are isomorphic.[53] Whatever is truly known is being, and being is what is known or remains to be known. Whatever is to be known is proportionate to human knowing, and so being is concrete because it is affirmed as virtually unconditioned in judgment. Being extends to whatever remains to be known, and so it is universal as the unrestricted desire to know that is the notion of being. Being is not conceived, and so it is not a concept. Therefore Lonergan's notion of being is neither the

---

Eschatology pushes out of the current state of affairs to imagine radically new possibilities for human being. This is also characteristic of the notion of being as it relates to the future. The issue Lonergan is dealing with here regards the concrete. If we fail to come to terms with the concrete, our hopes might head off in the wrong direction. The poet, after all, is not simply a dreamer but also a critic. The hopeful vision of the prophets is born out of their honesty with reality. Martin Luther King Jr.'s description of a dream is at the same time a condemnation of the current state of affairs. It is an act of judgment about the present reality. The concrete situation is our primary concern at this point. We will treat eschatological reality in chap. 5.

[51] Ibid., 385.

[52] Ibid.

[53] See Paul E. Kidder, "The Relation of Knowing and Being in Lonergan's Philosophy," (PhD diss., Boston College, 1987).

concept "with least connotation and greatest denotation" of Duns Scotus,[54] nor is it defined conceptually according to Platonic or Aristotelian categories.[55] Lonergan notes that Aquinas did not explicitly distinguish between the notion of being and the concept of being but argues that he was "aware of the implications of that distinction."[56] What are the implications?

Agreeing with Aristotle that "human intellect is a *potens omnia facere et fieri*," Aquinas held that the unrestricted desire to know is the origin of human intelligence.[57] The confirmation of this desire is our desire to know God. Having learned of God's existence in revelation, we want to know what God is, and so "by our nature we desire what by our nature we cannot achieve."[58] The desire aims toward the whole, being, whatever is to be known. Thus it is the question of being that drives Aquinas as much as it drives Heidegger.[59] While both explore the ramifications of Augustine's advertence to the questioning subject,[60] Aquinas is able to identify the source of our questions in the light of intelligence that is "a created participation of the

---

[54] Lonergan, *Insight*, 392.

[55] See ibid., 388–91, where Lonergan traces the theories of being in Greek philosophy. Briefly, he indicates that the problems the medievals inherited were largely based on the two well-known conflicting theories of being of Plato and Aristotle. According to Lonergan, Plato's theory of forms mistakes the "unconditioned of judgment" for a mere object of thought (p. 389), with the result that Plato is not able to relate the forms to the concrete universe except by a synthetic judgment. Aristotle inherited Plato's theory of judgment as synthesis but distinguished between the operations of the second and third levels of consciousness. However, while he identified being with the "concrete universe as in fact it is to be known," he maintained the Platonist idea that "the notion of being was a conceptual content" (p. 391). Lonergan explains that "Aristotle assigned the ontological principle 'form' as the ground of being in things and the cognitional act of grasping the form as the insight from which originates the conceptual content 'being'" (p. 391).

[56] Ibid., 394.

[57] Ibid., 393.

[58] Ibid., 394. Indeed, in this life the object of belief cannot be fully known; it remains a mystery. But it is a mystery that beckons us by unleashing our desire to know and placing it in an infinite horizon.

[59] Identifying being with a conceptual content seems to be the real target of Heidegger's critique. Insofar as Chauvet, echoing Heidegger, offers a conceptualist reading of the scholastic tradition, he finds a "family resemblance" that disappears on a careful reading of Aquinas.

[60] Augustine, *Confessions*, book 10, xxxiii (50): "*mihi quaestio factus sum.*" See Frederick Lawrence, "Expanding Challenge to Authenticity in *Insight*: Lonergan's Hermeneutics of Facticity (1953–1964)," *Divyadaan: Journal of Philosophy and Education* 15,

eternal and uncreated light."[61] The notion of being is a divine spark in us that anticipates the entire range of what remains to be known. Although it anticipates being in its totality, still we are able to "define being only at a second remove as whatever is to be known by intelligent grasp and reasonable affirmation."[62] Because it is the "whole of what intelligence anticipates," being is "open to all the incomplete and partial moments from which cognitional process suffers without ever renouncing its all-inclusive goal."[63] Still, being is known in the full term of cognitional process, not simply in understanding essence but in affirming existence.[64] This formulation raises the question of objectivity: How can one person's judgment be sufficient for the affirmation that something exists? How does judgment reach the real?

2.2. Objectivity

Normally when we think of objectivity we are apt to imagine something like an impartial observer who mirrors reality without involving his or her subjective interests in the correct recounting of events. Of course, the assumption fails to acknowledge the psychological and cultural historicity of the knower. The impartial observer is nowhere to be found. Then are we left without objectivity? Lonergan's answer is no. But his notion of objectivity goes beyond the naïve view of the mirror to the complexity of human cognitional process. Lonergan's notion of objectivity emerges from his cognitional theory, and therefore it is complex. Knowing is a process, not simply a look,

---

no. 3 (2004): 427–56. Lawrence notes Heidegger's narrow reading of Augustine, which contributes to his associating facticity with fallenness.

[61] Lonergan, *Insight*, 394.

[62] Ibid., 395.

[63] Ibid., 396.

[64] On the relevance of the distinction between essence and existence in Heidegger's interpretation of the scholastics, see John D. Caputo, *Heidegger and Aquinas: An Essay on Overcoming Metaphysics* (New York: Fordham University Press, 1982), 66–87. Caputo places this distinction at the heart of Heidegger's interpretation of metaphysics but highlights his misreading of Aquinas on this point. The distinction is fundamental for Lonergan's thinking here. If Aquinas holds "it is in and through essences that being has existence," then particular instances or things reveal being. Contrariwise, if being is conceived apart from essence it can have no existence, therefore being apart from essence is nothing. Because Scotus conceived knowing as looking, and since to look at nothing is clearly absurd, he supposed being to be that aspect of the real at which the intellect looks. Being is thereby reduced to a conceptual placeholder employed to avoid absurdity.

and so objectivity must obtain in different ways at different moments in the process. Lonergan distinguishes the principal notion of objectivity, absolute objectivity, normative objectivity, and experiential objectivity.[65]

There is a "principal notion" of objectivity that rests on the differentiation of objects, for example in the affirmations A is, B is, A is not B. Included among the series are such judgments as: I am a knower, this is a computer, I am not this computer.[66] Among the objects affirmed at this level is the subject doing the affirming. The result is a series of judgments that distinguish things from each other through these positive and negative affirmations. Among the properties of the principal notion of objectivity the first is the affirmed series of positive and negative judgments that distinguish the knowing subject from any of an entire range of things. Second, so defined, the principal notion of objectivity "is not contained in a single judgment, and still less in any experiential or normative factor that occurs in cognitional process prior to judgment."[67] Third, the principal notion of objectivity is valid if the pattern of judgments affirmed above is valid. Fourth, while distinction among things is commonly affirmed, it is frequently affirmed on the basis of an experiential objectivity that distinguishes between the sensible data that pertain to one thing and not another. A fifth property relates the principal notion of objectivity to the notion of being. If objectivity characterizes a set of judgments that distinguishes between things, "there is objectivity if there are distinct beings, some of which both know themselves and know others as others."[68]

Crucially, the subject is discovered within being, for objectivity does not mean standing outside being and looking at it. The subject is always implicated in the universe of being. After all, one has to exist before one can look.[69] Finally, the principal notion of objectivity elucidates the problem of transcendence, commonly articulated as a problem of "the bridge," i.e., how does the subject get outside of itself to reality "out there." Lonergan suggests the question is misleading because, for him, knowing intends being, not an *already-out-there-now-real*. The question, when proposed along the lines of

---

[65] See also *Method in Theology*, 262–65, for a synopsis of Lonergan's position on objectivity.

[66] Lonergan, *Insight*, 400.

[67] Ibid.

[68] Ibid., 401.

[69] Ibid.

Descartes' *cogito*, presupposes that the subject knows itself and asks how it can also know things "out there." Lonergan clarifies that it is in judgment that the subject knows itself as being and object. Therefore transcendence is not a matter of going outside oneself but of making a reasonable judgment, which includes objectivity and transcendence.

In addition to the principal notion of objectivity, Lonergan identifies three partial aspects of objectivity: absolute, normative, and experiential. Absolute objectivity is *de facto* absolute. It is not formally unconditioned and so necessary, but rather a conditioned whose conditions have been fulfilled and is known in a virtually unconditioned judgment. The content of that judgment is absolute because it is separable from the empirically residual aspects of the utterance—the place and time. Lonergan argues that this absolute objectivity is what gives our knowing its "publicity" insofar as our virtually unconditioned judgments are available to be shared by other knowers. Therefore judgments are not relative to space and time, because the unconditioned goes beyond space and time. What is true at one moment remains true at any other moment. In addition, there is a normative aspect of objectivity that is "constituted by the immanent exigence of the pure desire to know."[70] The normative sense pertains to the operations of our conscious intending. To be objective in the normative sense is a matter of giving "free rein to the pure desire, to its questions for intelligence, and its questions for reflection."[71] Anything less would involve an intrusion of bias into thinking.

Finally, there is an experiential aspect of objectivity that recognizes reality as given. The given is the entire range of data on which intelligence operates in understanding and to which reflective understanding returns for verification. This includes not only "the materials into which the natural scientist inquires but also the materials into which the psychologist or methodologist or cultural historian inquires."[72] The given is equally unquestionable and indubitable, residual and diffuse, because it is prior to questioning and remains after intelligence abstracts from it. Like his notion of being, Lonergan's notion of objectivity is minimal and open. It rests on the self-appropriation of intelligent and rational consciousness for its verification.

[70] Ibid., 404.
[71] Ibid.
[72] Ibid., 407.

2.3. Summary

Lonergan's reflection on objectivity concludes the section of *Insight* that deals with epistemology, preceding the chapters on metaphysics. In the previous sections we have identified the role of judgment, which brings the cognitional process to its term in the virtually unconditioned. We have witnessed a performative verification of judgment in the self-affirmation of the knower. By attending to being and the notion of being, we have identified the proper object of the intellect with the to-be-known that is being, and the dynamism of human knowing with the pure desire that is the notion of being. These reflections led us to consider objectivity in terms of the virtually unconditioned judgment that distinguishes between objects within the universe of being and the partial aspects of objectivity that correspond to cognitional process.

It remains for us, in this chapter, to consider the question of metaphysics. Though brevity would have dictated our beginning with metaphysics, we would also have overlooked the unique approach Lonergan brings to the question through his analysis of human conscious intentionality and been too easily tempted to suggest that his approach is another instance of the onto-theo-logical. In addition, we might have missed the fact that for Lonergan metaphysics is derived and decentered, and so is both critical and heuristic.

3. Lonergan's Metaphysics:
The Integral Heuristic Structure of Proportionate Being

Because Lonergan identifies being through an isomorphism with knowing, his critical realist metaphysics is heuristic. It identifies only whatever is to be known, not in its content but in its intelligibility. Intelligibility is intrinsic to being, since being includes whatever is intelligently grasped and rationally affirmed. This does not mean that being is some content underlying everything, the Scotist concept; it is simply a heuristic identification of whatever is known and remains to be known. Starting from the basic affirmation of being as the objective of the pure desire to know, Lonergan can use a methodical approach to metaphysics that makes explicit what otherwise remains implicit, and frequently problematic.

3.1. The Method of Metaphysics

a. Toward Explicit Metaphysics

At the outset of his treatment of metaphysics Lonergan introduces an underlying problem. He acknowledges that his epistemology will be assailed by those who claim that objectivity is a matter of taking a look, the concrete universe of being is equivalent to the already out there now, and the self is the bewildered existential subject, thrown into an apparently indifferent universe.[73] He suggests that each of these criticisms has its ground in the "concrete unity-in-tension that is man."[74] The phrase "unity-in-tension that is man" indicates the polymorphism of human consciousness and its patterns. Rarely, if ever, do we find ourselves wholly absorbed in the flow of a single pattern, and so our experience of ourselves is of a concrete unity-in-tension. Lonergan explains:

> These patterns alternate; they blend or mix; they can interfere, conflict, lose their way, break down. The intellectual pattern of experience is supposed and expressed by our account of self-affirmation, of being, and of objectivity. But no man is born in that pattern; no one reaches it easily; no one remains in it permanently; and when some other pattern is dominant, then the self of our self-affirmation seems quite different from one's actual self, the universe of being seems as unreal as Plato's noetic heaven, and objectivity spontaneously becomes a matter of meeting persons and dealing with things that are "really out there."[75]

These antitheses highlight the very real problems that emerge in the many contradictory and disparate philosophies that Lonergan distinguishes as "positions" and "counterpositions."

Lonergan's critique of philosophy aims at understanding philosophy's history as a series of contradictory contributions to what is ultimately a common goal. His dialectical analysis groups philosophies according to their basis in cognitional theory and their expansion into other questions. Insofar as philosophies hold positions, they invite development, while those that hold counterpositions invite reversal. The basic position is specified

[73] Ibid., 410.
[74] Ibid.
[75] Ibid., 410–11.

by the three categories that occupy Lonergan's cognitional theory. A philosophical basis in cognitional theory is revealed to be a basic position. A basic position exhibits the following criteria: "(1) if the real is the concrete universe of being and not a subdivision of the 'already out there now'; (2) if the subject becomes known when it affirms itself intelligently and reasonably and so is not known yet in any prior 'existential' state; and (3) if objectivity is conceived as a consequence of intelligent inquiry and critical reflection, and not as a property of vital anticipation, extroversion, and satisfaction."[76] It is revealed to be a basic counterposition if it contradicts one or more of the basic conditions. While positions invite development, counterpositions invite their own reversal because they frequently enact a performative contradiction. With the dialectic mapped out, Lonergan can define metaphysics.

Like his definitions of being and objectivity treated above, Lonergan's definition of metaphysics is derived and therefore heuristic and open. He argues that metaphysics is the department of human knowledge that underlies, penetrates, transforms, and unifies all other departments.[77] What can this possibly mean? Metaphysics underlies all other departments of knowledge because metaphysics has as its principles the "detached and disinterested drive of the pure desire to know and its unfolding in empirical, intellectual, and rational consciousness of the self-affirming subject."[78] It penetrates all other departments because all particular departments "spring from a common source and seek a common compatibility and coherence."[79] It transforms all other departments because, being free from particular viewpoints, it develops positions and reverses counterpositions.[80] It unifies all other departments because it is the original and total question and moves toward a total answer. Metaphysics deals with the whole *in* knowledge, not the whole *of* knowledge. Consequently, we can distinguish three stages of metaphysics: latent, problematic, and explicit. Metaphysics is latent in the operating human desire to know that seeks coherence and unity but remains undifferentiated. It is problematic insofar as it is involved in the "disarray

---

[76] Ibid., 413.
[77] Ibid., 415.
[78] Ibid.
[79] Ibid.
[80] Ibid.

of the positions and counterpositions that result from the polymorphic consciousness of man."[81] When latent metaphysics succeeds in conceiving itself and affirming its conception, it becomes explicit.

Lonergan defines explicit metaphysics as "the conception, affirmation, and implementation of the integral heuristic structure of proportionate being."[82] By proportionate being Lonergan means "whatever is to be known by human experience, intelligent grasp, and reasonable affirmation."[83] He avoids onto-theology by restricting his initial exploration of metaphysics to what is proportionate to the dynamic structure of human conscious intending, leaving aside the question of transcendent being. By "integral heuristic structure" Lonergan means the ordered set of all heuristic notions, where "heuristic notion" refers to unknown content that is "determined by anticipating the type of act through which the unknown would become known."[84] Lonergan builds a critical metaphysics on his cognitional theory, emphasizing that "prior to the understanding that issues in answers, there are the questions that anticipate answers; and as has been seen, such anticipation may be employed systematically in the determination of answers that as yet are unknown."[85] Again, the definition Lonergan develops is open or heuristic. It anticipates answers to questions but resists the temptation to fill in the empty spaces with conceptual content or categorical specification before the further acts of understanding and judging have occurred.

Further, latent metaphysics becomes explicit in the conception, affirmation, and implementation of the integral heuristic structure. If latent metaphysics is "the dynamic unity of empirical, rational, and intellectual consciousness as underlying, penetrating, transforming, and unifying the other departments of knowledge," then, Lonergan suggests, "an integral heuristic structure of proportionate being would perform these offices in an explicit manner."[86] Explicit metaphysics is heuristic because it underlies all fields. It penetrates other fields as the questions those fields answer. It transforms answers through a dialectic that distinguishes positions from

---

[81] Ibid., 416.
[82] Ibid.
[83] Ibid.
[84] Ibid., 417.
[85] Ibid.
[86] Ibid.

counterpositions and drives the development of positions. As an integral structure, it brings fields into "a single intelligible whole."[87]

Explicit metaphysics is the goal, but it remains an open project, for explicit metaphysics is progressive, nuanced, and factual. It is progressive because unknown contents, or heuristic notions, emerge only in the process of subjecting the operations of consciousness to critical analysis. Explicit metaphysics "advances by adding these discoveries to its account of the integral heuristic structure of proportionate being."[88] Explicit metaphysics is nuanced. It is not perfect knowledge of the whole but admits varying degrees of clarity and precision, of evidence and inevitability. It has made its peace with the scientific breakthrough to probability and refuses to speak in terms of universal and necessary causes. Finally, explicit metaphysics is factual. It does not concern itself with all possible worlds or necessary causes, but with the contingent events that happen to be the case. It both precedes and unifies the empirical sciences and common sense that aim at what is in fact the case.

Metaphysics depends formally on cognitional theory and materially on the sciences and common sense.[89] This dependence is not in the manner of an effect on a cause but that of a unifying principle on what it "generates, transforms, and unifies."[90] Metaphysics is not a separate department with its own particular set of data for inquiry, for "it does not pretend to know the universe of proportionate being independently of science and common sense"; rather, it unifies the results of these distinct inquiries by reversing counterpositions and by "discerning in them the concrete prolongations of the integral heuristic structure which it itself is."[91] Consequently this metaphysics is stable because "a merely heuristic account is not open to revision."[92]

Lonergan states a final and crucial implication of his definition of metaphysics. Metaphysics is primarily a matter of explanation, and only secondarily a matter of description.[93] The distinction between description and

[87] Ibid.
[88] Ibid., 418.
[89] Ibid., 421.
[90] Ibid., 418.
[91] Ibid.
[92] Ibid., 419.
[93] Ibid.

explanation recalls our discussion of the two orientations toward things with which we began our examination of *Insight*. While it is true that explanation relates things to one another and description relates things to us, still we are things. Therefore some descriptive relations will be identical with explanatory relations. Descriptive relations, however, remain secondary, for their relevance is discovered in relation to things as explained. Lonergan notes that the ten categories ascribed to Aristotle, which have a long history in considerations of metaphysics, are in fact descriptive and so "do not pertain to the constitutive structure of metaphysics."[94] Explicit metaphysics is the conception, affirmation, and implementation of what otherwise remains latent in the operations of consciousness and problematic because of the polymorphism of that consciousness. Lonergan clarifies his position through a discussion of methods.

b. Method and the Dialectic of Method

If the preceding task of defining has left any doubt whether or not Lonergan's understanding of metaphysics is simply one more conceptual system, he quickly dispatches that misunderstanding by reminding the reader that metaphysics is something in a mind.[95] If explicit metaphysics is the conception, affirmation, and implementation of the integral heuristic structure of proportionate being, then "it exists only in the empirical, intellectual, and rational consciousness of the self-affirming subject."[96] This means that the process toward explicit metaphysics is toward self-knowledge. The subject in question is not the transcendental or absolute subject of idealism but any subject that experiences, understands, and judges. Consequently, "the starting point of metaphysics is people as they are" in their polymorphism, "their native disorientation and bewilderment," their *facticity*.[97]

The method of metaphysics is primarily pedagogical because it appeals to the native desire existing and operative in the human subject that aims toward knowing. In the beginning of *Insight*, Lonergan's attention to the desire to know is precisely this kind of pedagogy, in which the reader

---

[94] Ibid., 420.
[95] Ibid., 421.
[96] Ibid.
[97] Ibid., 422. See Martin Heidegger, *Ontology: The Hermeneutics of Facticity*, trans. John van Buren (Bloomington: Indiana University Press, 1999).

begins to recognize both the tension that attends questions and the release of tension that accompanies insights. In addition, his identification of the subjective and objective fields of common sense highlights the possibility of disorientation and bewilderment in a subject whose native desire is crushed under the weight of bias. The outcome of this pedagogical method is the self-affirming subject.

The arrival at self-affirmation from out of the disorientation and bewilderment of polymorphic consciousness calls for a reorientation and integration of the subject. The reorientation involves advertence to the polymorphism of human consciousness and the development of a critical capacity to identify the intrusion of bias into the claims of common sense and of science. Furthermore, as "the subject's advertence to the polymorphism of his consciousness leads to a transforming reorientation of his scientific opinions and his common sense, so his advertence both to his detached and disinterested desire to know and to the immanent structure of its unfolding leads to an integration of what is known and what is to be known of the universe of proportionate being."[98] It is in this integration of knower and known that we find the transition from latent to explicit metaphysics.

Lonergan's dialectical reading of the history of metaphysics attends to methods, because in metaphysics "methods and their results are of equal generality and tend to be coincident."[99] Among the methods Lonergan regards as failing to articulate a critical metaphysics grounded in the isomorphism of knower and known are deductive methods, universal doubt, empiricism, commonsense eclecticism, absolute idealism, and scientism.[100] Each of these methods is rooted in one of the distorted assumptions about knowing with which we began our exposition of Lonergan's thought. Rather than repeat that analysis here, we simply call the reader's attention to the following problems: (1) the influence of picture thinking, or the primacy of the ocular metaphor for knowing that omits the discursive character of human cognition, (2) claims about the transparency of the subject to itself that fail to advert to the polymorphism of human consciousness and therefore are not sufficiently critical, (3) extroverted consciousness, or thinking of the real as a subdivision of the already-out-there-now. Each of these problems is connected with the polymorphism of human consciousness, leading to

---

[98] Lonergan, *Insight*, 424.
[99] Ibid., 427.
[100] See ibid., 426–55.

what Lonergan calls problematic metaphysics.[101] The resolution of these problems requires the transition (articulated above) from latent, through problematic, to explicit metaphysics.

There is one method that is worthy of our attention here because in Lonergan's discussion of it we find the crux of his agreement and disagreement with Chauvet. Chauvet's reading of Western metaphysics, borrowing heavily from Heidegger, criticizes that tradition for presupposing (1) a static notion of presence and (2) a mechanistic understanding of causality. It seems Lonergan would agree with these criticisms, but on different grounds. In his analysis of deductive methods Lonergan isolates a particular aspect of the polymorphism of consciousness in scholastic metaphysics that renders it problematic. We find it especially in Scotus but also, in a more limited sense, in Thomas.

Lonergan calls our attention to the fact that abstract deductivism begs the question by relying on self-evident propositions. The problem is not deduction but the assertion that universal and necessary propositions govern the deduction. The assertion of universal and necessary truths as self-evident yields abstract categories through which experience is apprehended. For Scotus, and those who follow him, the particular is only known in the light of the universal, especially the most universal, the concept of being. All beings have their being by participation in being as a foundational concept. Scotus affirms the particular by positing an "intuition of the existing and present as existing and present,"[102] which he describes as *haecceitas*. It is Scotus's category of *haecceitas* that Heidegger applies in his reflection on *Dasein*'s experience of temporal extension. Being in its universality always remains hidden behind the temporally extended particular, so that every presence is also an absence. *Dasein* experiences its *haecceitas* against the background of Being's absence. In his appropriation of Heidegger, Chauvet employs the notion of *haecceitas* transposed in Heidegger's emphasis on absence and truth as unconcealment without ever adverting to the influence of Scotus on Heidegger's thinking about language and being.[103]

---

[101] "The polymorphism of human consciousness seems relevant to the problems of philosophy, for philosophy is concerned with knowledge, reality, and objectivity, and these terms take on different meanings as consciousness shifts from one pattern or blend of patterns of experience to another" (ibid., 451).

[102] Ibid., 428.

[103] For an exploration of Scotist influence in Heidegger, see Sean J. McGrath, "Heidegger and Duns Scotus on Truth and Language," *Review of Metaphysics* 57 (December 2003): 339–58.

What Lonergan finds in Scotus is a problematic metaphysics that operates under the assumption that knowing is like taking a look. In the case of Scotus the looking is a perception of conceptual contents paired with an intuition or encounter with *haecceitas*, the "thisness" of a thing.[104] Scotus separates the intelligible and universal from the particular encounter with the *haecceitas* of a thing. Each thing is taken as a particular, not an instance of a universal. Instead, universals reside in concepts. Lonergan traces the activities of intelligence in its encounter with the real in Scotus's epistemology as follows:

> The first step was abstraction; it occurs unconsciously; it consists in the impression upon intellect of a universal conceptual content. The second step was intellection: intellect takes a look at the conceptual content. The third step was a comparison of different contents, with the result that intellect saw which concepts were conjoined necessarily and which were incompatible. There follows a deduction of the abstract metaphysics of all possible worlds, and to it one adds an intuition of the existing and present as existing and present, to attain knowledge of the actual world.[105]

It is the formation of concepts that remains particularly mysterious in Scotus. Concepts impress themselves on intellect. From where is not clear. But that they are not generated by the subject seems to be what preserves their objectivity for Scotus, for concepts deal with all possible worlds.

Clearly, Aristotle and Thomas took a different tack. Lonergan admits that both remained tied to a faculty psychology, but "both affirmed the fact of insight as clearly and effectively as can be expected."[106] Both the sensible and the intelligible remain in potency in the object or image respectively. The faculties of sensing and intellect operate to bring potency to act. Therefore the sensible in act is sense in act and the intelligible in act is intellect in act. Intellect abstracts from sense data to form an adequate image that indicates

---

[104] The idea of *haecceitas* is in the background of the phenomenological turn in continental philosophy and makes its way into sacramental theology. See Kenan Osborne, *Christian Sacraments in a Postmodern World: A Theology for the Third Milllenium* (New York: Paulist Press, 1999). Osborne uses the category to preserve the particular character of each sacramental encounter as an instance of "sacramental *Haecceitas*" (see pp. 58–60).

[105] Lonergan, *Insight*, 431.

[106] Ibid.

the intelligible relations in the data; once it has an insight into the intelligibility it forms a concept to express the intelligibility. The concept is generated in intellect, not impressed from without. The concept, because it abstracts intelligible relations from the data, communicates a universal. So a circle can be defined in a concept. The concept does not change, even as every actually existing occurrence of circularity is never a perfect representation of the concept. But when you are at highway speeds you hope the wheels on your car are as close to round as they can get. This way of proceeding has little interest in a metaphysics of all possible worlds; it is comfortable with contingent occurrences. This does not mean that Thomas abandons universals or first principles, but the principles are not the beginning of a deductive account of reality as in Scotus. Lonergan's first principles are the concrete operations of the subject that indicate the integral heuristic structure of proportionate being.

3.2. Elements of Metaphysics: Central and Conjugate Potency, Form, and Act

In the preceding section we discovered that Lonergan's metaphysics is derived from the threefold structure of human knowing, because that structure implies an ordered set of all heuristic notions that constitute the integral heuristic structure of proportionate being. In the present section our task will be to define the elements of the heuristic structure and explain their relations. The six elements are central potency, central form, and central act, conjugate potency, conjugate form, and conjugate act.

First, we turn to the triad of potency, form, act. The terms are borrowed from Aristotle and Aquinas but are defined according to the structure of a derived metaphysics of proportionate being.[107] "Potency" indicates whatever is "to be known in fully explanatory knowledge by an intellectually patterned experience of the empirical residue."[108] "Form" refers to whatever is to be known about things in relation to one another. "Act" is whatever

---

[107] Lonergan identifies the conflict with modern science that results from Aristotle's use of the terms in a descriptive account of physical science, particularly his notion of sensible forms (*Insight*, 458–59). The sensible forms color, sound, heat and cold, wet and dry, hard and soft, heavy and light, etc., Lonergan says, are "extremely ambiguous" (p. 459). For modern science and a critical metaphysics all of these categories pertain not to form but to potency.

[108] Ibid., 457.

is to be known "by uttering the virtually unconditioned yes of reasonable judgment."[109] Therefore potency, form, and act constitute a unity, because the three components coalesce into a single known, for "what is experienced is what is understood; and what is understood is what is affirmed."[110] Lonergan further distinguishes two instances of potency, form, and act by applying the modifiers "conjugate" and "central."

Conjugates are traditionally named properties or characteristics or, in scholastic terminology, accidents. Specifically, Lonergan is calling our attention to these properties as they relate to each other. For example, we have distinguished heat "as felt" from heat "as defined." The former is an *experiential* conjugate, related directly to our senses. The latter is an *explanatory* conjugate that relates temperature to other temperatures. The metaphysical elements are concerned with the latter. Insofar as these properties are understood, they are conjugate forms. Because they are forms they stand in relation to potency and act in the composition of a single unity. Finally, conjugate act is the actual occurrence of a given property. Such is the meaning of conjugate potency, conjugate form, and conjugate act. As conjugate form stands in relation to conjugate potency and conjugate act, so central form stands to central potency and central act.

If there are conjugate potency, form, and act, of necessity there is a thing that these conjugates depend on; there is no such thing as free-floating temperature or mass, since explanatory conjugates pertain to things. In terms of the elements of metaphysics *unity-identity-wholes* are designated as central forms. Central form is identified by the demonstrative "this," which "can be used only inasmuch as there is a link between concepts and data as individual."[111] "This" identifies the *unity-identity-whole* that undergoes change; "it consists in the same concrete, intelligible unity providing the unification for successively different data; and so without the unity there is no change."[112] While Lonergan applies his argument to the hard sciences, which observe changes in data that pertain to a single thing in order to understand each of its properties, the distinction is a metaphysical one. "This" refers to the concrete and intelligible unity that undergoes change. Without a central form that provides the

[109] Ibid.
[110] Ibid.
[111] Ibid., 461.
[112] Ibid.

unification of the data there is no such thing as change. Instead, each thing is a new creation. For example, a human being exists in multiple phases and yet remains the same thing. When my four-year-old was an infant he neither spoke nor walked. Now he speaks and walks and much more. This is the same person, not a new person at each stage but a human being in the process of development. When I introduce my son to friends, saying, "This is my son," I do not mean simply the phenomenon standing next to me, extending his hand in greeting. Rather, I am referring to the totality of data that pertains to the "thing" my son is, his entire biography. Or take for another example you, the reader. As you read, your body is abuzz with activity, with processes, movements, and changes that are essential for your survival. However, from moment to moment you are not a *new* person, but the same person undergoing change. If you were not the same person you would not be undergoing change; you would simply be a new creation at each moment.

From the preceding discussion the connection between Lonergan's understanding of central form as the concrete and intelligible unity, identity, whole undergoing change and the classical category of "substance" is clear. Lonergan explains:

> The difference between our central form and Aristotle's substantial form is merely nominal, for the Aristotelian substantial form is what is known by grasping an intelligible unity, an *unum per se*. However, since the meaning of the English word "substance" has been influenced profoundly by Locke, since the Cartesian confusion of "body" and thing led to an identification of substance and extension and then to the riposte that substance is underneath extension, I have thought it advisable, at least temporarily, to cut myself off from this verbal tangle.[113]

The confusion continues into our own day, when "substance," in common-sense use, refers exclusively to material stuff.

The difference between Lonergan's conjugates and Aristotle's accidental forms is partly nominal and partly real. It is a nominal difference inasmuch as the word accidental suggests "merely incidental," a connotation that is problematic.[114] The difference is real in that Aristotle relates accidental form

---

[113] Ibid., 462.

[114] This is especially the case in eucharistic theology, since it can be taken to mean that the bread and wine of the Eucharist have no meaning of their own but function as mere

to sensible qualities as sensed, while for Lonergan form is only known by understanding, and sensible qualities stand in potency to understanding. Lonergan's conjugate form indicates the pattern or meaning in the sensible data. For example, Fido presents a range of sense data. At the level of experience they are merely sensed: soft fur, warm breath, etc. But understanding attends to the relations among these individual data in trying to understand an intelligibility in the data. Conjugate form is therefore related to understanding as answering a series of questions by identifying an intelligible pattern in data, whereas Aristotle's accidental form tends to reduce the meaning of the sensible to its being sensed. Central form, or substance, answers the further question, "what is this?" The answer begins as a hypothesis, or a definition proposed for understanding conjugate forms. The intelligibility as defined is central form. As affirmed by judgment it is central act.

If central form is a transposition of substance or essence, central act is a transposition of existence. Central act corresponds to the affirmation of the existence of central form or essence. Recalling that Lonergan's metaphysics develops from an isomorphism between knowing and known, the distinction between essence and existence in metaphysics is correlative with the distinction between understanding and judging in cognitional theory. Judgment affirms or denies that the conditions have been fulfilled for the form as understood to exist. What is understood is only a guess, hypothesis, or possibly relevant understanding of the data. Judgment affirms the existent in act, which means a conditioned central form whose conditions have in fact been fulfilled. "Existence is the act of being. . . . [T]he notion of existence emerged with the question whether the particularized concept, this thing, was anything more than an object of thought."[115] The affirmation of existence answers the question "is it so?" with a positing of the known in a reflective grasp of the unconditioned. The conditions for this thing's being what it is have been fulfilled.[116] Existence is always contingent. Affirming

---

ciphers. As we will see below, the idea that "accidents" are reduced to empty carriers is a correlate in a theory of eucharistic change through annihilation of the substances of bread and wine. In contrast, transubstantiation preserves the significance of the bread and wine as the appropriate symbols of the presence of the Incarnate Word.

[115] Lonergan, "*Insight*: Preface to a Discussion," 142–52, in *Collection*, CWBL 4, at 150–51.

[116] See ibid., 152n21.

that such and such is actually the case does not entail that it is necessarily the case. Lonergan's critical metaphysics of proportionate being affirms the contingency of things by distinguishing between essence and existence.

3.3. Causality in Lonergan: The Analogy of Contingent Predication

The metaphysical element "act" involves causality. A cause brings about the occurrence or existence of a thing. To affirm a thing as existing implies an intelligible relation between the existing thing and the ground of its existence. Thomas Aquinas's transformation of Aristotelian causality derives from a major distinction between ancient Greek and Christian cosmologies that clarifies the relationship of existing realities to their ground in a theology of creation. For Thomas, God is related to created things as an efficient cause. If God creates the universe, then the created order stands in relation to God as instrument to agent. Every change is therefore an instance of instrumental causality wherein the instrument is moved by a divine agent to effect a change.[117] This basic Christian theological doctrine is complicated by questions of fate and free will, which lead to dissatisfaction with the category of causality generally among some contemporary theologians. Insofar as causality is misunderstood, so also are issues surrounding free will and fate. Lonergan worked through these questions in his interpretation of Aquinas in his doctoral dissertation, later published under the title *Grace and Freedom: Operative Grace in the Thought of Saint Thomas Aquinas*.[118] Lonergan's clarification of the relation between grace and freedom helps us understand both the meaning of the metaphysical element "act" and sacramental causality.

The relevant theological insight regarding sacramental causality concerns the distinction between operative and cooperative grace. The intelligible relation of dependence of one thing on another articulated in Thomas's theory of sacraments explains that the recipient of the sacrament is made holy through both operative and cooperative grace, insofar as one receives

---

[117] See Lonergan, "On God and Secondary Causes," 53–65, in *Collection*, CWBL 4.

[118] Bernard Lonergan, *Grace and Freedom: Operative Grace in the Thought of Saint Thomas Aquinas*, CWBL 1, ed. Frederick E. Crowe and Robert M. Doran (Toronto: University of Toronto Press, 2000). Lonergan's analysis is applied to the sacraments in Philip McShane, "On the Causality of the Sacraments," *Theological Studies* 24, no. 3 (1963): 423–36.

the sacrament in order to partake of its effect. For example, Thomas argues that "sound and hearing, instances of action and passion, must be one and the same reality, else every mover would also be moved."[119] Causation as a relation of dependence of B on A is "the common feature of both operation and cooperation."[120] Accordingly, in a relation of dependence, A operates by moving and B cooperates by being moved. The mistaken assumption is that causality is something *in between* cause and effect. Even if this mistake, which often shapes discussions of sacramental causality, were correct, it is not relevant in the case of divine causation, for "in God substance and principle of action are one."[121] Lonergan shows that for Thomas what is moved is moved more by the primary mover than the secondary instrument, because the instrument is moved by the one moving. It is what Lonergan called a "caused causation."[122] For example, each keystroke that puts a piano into action is the act of the one striking the key rather than the mechanism of the piano acting on its own. Lonergan encapsulates this relationship in the Latin phrase "*actio est in passio.*"[123] The action of the one moving is present in the act of the one moved. The action involves no change in the mover, but only the change in the one being moved. Frequently the imagination reverses this, so that the change in the patient is attributed to a change in the agent. But this way of formulating the relationship would require a further action that would move the agent to act, and so on to infinity.

The challenge, then, is to avoid thinking of causation as a change in the one causing, for causation is only an intelligible relation of the change in the patient to the cause, which does not involve any real change in the cause as cause, viz., "on the Thomist view action is a formal content attributed to the cause as causing."[124] As the doctrine of creation implies, if every change requires a prior change in a causal series, then the universe would depend on an eternal and infinite series of causal changes without a first change. As Lonergan argued, "St. Thomas refuted this conclusion, not by substituting a premotion that was *natura prius*, but by arguing that what came first was not in the category of change but creation, and that creation,

[119] Lonergan, *Grace and Freedom*, 69.
[120] Ibid., 67.
[121] Ibid., 87.
[122] Ibid., 88.
[123] Ibid., 264.
[124] Ibid., 72.

so far from taking place in time, includes the production of time itself."[125] If God applies all agents to their activity, then sacraments stand within the intelligible universe of instrumental causes in relation to God. Sacraments offer a unique case—because disproportionate to human agency alone—of cooperation with the divine action in worship.

4. Conclusion

Lonergan's elaboration of the elements of metaphysics is a transposition of the scholastic categories of substance and accidents into terms derived from an explanatory metaphysics grounded in intentionality analysis. Why is any of this important to a study of sacramental theology? Lonergan's diagnosis of the problem confronting a culture caught in decline, and confronting any theologian who attempts to respond to systematic theological questions in that culture, means that the explanation of doctrines has first to cut through significant oversights due to a flight from understanding. In sacramental theology we use terms like "real," "substance," "presence," "appearance," "cause," and "effect." Commonsense eclecticism employs these technical terms facilely, as when we talk about the real world, about substance abuse or banned substances. [126] Our presence is requested, and so we keep up appearances. Whether playing billiards or bowling, driving or building, we are constantly engaged with the experience of cause and effect. In every case the connotation and denotation are reduced or expanded in order to meet the respective demands of everyday language. The polymorphism of human consciousness also affects the uncritical deployment of these terms in eucharistic theologies. Typically the terms are defined by their usage in either the biological or the dramatic patterns of experience. In the intellectual pattern, however, these terms can be understood within the explanatory context of statements accepted in faith. Therefore the theologian cannot take the meanings of these terms for granted, especially as they are employed in eucharistic doctrines.

Chauvet was correct in arguing that the meanings of such terms are in fact frequently distorted in dramatic ways, with quite destructive pastoral consequences. Not only this, but (with a nod to Chauvet and Heidegger)

---

[125] Ibid., 74.
[126] On commonsense eclecticism, see Lonergan, *Insight*, 441–45.

when a "commonsense eclectic" uses these terms they become caricatures of the language of metaphysics vis-à-vis our being-in-the-world, as operating in the dramatic pattern of experience. For example, Chauvet was right to point out that presence is often conceived as a permanent presence, as referring to an *already-out-there-now-real*. But that does not justify a wholesale rejection of metaphysics in the name of eliminating onto-theology; rather, it requires the very delicate procedure of removing the tumor of the flight from understanding without destroying the organs of intelligence. Our exploration of *Insight* has tried to demonstrate that this is in fact what Lonergan has achieved.

Chapter Four

From Metaphysics
to Categories of Meaning

The previous chapters highlight methodological differences between Lonergan's *explicit* cognitional theory, epistemology, and metaphysics and Chauvet's *implicit* cognitional theory, epistemology, and metaphysics. The remaining chapters move toward an interpretation of eucharistic doctrines, building on Lonergan's explicit metaphysics. In order to understand eucharistic doctrines on the level of our time, a transposition into categories consonant with intellectual conversion is desirable. If the metaphysical categories that traditionally inform theologies of the Eucharist have been roundly criticized by Chauvet (because they obscure the symbolic dimension of sacramental mediation by speaking in terms of instrumentality, causality, presence, substance, and accident) the doctrinal tradition contains genuine insights that are simply expressed in metaphysical terminology and can be expressed otherwise.

The key to understanding doctrines is to experience the insights that are affirmed to be true in the statements of faith. Chauvet's criticisms too often obscure this aspect of doctrines. Doctrines answer questions that arise in the Christian community. Historically those answers have frequently employed technical language, even inventing terms in order to communicate insights into revealed intelligibilities that push language to its limits. Chauvet criticizes this procedure, preferring a method of permanent questioning. Of course, the technical language of doctrine is prone to a superficial assent, but that alone does not disqualify the intelligibility a doctrine expresses. Simply because people deploy the term "transubstantiation" as a kind of shibboleth does not mean that the intelligibility it communicates ceases to exist. It simply means that human beings are prone to commonsense eclecticism. Chauvet is right to highlight this frequently uncritical employment of the metaphysical language of doctrine among theologians and pastors who assume they understand what doctrines mean. The result of uncritical use of technical language is confusion and skepticism among the faithful about what doctrines could possibly mean. However, if we can recover the insights that led to the dogmatic statements about the Eucharist we can begin to transpose those statements into categories derived from critical realist interpretations of traditional metaphysical terms like instrumentality, causality, substance, and accident. In order to execute that transposition we have endured a rather lengthy investigation of Lonergan's cognitional theory, epistemology, and metaphysics.

The present chapter turns to Lonergan's analysis of meaning. It has two primary tasks: (1) to elaborate Lonergan's understanding of foundations in theological reflection, paying particular attention to the role of intellectual conversion; and (2) to indicate the carriers, elements, and functions of meaning, the ontological status of meaning, and the realms within which meaning unfolds. Before we turn to Lonergan's foundations it will help to explain his understanding of dialectic.

1. Dialectic

Between *Insight* and *Method in Theology*, works that had originally been conceived as a single effort, Lonergan experienced a major breakthrough in theological method: functional specialization. This vision of theological method employs the levels of conscious intentionality to identify particular functions in the theological enterprise: research, interpretation, history, dialectic, foundations, doctrines, systematics, and communications. The eight specializations indicate ranges of inquiry corresponding to levels of operation. Briefly, in the mediating phase, research assembles the relevant data for experience. Interpretation proposes an understanding of the data. History renders a judgment about what was developing at a particular time. Dialectic distinguishes between positions and counterpositions in the tradition. Turning to the mediated phase, foundations objectifies conversion as the horizon of the theologian and develops categories consistent with that horizon. Doctrines express judgments consonant with conversion. Systematics deals with understanding the realities affirmed in judgments. Communications relates theological understanding in various contexts, building up the Christian community through common meaning.[1] For the moment our concern is with dialectic.

Lonergan's elaboration of the structure of dialectic has two levels; on the upper level are the operators, and on the lower level are the data. He explains:

> The operators are two precepts: develop positions; reverse counter-positions. Positions are statements compatible with intellectual, moral, and religious conversion; they are developed by being integrated with fresh data and further discovery. Counter-positions are statements incompatible with intellectual, or moral, or religious conversion; they are reversed when the incompatible elements are removed.[2]

Lonergan distinguishes between differences that are perspectival and those that are more fundamental. The fundamental differences are dialectical because they derive from failures of intellectual, moral, or religious conversion.[3] Dialectic involves identifying these fundamental differences. The previous three chapters brought to light a dialectical opposition between the Heideggerian critique of metaphysics we find in Chauvet, with its implicit cognitional theory, and a transposition of the Thomist position on knowing and being in Lonergan. A brief summary will clarify the dialectic opposition.

1.1. Postmodern Method and Metaphysics

In chapter 1 we explored Chauvet's method and his application of that method in relation to doctrines dealing with eucharistic presence and sacrifice at length. Chauvet leans heavily on Heidegger's critique of the Western metaphysical tradition, separating himself from that tradition in order to articulate a fundamental theology of the sacramental. His brief against metaphysics calls it to account for confusing the real with discourse about the real and reducing the sacraments to the metaphysical categories of cause and effect. Freeing the sacraments from the logic of cause and effect, he feels, allows them to retain their full symbolic depth as revelers of the "already-there of grace" and operators of the symbolic order. For Chauvet the symbolic order is the horizon of *Dasein*, so that what happens in the

---

[1] Bernard Lonergan, *Method in Theology* (Toronto: University of Toronto Press, 1990), 127–33.

[2] Ibid., 249.

[3] Ibid., 235.

sacraments "is not of the physical, moral, or metaphysical but of the symbolic order. . . . Clearly, the whole problem here lies in the manner in which
one thinks of reality: it is not of the order of subsistent entities, but of the
order of the on-going transformation of subjects into believers."[4] Chauvet
identifies the problem accurately by raising the question about the real, but
he juxtaposes the world of things to the human world in such a way that he
unnecessarily severs the metaphysical from the symbolic.[5] Recall Chauvet's
position: "Emphasis on [the sacraments as operators] can free itself from
the productionist scheme . . . only if we 'overcome' the metaphysical view
of the world (characterized by instrumentality and causality) and move
into the symbolic (characterized by the mediation through language and
symbol, where 'revealer' and 'operator' are indissolubly linked insofar as
they are homogeneous)."[6] Overcoming the metaphysical view is a matter of
choosing another starting point.

Chauvet's symbolic approach leads him to interpret the eucharistic presence of Christ as *ad-esse*, as a "being for." Consequently he argues that the
eucharistic bread not only remains bread after the consecration but is "never
so much bread" as in this mystery.[7] By shifting the terrain to the symbolic,

---

[4] Louis-Marie Chauvet, *Symbol and Sacrament: A Sacramental Reinterpretation of
Christian Existence* [= *SS*], trans. Patrick Madigan and Madeleine Beaumont (Collegeville, MN: Liturgical Press, 1995), 438.

[5] Giovani Sala identifies a similar separation in Edward Schillebeeckx's notion of
transignification. See Giovani Sala, "Transubstantiation oder Transignifikation: Gedenken zu einem Dilemma," *Zeitschrift fur Katholische Theologie* 92 (1970): 1–34.

[6] *SS*, 544.

[7] "Because the mystery of the Eucharistic body of the Lord cannot be expressed on
this [symbolic] terrain unless it carries with it the symbolic richness of bread evoked
all along the journey, it is clear that to express all its radicalness, not only can one no
longer say but one must no longer say, 'This bread is no longer bread.' On the contrary,
such a statement had to be made on the terrain of metaphysical substance since on
this level it expressed the necessary implication of the *conversio totius substantiae*
formulated dogmatically at the Council of Trent. On the altogether different terrain of
symbolism and due to the fact it is so different that the verb *'be' no longer has the same
status it had at its origin* because the *Sein* is inseparable from the human *Da-Sein* and
thus from language, from which it nevertheless remains distinct, to say that 'this bread
is the body of Christ' requires that one emphasize all the more it is indeed still bread,
but now essential bread, bread which is never so much bread as it is in this mystery.
We find again the biblical language of John 6: This is THE bread, the 'true bread,' the
artos alethinos where the truth of bread, always forgotten (*a-letheia*), is revealed" (*SS*,

Chauvet attempts to fortify his interpretation of eucharistic presence against criticism. However, he seems unaware that his disjunction of the symbolic and the metaphysical orders is a false one. The disjunction is again apparent in his defense of his interpretation: "Here, it is fitting to recall that the real, according to our symbolic approach, resists every attempt at a definitive understanding by the subject. Not coming to the subject except as mediated by language, the real is even, in the last analysis, what is always absent."[8] And further he argues, as we noted previously: "In this perspective, *the symbolic order is the most radical mediation of the real's resistance to every attempt at a subjectivist reduction.* Hence . . . one's taking all aspects of the Eucharistic presence into account *does not necessarily require that one conceive it in the mode of metaphysical substance.*"[9] We cannot but agree that the real is mediated for human beings by language and that a full account of eucharistic presence does not end with identifying metaphysical substances.

As regards the meaning of Christ's passion, Chauvet employs Heidegger's notion of *Gelassenheit.* The Son is the exemplar of "letting-be" to the point of self-sacrifice of his divine authority, in filial trust, to the Father. Chauvet draws on the *kenosis* of Christ described in Philippians 2 as the paradigm for understanding the passion. Christ's *kenosis* is understood as "the *consent to his condition as Son-in-humanity and as Brother of humanity.*"[10] The Son's kenotic self-giving is a reversal of Adam's sin, in which humanity finds itself in competition with God, "a pattern whose typical representation is the *slave* trying to seize for him or herself the omnipotence of the *master* and to take the master's place."[11] While Chauvet retains an understanding of Christ's work as a sacrifice, he does so in terms of an existential rather than a ritual modality. Christ "consents to taste humanity to its extreme limit, death experienced in the silence of a God who would not even intervene to spare the Just One this death."[12] Christ does not perform a ritual sacrifice; rather, Chauvet interprets his sacrifice as anti-sacrifice, as inaugurating a

---

400). In his review of *Symbol and Sacrament,* Raymond Moloney suggests that Chauvet's position recalls theories of consubstantiation. See Moloney's "*Symbol and Sacrament,*" in *Milltown Studies* 38 (Autumn 1996): 146–49, at 146.

[8] *SS*, 400–401.
[9] Ibid., 401.
[10] Ibid., 301.
[11] Ibid., 299.
[12] Ibid., 301.

new understanding of sacrifice demarcated by the rending of the temple curtain, which renders ritual sacrifice obsolete.

This "anti-sacrificial" interpretation of the cross opens up a new path for thinking through the relation of the church to the work of Christ. In moving beyond the *quid pro quo* economy of expiatory or propitiatory sacrifice informed by the metaphysics of cause and effect, Chauvet interprets the Eucharist in terms of symbolic gift exchange: "The Eucharist gives us back to ourselves and to others (its dimension of reconciliation) in the very act where we give ourselves back to God in offering God our filial thanksgiving (its [always primary] dimension of 'sacrifice of thanksgiving')."[13] Through eucharistic communion in the mode of symbolic exchange the church becomes a community of sisters and brothers of Christ, adopted children of the Father, a "eucharistic people" who give flesh here and now to the crucified God by loving God and neighbor, which is the "true sacrifice" of the Eucharist.[14]

Chauvet wants to get beyond the confines of a metaphysics that reduces grace to a commodity purchased by ritual sacrifice and supports an image of material permanence regarding Christ's presence in the Eucharist, to attain to a symbolic framework that is open to the gratuitousness of grace and an eschatological awareness of "real absence" in the Eucharist. This opening to the symbolic, Chauvet believes, will enable a theology of the sacramental that integrates Scripture, sacrament, and ethics in a work of mourning the absence of God who asks that the church give God a body in history: "The element 'Sacrament' is thus the symbolic place of the on-going transition between Scripture and Ethics, from the letter to the body. The liturgy is the powerful pedagogy where we learn to consent to the presence of the absence of God, who obliges us to give him a body in the world, thereby giving the sacraments their plenitude in the 'liturgy of the neighbor' and giving the ritual memory of Jesus Christ its plenitude in our existential memory."[15]

Chauvet's impulse to integrate Scripture, sacrament, and ethics in a fundamental theology of the sacramental is certainly the right one. Any attempt to isolate these aspects of Christian living from one another results in a distorted practice. In addition, his shift to a concrete foundation in human

---

[13] Ibid., 314.
[14] Ibid., 315.
[15] Ibid., 265.

performance coheres with a critical-realist understanding of contingency and verification. Chauvet's questions for the tradition are important, but his method of answering them is problematic. The result is that while he does manage to articulate a new way of thinking about the relationships between Scripture, sacrament, and ethics in terms of the arch-symbol of the Christian body born in symbolic gift exchange, Chauvet never actually breaks the cause-effect schema and is trapped by an artificial disjunction of the symbolic and the metaphysical without ever being explicit about how he understands the latter. In failing to be explicit, Chauvet employs a problematic metaphysics in which the real remains *already-out-there-now-real*, even if he describes it in terms of absence rather than presence. Indeed, Chauvet hopes to protect the exteriority of the real against the logic of the same by holding up its dimension of absence. Absence preserves the other from reduction to the same. But again we find a performative contradiction: after articulating what purports to be a definitive statement in regard to the eucharistic bread, i.e., that this bread is the "true bread" of John 6,[16] Chauvet emphasizes the retreat of the real from the subject. How can we distinguish "true bread" or "true sacrifice" within this methodology? In what sense are they true? What are the criteria? Is it because of their absence? In what sense does absence preserve the truth of a thing? Granted, Chauvet has admitted his intention to sidestep all such questions by operating on the terrain of the symbolic. But even identifying such a terrain is saying something about the nature of reality, especially the reality of human beings. He means something, indeed, something very important, but his method militates against his saying it. He is trapped in a methodological blind alley because he fails to pay attention to his own performance.

This is why Chauvet can advocate for a position of permanent questioning while interdicting all questions that demand "is it so?" Questions that move toward knowledge of truth belong to the realm of metaphysics, which he has abandoned for the symbolic. In addition, he fails to grasp the point about causality that it is an explanation of all temporal change in terms of a real relation of dependence. In fact, Aquinas explains that, in the order of the universe that actually exists, all change is causally related to divine agency, and therefore *everything,* aside from the divine, functions on the order of secondary or instrumental causality, including grace. But more on

---

[16] Ibid., 400.

this later. Each of these oversights is indicative of what Lonergan identifies as a lack of intellectual conversion, and Chauvet is not alone. The tendency in much postmodern thought to conflate the search for understanding with the modern materialist position on knowing as a matter of prediction and control is misleading and inaccurate. The result is that some contemporary theologians suggest that the very desire to know involves the knower in a conceptual idolatry in need of deconstruction.

In his review of the English edition of *Symbol and Sacrament*, the Irish Jesuit Raymond Moloney highlights the key problems in Chauvet's treatise while commending many of the more fruitful portions of the work, which he describes as "a force to be reckoned with."[17] Moloney suggests that Chauvet's Heideggerian criticisms of metaphysics "will find their mark in [Platonic and Scotist] metaphysics, but there is another kind, closer to that built into the nature of the mind as such, to which Heidegger and Chauvet scarcely do justice."[18] That such a built-in metaphysics, fully elaborated by Lonergan, continues to form Chauvet's thinking "is perhaps suggested by the fact that when Chauvet comes to speak of the operative nature of the sacramental sign, he cannot do so without himself falling back into the language of 'efficacy.'"[19]

Identifying the metaphysics to which Moloney refers is a matter of self-appropriation and intellectual conversion. Without self-appropriation and intellectual conversion, metaphysics remains latent, and a counterpositional cognitional theory is almost inevitable. Moloney suggests a possible remedy to Chauvet's counterpositional argument in Lonergan's distinction between common sense, theory, and interiority: "Chauvet presumably never read Bernard Lonergan; certainly he never refers to him; but the categories of the Canadian author undoubtedly help one in approaching some of the key problems raised in this book. One might start with Lonergan's notion of the differentiation of consciousness, and so distinguish between the worlds of common sense, theory and interiority. Chauvet's positive points are to be found in the first and third of these worlds."[20] Indeed, Chauvet's turn to the symbolic is precisely the kind of work that needs to be done in

[17] Moloney, "*Symbol and Sacrament*," 146.
[18] Ibid., 148.
[19] Ibid.
[20] Ibid.

sacramental theology in the third stage of meaning, in which theology is communicated in categories of interiority; however, this turn to the symbol, if it remains detached from theory, merely reinforces the symbol/real split that has plagued eucharistic theology since at the least the eleventh-century condemnation of Berengar. There is another possibility.

1.2. Differentiating the Metaphysical and the Symbolic

When Lonergan distinguishes common sense, theory, and interiority he invokes the idea of stages of meaning in history.[21] The turn to theory in Western philosophy is a turn from commonsense meaning to a theoretical control in which rigorous definition overcomes the ambiguity of commonsense thinking. Plato's dialogues consistently pursue this kind of theoretical rigor as Socrates prods his interlocutors to transcend the common sense of the *agora* in order to clarify what they mean when they refer to such things as virtue or happiness. Theory is important for overcoming the ambiguities that may otherwise come to dominate human discourse and confound genuine conversation. While Chauvet slides into these ambiguities through a persistent assertion of the symbolic over the metaphysical, Moloney, following Lonergan, raises another possible understanding of theory: "Distinguishing the realm of theory from the other two realms is one of the first steps in vindicating this realm in the face of the kind of criticism raised by Chauvet. Metaphysics and symbolism are not two competing explanations but two different levels of discourse, with the former capable of illuminating the intelligibility of the latter. I say 'capable' advisedly, since not all metaphysics is of equal value."[22] Chauvet's division of "metaphysical" and "symbolic" only makes sense if the metaphysical side is a particular variation of decadent scholastic emphasis on certitude peculiar to a certain kind of Platonizing philosophy as practiced

---

[21] Lonergan, *Method in Theology*, 85: "The stages in question are ideal constructs, and the key to the constructing is undifferentiation or differentiation of consciousness. In the main we have in mind the Western tradition and we distinguish three stages. In the first stage conscious and intentional operations follow the mode of common sense. In a second stage besides the mode of common sense there is also the mode of theory, where the theory is controlled by a logic. In a third stage the modes of common sense and theory remain, science asserts its autonomy from philosophy, and there occur philosophies that leave theory to science and take their stand on interiority."

[22] Moloney, *"Symbol and Sacrament,"* 148.

by Ockhamist and post-Enlightenment neoscholasticisms.[23] That way of thinking, because it emphasizes concepts to the neglect of understanding, is governed by an exorbitant use of the logical control of meaning and issues in the conceptualist certitude that informed the theology of the manuals. When the term "metaphysics" is employed to indicate this kind of logical control as opposed to a symbolic approach it usually suggests that metaphysics deals exclusively with the truth of reality and relegates the symbolic realm of metaphors and myths to falsehood and unreality. It was this theology that Heidegger left behind when he abandoned "the system of Catholicism." Indeed, much of the twentieth-century rehabilitation of the symbolic, including Chauvet's, is carried out in reaction to this scholastic mentality in order to vindicate the symbolic—an effort that is critical to sacramental theology. But there are other philosophical methods and other modes of Catholic theology. Moloney pinpoints the difference in Chauvet's use of Heidegger: "For all his polemic against the subject-object schema, Heidegger himself could never finally overcome the dichotomy between thought and experience as long as he failed to analyse adequately the problem of objectivity. Thus Lonergan once remarked that Heidegger ended up half-way between empiricism and idealism (*Method in Theology*: Toronto Summer School 1969, vol. 2, p. 516). Objectivity in *Being and Time* is a point of reference at the origin of the processes of knowledge rather than the fruit of their authentic implementation."[24] Chauvet's disjunction of the symbolic and the metaphysical reflects "the same unresolved dichotomy."[25] Moloney argues, "A notion of objectivity such as that of Lonergan, seeing it as the attribute of true judgment and the fruit of authentic subjectivity, cuts through a lot of Chauvet's criticisms and helps to obviate the need for his post-modern deconstruction."[26] The metaphysical and the symbolic together make up the real world.

[23] See Louis Dupré, *Passage to Modernity: An Essay in the Hermeneutics of Nature and Culture* (New Haven, CT: Yale University Press, 1993); Susan Schreiner, *Are You Alone Wise? The Search for Certainty in the Early Modern Era* (New York: Oxford University Press, 2011). See also Gerald A. McCool, *Nineteenth-Century Scholasticism: The Search for a Unitary Method* (New York: Fordham University Press, 1989).

[24] Moloney, "*Symbol and Sacrament*," 149. The document to which Moloney refers is available online. See *1969 Institute on Method Lecture* 1B,17–18. Website accessed December 2, 2013, http://www.bernardlonergan.com/pdf/51600DTE060.pdf.

[25] Ibid.

[26] Ibid.

Lonergan resists polarizing the metaphysical and symbolic orders because he holds that the real world in which human beings live is one mediated by meaning and motivated by values and for the most part known through language. For Lonergan metaphysics is not knowledge of things by their universal and necessary causes, but a heuristic structure of what is "to be known." And in the human world what is "to be known" is meaning. Lonergan consistently affirms that what we mean by the "real world" is a world mediated by meaning. The real is not the already-out-there-now, because in the world of meaning the real is known in a judgment regarding the truth of particular meanings or values. In the world mediated by meaning the integral heuristic structure of metaphysics is applicable to human acts of meaning, to symbols and rituals as explicated hermeneutically. By identifying metaphysics as the integral heuristic structure of proportionate being that is isomorphic with the structure of human cognition Lonergan's understanding of metaphysics becomes relevant to symbols as carriers of meaning more than to any abstract category of being.

What Chauvet strove to accomplish through Heideggerian *Destruktion*, Lonergan did by returning to Thomas and undertaking to expand and clarify the old by means of the new, *vetera novis augere et perficere*. Clearly, the philosophical consensus that informed scholasticism is long gone. Nothing has emerged to replace it. And while the postmodern criticism of foundations may be warranted in response to the overreaching rationalism of modernity, its purported openness appears to open in only one direction. But Lonergan was convinced that insights of the past could help illumine the future. He was not content with an eclectic solution; he was certain that the new synthesis should ascend to the level of what Thomas achieved for medieval theology in order to enable a limited and analogical understanding of the mysteries of faith that renders their meaning transformative in history. This synthesis would include

> First, an understanding of modern science, secondly, an understanding of modern scholarship, and thirdly, a philosophy that is at home in modern science and modern scholarship. Next, continuity with what is old will be a matter of analogy, and, indeed, of analogy of proportion; so a theology will be continuous with Thomism . . . if it stands to modern science, modern scholarship and an associated philosophy as Thomism stood to Aristotelianism. Finally, the theology will be dialectical if it distinguishes systematically between the authentic and

the unauthentic, between positions and counterpositions, and if it can settle issues by appealing to this distinction.[27]

Lonergan was not content to repeat what Thomas had said; rather, he wanted to do for our time what Thomas had done in his. Lonergan's life-work was to develop the total and basic science of generalized empirical method—what he called "foundational methodology"—and an empirically grounded metaphysics that could inform an explanatory theology. If the implementation of that work and the emergence of a subsequent theological and philosophical consensus is indeed a long way off, I am convinced that applying Lonergan's thought to eucharistic doctrines can overcome the impasse between objectivist and subjectivist interpretations of those doctrines and thus contribute to that implementation.[28]

2. Foundations in Lonergan

Lonergan and Chauvet agree on the need for a shift from abstract to concrete foundations in theology. Chauvet's foundation in "thinking" as meditating on the difference between the real and discourse about the real raises the problem of cognitional theory but does not provide a sufficient account of what we are doing when we are knowing. Lonergan elaborates how "thinking" unfolds in its intending and can even lead to affirming concrete foundations without anxieties over uncritically grounded notions of objectivity or metaphysics. Lonergan's metaphysics, as a part of the foundational reality, does not function as abstract premises from which we can deduce conclusions but as the concrete universal elaborated in terms of the notion of being.

2.1. Conversion and Authenticity

For Lonergan the notion of being, as illumined by faith, is the source of theological reflection. Recall that the notion of being is the unrestricted desire

---

[27] Lonergan, "The Scope of Renewal," *Philosophical and Theological Papers, 1965–1980,* CWBL 17, 282–98, at 293.

[28] This is Chauvet's description of the two primary orientations in eucharistic theology. See *SS,* 410–25, as well as Chauvet, *Sacraments: The Word of God at the Mercy of the Body,* trans. Madeleine Beaumont (Collegeville, MN: Liturgical Press, 2001), xiii–xxi.

to know, operative in the human subject. In the theological context the notion of being operates in a horizon transformed by grace. Lonergan elaborates the roots of this horizon in terms of three conversions that constitute the foundational reality for authentic theological reflection. In the experience of religious conversion the love of God elicits a conversion through which one falls in love with God in an unrestricted fashion and begins to operate in a horizon suffused with divine love. Within that horizon one's own good is transcended by the good revealed by God's love, so that, normally, a moral conversion follows religious conversion. The experience of divine love as the supreme good transforms all our human questioning in such a way that the philosophical question about being is transposed into a new horizon in which it ultimately becomes a question about God. An intellectual conversion may result, so that reality is no longer just a collection of sense data but an order that has a meaning and an intelligent ground. In this context the universe is neither foreign and threatening nor the source of existential anxiety into which we are thrown, but a revelation of the goodness that is divine love. These three conversions constitute the foundational reality for Lonergan. The foundation is nothing other than human consciousness operating in a new horizon shaped by the three conversions that, for Lonergan, constitute human authenticity.

This may sound flimsy if we fail to take into account Lonergan's understanding of authenticity. It is not "being yourself" in any ordinary commonsense understanding of the term, nor is it equivalent to Heidegger's or Charles Taylor's usage.[29] Authenticity refers to consciousness operating in the horizon of religious, moral, and intellectual conversion. If in much theological reflection the aspects of religious and moral conversion receive significant attention today, this occurs in a rather undifferentiated way, so that intellectual conversion and the attendant theoretical differentiation of consciousness is nearly forgotten. As a result, theology is frequently dominated by narrative and rhetoric. This is not necessarily a bad thing. Indeed, the Second Vatican Council took a more scripturally grounded approach. However, narrative alone cannot deal adequately with parties arguing that

---

[29] For an analysis of the differences and similarities between Lonergan and Taylor, see Brian J. Braman, Meaning and Authenticity: *Bernard Lonergan and Charles Taylor on the Drama of Authentic Human Existence* (Toronto: University of Toronto Press, 2008).

"my story describes my experience of reality better than your story."[30] How
are we to assess rival descriptions of reality? In eucharistic theology this
issue arises whenever some argue that Christ is "really present" in the Eucharist and others contend, apparently to the contrary, that the Eucharist
is a "symbol" of Christ's presence, or again when some stipulate that the
Eucharist is a "sacrifice" and others argue, apparently to the contrary, that
the Eucharist is a "meal." In the end we have to do not with opposed positions but with possibly complementary descriptive ways of working out
the meaning of a ritual that are usually employed by persons innocent of
intellectual conversion and hence confined to commonsense eclecticism.[31]
This does not mean that the people who argue these positions are acting
in bad faith or that they are unintelligent; it means only that an intellectual
conversion preparatory to answering to the question "what is reality?" is
not frequent.[32]

The sacraments are perhaps the paradigmatic case of the need for intellectual conversion in theological understanding.[33] In previous centuries when
questions about the nature of the Trinity or the two natures of Christ were
of major concern, new explanatory dogmatic statements informed those
impelled by the Socratic turn to theory and the systematic differentiation of

---

[30] This form of narrative agonistics dominates the interpretive program of John
Milbank and the theological movement centered on his work, "radical orthodoxy." See
Oliver Davies, "Revelation and the Politics of Culture: A Critical Assessment of the The-
ology of John Milbank," 112–25, in *Radical Orthodoxy? A Catholic Enquiry*, ed. Laurence
Paul Hemming (Burlington, VT: Ashgate, 2000).

[31] What is so problematic about surveys that inquire into beliefs about the Eucharist is that they tend to reinforce these disagreements between forms of commonsense
eclecticism among respondents. What a given person thinks about a doctrine depends
on a massive polymorphism of human consciousness, which a survey cannot possibly
consider.

[32] As we noted above, it was precisely this question Schillebeeckx was trying to answer in *The Eucharist*, but his primarily Kantian intellectual resources did not allow him
to arrive at the critical realist position, so he was pulled in two between transignification
on the one side and transubstantiation on the other.

[33] Absence of intellectual conversion does not preclude meaningful participation in
sacramental worship, but a version of it is continually referenced in the church fathers,
who describe an invisible meaning to be understood through the mediation of the sensible
signs of the sacraments. The presence or absence of that conversion can be related to
two ways of participating in the Eucharist; Saint Thomas Aquinas calls these "spiritual
eating" and "sacramental eating."

consciousness provided answers by working out terms like *homoousios* or *hypostasis* to explain revealed truths. Similarly, early eucharistic doctrines offered answers to questions about the mode of Christ's presence in the Eucharist and were codified in conciliar decrees that clarified the matter.[34] But just as the categories "person" and "nature" have undergone radical redefinition in modern and postmodern philosophy, so have the categories "substance" and "causality." Consequently, understanding conciliar decrees on the Eucharist is exceedingly difficult for contemporary Christians, but especially in the absence of either the systematic differentiation of consciousness or intellectual conversion. However, if any aspect of Christian life can awaken us significantly to the need for intellectual conversion it is sacramental worship.

Sacramental worship confounds picture thinking or the image of knowing as taking a look at what is there to be seen, because what is at stake in the mystery of sacramental action is religious and moral conversion. Giving an account of sacramental activity requires an intellectual conversion, which is lacking in much contemporary sacramental theology. Although Chauvet moves in the right direction, his presentation is not sufficiently differentiated to handle the real problems in scholastic theology. As a result, categories like causality creep back in without being critically grounded. His interpretations of key doctrines use Heidegger to gloss, rather than critically analyze, the underlying issues proper to the doctrinal statements.

Lonergan's different approach can accommodate a point of departure similar to Chauvet's. Lonergan is more specific about the problem of the subject that is foundational for both himself and Chauvet. The latter helpfully calls our attention to the linguistic mediation of human culture and to the body as the locus of linguistic mediation that becomes an arch-symbol by its performative acts of meaning. These insights demand that we think about sacraments and sacramentality in a more critical way. By arguing that in fact we go beyond thinking to knowing in our intending, Lonergan pushes even further in the critical direction. While our knowing attains not the totally unconditioned, but virtually unconditioned contingent facts, it still is knowing nonetheless, and we must be responsible for what we know and how we know. By pushing beyond thinking to knowing, Lonergan

[34] See Edward J. Kilmartin, *The Eucharist in the West: History and Theology*, ed. Robert J. Daly (Collegeville, MN: Liturgical Press, 1998), 143–53.

arrives at a notion of objectivity grounded in human conscious performance. *Insight* and *Method in Theology* "develop a doctrine of objectivity that [is] relevant to the world mediated by meaning and motivated by values."[35] The notion of objectivity Lonergan develops is grounded in the performance of the subject operating in the horizon of authenticity: "Objectivity [is] the fruit of authentic subjectivity."[36] Lonergan clarifies, "Insofar as one is inauthentic, there is needed an about-turn, a conversion—indeed, a threefold conversion: an intellectual conversion by which without reserves one enters the world mediated by meaning; a moral conversion by which one comes to live in a world motivated by values; and a religious conversion when one accepts God's gift of his love bestowed through the Holy Spirit."[37] Intellectual conversion identifies reality with a world mediated by meaning.

To be fully responsible for our knowing demands self-appropriation and intellectual conversion, no less in theology than in philosophy. But the key point here is Lonergan's emphasis that intellectual conversion involves entering into the world mediated by meaning *"without reserves."* It is frequently the case that, when interpreting eucharistic doctrines, theologians and church authorities alike fail to concede this because they feel the need to still hold on to some aspect of reality that is putatively "objectively" out there.[38] Intellectual conversion abandons the intransigent mythic notion of objectivity as "seeing what is there to be seen, and not seeing what is not there, and that the real is what is out there now to be looked at."[39] Intellectual conversion is essential for gaining a fruitful analogical understanding of the mystery of Christ's presence in the Eucharist. To be sure, according to the tradition, discerning the presence of Christ in the Eucharist is no mere intellectual exercise. If one is not intellectually converted, however, one can be greatly impeded from understanding adequately the experience of this great Christian mystery. This is more a problem for those who talk about the mystery, theologians and teachers, than for those who experience it. But

---

[35] Lonergan, "Reality, Myth, Symbol," 384–90, in *Philosophical and Theological Papers, 1965–1980*, CWBL 17, at 389.

[36] Ibid.

[37] Ibid, 389–90.

[38] This is precisely what leaves Schillebeeckx in the compromised position of holding both transignification and transubstantiation. The same perspective is apparent in Paul VI's response to Schillebeeckx in *Mysterium Fidei*, which we will review presently.

[39] Lonergan, *Method in Theology*, 238.

the transformative potential of encounter with Christ in the Eucharist can only benefit from intellectual conversion.

The theologian operating in virtue of intellectual, moral, and religious conversion is foundational for theological reflection, according to Lonergan. However much some might wish for the security of a foundation in a set of premises from which theological conclusions could be deduced automatically, in the present context we are faced with the reality that such a theology is "notoriously insufficient."[40] Lonergan argues: "It does seem necessary to insist that the threefold conversion is not foundational in the sense that it offers the premises from which all desirable conclusions are to be drawn. The threefold conversion is, not a set of propositions that a theologian utters, but a fundamental and momentous change in the human reality that a theologian is."[41] The theological statements of the triply converted theologian will not necessarily reflect authenticity, however, because differentiations of consciousness also lead to "pluralism of expression."[42]

2.2. Differentiations of Consciousness

Lonergan distinguishes between differentiated and undifferentiated consciousness in his analysis of the pluralism of expression in the history of theology. If conversion is foundational for theological reflection, "that manifestation will vary with the presence or absence of differentiated consciousness."[43] Differentiations of consciousness combine distinct groups of operations identified in *Method in Theology* as common sense, theory, interiority, and transcendence, to which he adds scholarship and art. Undifferentiated consciousness is content with commonsense understanding. It tends to resist the more theoretical manner of speaking, and sometimes even forms of artistic meaning. For undifferentiated consciousness the doctrine of transubstantiation may be as opaque as the ritual in which it is enacted. Undifferentiated consciousness is not necessarily antagonistic toward these more specialized domains, although often it is;[44] rather, it simply subsumes theory and ritual under the domain of common sense.

---

[40] Ibid., 270.
[41] Ibid.
[42] Ibid., 271.
[43] Ibid.
[44] See ibid., 273: "Less differentiated consciousness finds more differentiated consciousness beyond its horizon and, in self-defence, may tend to regard the more differentiated

Differentiations of consciousness, on the other hand, will take manifold combinations whenever common sense enters other realms of meaning. Lonergan identifies religiously, artistically, theoretically, scholarly, and interiorly differentiated consciousness. Religiously differentiated consciousness is found in the mystic who withdraws "from the world mediated by meaning into a silent and all-absorbing self-surrender in response to God's gift of his love."[45] Artistically differentiated consciousness "promptly recognizes and responds to beautiful objects," and its "higher attainment is creating: it invents commanding forms; works out their implications; conceives and produces their embodiment."[46] Theoretically differentiated consciousness develops in two phases in which objects are understood in their relations to each other, not in their relations to us. In the first phase "basic terms and relations pertain to philosophy, and the sciences are conceived as further and fuller determinations of the objects of philosophy, as in Aristotelianism."[47] But in the second phase the sciences are liberated from the philosophers' terms and relations to discover their own,[48] "and as that discovery matures, there occurs in a new setting the distinction Aristotle drew between the *priora quoad nos* and the *priora quoad se.*"[49] The scholarly differentiation of consciousness studies the common sense of different cultures and different historical periods in order "to understand the meaning intended in particular statements and the intentions embodied in particular deeds."[50] It is, therefore, distinct from the theoretical differentiation that aims toward

---

with that pervasive, belittling hostility that Max Scheler named *ressentiment*." For many in the contemporary American context *ressentiment* is considered a public virtue, so much so that any whiff of theory is deemed effete. This pattern presents a serious challenge for theologians who have recourse to theoretical rather than rhetorical tools, the former being called increasingly into question while the latter dominate the narrative agonistics of American public religious discourse.

[45] Lonergan, *Method in Theology*, 273.

[46] Ibid.

[47] Ibid., 274.

[48] The theological debate between Filippo Selvaggi and Carlo Colombo over the proper place of science in understanding transubstantiation could have benefited from this basic distinction. The temptation among theologians to continue to operate in the first phase, where science uses only philosophy's terms, has led to rather bizarre claims in regard to the Eucharist. See Richard G. Cipolla, "Selvaggi Revisited: Transubstantiation and Contemporary Science," *Theological Studies* 35 (1974): 667–91.

[49] Lonergan, *Method in Theology*, 274.

[50] Ibid.

universal principles. Finally, interiorly differentiated consciousness "operates in the realms of common sense and interiority."[51] While it begins, like theoretically differentiated consciousness, with sense experience, it quickly moves to a consideration of the data of consciousness, namely, the conscious operations through which sensible data are understood and judged. It is on the basis of interiorly differentiated consciousness that Lonergan's method is erected: "It has been toward such a basis that modern philosophy has been groping in its efforts to overcome fourteenth-century skepticism, to discover the relationship to the natural and human sciences, to work out a critique of common sense which so readily blends with common nonsense, and to place abstractly apprehended cognitional activity within the concrete and sublating context of human feeling and moral deliberation, evaluation, and decision."[52]

The key point to distinguishing the various differentiations of consciousness in regard to the foundations of theological reflection is that "theoretically differentiated consciousness enriches religion with a systematic theology, but it also liberates natural science from philosophic bondage."[53] And while scholarship "builds an impenetrable wall between systematic theology and its historical religious sources . . . this development invites philosophy and theology to migrate from a basis in theory to a basis in interiority."[54] A basis in interiority is what Lonergan's understanding of foundations offers. As with Chauvet, that foundation is to be found in human consciousness, but in a more differentiated way that includes thinking in a larger process of knowing and stakes its claims on a critical objectivity grounded in authentic subjectivity characteristic of religiously, morally, and intellectually converted persons.

2.3. *Categories*

From a foundation formulated in terms of conversion and interiorly differentiated consciousness Lonergan derives general and special categories that are to orient theological reflection. The categories he proposes have a transcultural base because they are not derived from abstract philosophical

[51] Ibid.
[52] Ibid., 274–75.
[53] Ibid., 275–76.
[54] Ibid., 276.

premises but from a transcendental method that accounts empirically for the basic operations of human intelligence in asking and answering questions. Though transcendental method is not transcultural in its articulation, it is so in its performative reality. Human beings wonder. They ask questions for understanding, for judgment, and for deliberation. In addition, the gift of God's love is given to all human beings and so it, too, has a transcultural aspect, not inasmuch as it is manifested differently in different cultures but as a gift, because "God's gift of his love is free. It is not conditioned by human knowledge; rather it is the cause that leads man to seek knowledge of God."[55] These two principles provide the bases for categories that are transcultural. General theological categories are grounded in transcendental method, and special categories are grounded in God's gift of love operative in human beings in love with God. Here, Lonergan introduces an important clarification that brings his treatment of the polymorphism of human consciousness in *Insight* to bear on theological reflection.

Being in love with God as defined is "the habitual actuation of man's capacity for self-transcendence; it is the religious conversion that grounds both moral and intellectual conversion; it provides the real criterion by which all else is to be judged; and consequently one has only to experience it in oneself or witness it in others, to find in it its own justification."[56] In its pure state, however, the experience of being in love with God is rare, since it is often mixed into the messiness of human historicity. Authenticity is always dialectical. "It is authenticity as a withdrawal from unauthenticity, and the withdrawal is *never complete and always precarious*."[57] Just as Lonergan was not naïve about the perfect functioning of human conscious intentionality in his discussion of cognitional theory, neither is he naïve about the achievement of a perfect being in love with God that would offer theology the most secure foundation. For Christians this degree of perfection is found only in Jesus, but even his articulation involved withdrawal from unauthenticity, processes of discovery, trial and error.

The general theological categories, then, will be derived from the base of the attending, inquiring, reflecting, deliberating subject. But because knowing is isomorphic with being, the structure of human conscious intentionality as

---

[55] Ibid., 283.
[56] Ibid., 283–84.
[57] Ibid., 284. Emphasis added.

verified in the process of self-appropriation reveals both objects insofar as they are compound unities, identities, and wholes, along with their conjugate forms, and the subject as subject in a verifiable account of human knowing. From these basic terms and relations one can derive a series of differentiations that enrich our understanding of human conscious intentionality, as occurs in the course of reading *Insight* and the early chapters of *Method*.

Turning to special theological categories, Lonergan advocates a transposition of medieval categories, which were developed in the terms of a theoretical theology, into categories that apply to a methodical theology. A transposition of medieval categories into a new key will help us to reinterpret eucharistic doctrines without abandoning important insights. Lonergan offers an example of a special theological category transposed from medieval theology when he moves from talking about "sanctifying grace" to talking about the dynamic state of being in love with God as other-worldly love. "It is this other-worldly love," Lonergan explains, "not this or that act, not a series of acts, but as a dynamic state whence proceed the acts, that constitutes in a methodical theology what in a theoretical theology is named sanctifying grace."[58] What medieval theology explained in terms of a "supernatural entitative habit," Lonergan explains in terms of the gift of God's love experienced as a dynamic state. That dynamic state makes acts of continuous self-transcendence like religious, moral, and intellectual conversion possible. The data of that dynamic state "are the data on a process of conversion and development."[59] In addition, there are inner and outer determinants of that love: "The inner determinants are God's gift of his love and man's consent, but there are also outer determinants in the store of experience and in the accumulated wisdom of the religious tradition."[60] These outer determinants offer the word of a religious tradition and that outer word is indispensible for growing in relationship with God.

The outer word of tradition is analogous to the avowal of love between two lovers whose love had hitherto remained unfulfilled because it did not reach the point of declaration. "It is the love that each freely and fully reveals to the other that brings about the radically new situation of being in love."[61]

---

[58] Ibid., 289.
[59] Ibid.
[60] Ibid.
[61] Ibid., 113.

The outer word of love has the same role in the experience of divine love. "Ordinarily the experience of the mystery of love and awe is not objectified. It remains within subjectivity as a vector, an undertow, a fateful call to a dreaded holiness."[62] But that pull intends an outer word, "the word of tradition that has accumulated religious wisdom, the word of fellowship that unites those that share the gift of God's love, the word of the gospel that announces that God has loved us first and, in the fulness of time, has revealed that love in Christ crucified, dead, and risen."[63] These outer words constitute a relationship with God of mutual self-donation made possible by the *kenosis* of Christ, who communicates through his mission the fullness of divine love in self-offering. Lonergan explains that the word of tradition is personal and social:

> The word, then, is personal. *Cor ad cor loquitur*: love speaks to love, and its speech is powerful. The religious leader, the prophet, the Christ, the apostle, the priest, the preacher announces in signs and symbols what is congruent with the gift of love that God works within us. The word, too, is social: it brings into a single fold the scattered sheep that belong together because at the depth of their hearts they respond to the same mystery of love and awe.[64]

In addition, the word is historical, and so as contexts change the expression of the same word of love changes to meet the demands of language and culture.

The implications of Lonergan's identification of the inner and outer words of love for sacramental theology are apparent and will be explicated in subsequent sections of this chapter. Lonergan's transposition of sanctifying grace offers an example of the kinds of categories his new understanding of foundations makes possible. The special theological categories to be derived involve: (1) religious experience or spirituality—religious interiority as it shapes the prophet, the mystic, the doctor, the theologian; (2) "the history of the salvation that is rooted in a being-in-love, and the function of this history in promoting the kingdom of God"; (3) the Trinity as "the

[62] Ibid.
[63] Ibid.
[64] Ibid.

loving source of our love" and our eschatological home;[65] (4) the church as an emerging concrete reality of authentic Christian witness;[66] (5) the vectors of progress, decline, and redemption wherein redemption is understood as a divine solution to the problem of evil by overcoming evil with good.[67]

3. Meaning

An additional set of general categories that will be helpful for interpreting eucharistic doctrines in a new key appear in Lonergan's analysis of meaning. If the real world is a world mediated by meaning, then we need to explicate further how meaning mediates a world. In *Method in Theology* Lonergan develops a theory of meaning, in which he identifies the carriers, elements, functions, and realms of meaning.

3.1. Carriers of Meaning

Lonergan emphasizes that the "real world" is one mediated by meaning and motivated by values, but what does he mean by meaning, and how is meaning mediated? First, meaning is intersubjective: for example, a smile communicates a meaning spontaneously. Our smiling is usually not calculated except perhaps when it is used to deceive. A smile reveals our feelings as much as do tears and weeping. Insofar as these spontaneous acts reveal our feelings they carry a meaning, so that originally meaning is mediated through our bodies in postures, gestures, facial movements, or the tone and pitch of the voice. Prior to any more complex constructions of meaning, these movements and sounds communicate, as when parents communicate love to an infant child, for whom words are mere sounds but a smile is security and comfort.

[65] Lonergan explains: "The Christian tradition makes explicit our implicit intending of God in all our intending by speaking of the Spirit that is given to us, of the Son who redeemed us, of the Father who sent the Son and with the Son sends the Spirit, and of our future destiny when we shall know, not in a glass darkly, but face to face" (ibid., 291).

[66] On *authentic* Christian witness Lonergan writes, "Just as one's humanity, so too one's Christianity may be authentic or unauthentic or some blend of the two. What is worse, to the unauthentic man or Christian, what appears authentic, is the unauthentic. Here, then, is the root of division, opposition, controversy, denunciation, bitterness, hatred, violence" (ibid., 291).

[67] Ibid.

Just as bodily movements communicate on a prelinguistic level, so art communicates meaning prior to its objectification in the language of the critic or commentator. Artistic meaning is purely experiential, or elemental.[68] The work of art communicates the freedom through which the artist and her world are transformed: "[The artist] has been liberated from being a replaceable part adjusted to a ready-made world and integrated within it. He has ceased to be a responsible inquirer investigating some aspect of the universe or seeking a view of the whole. He has become just himself: emergent, ecstatic, originating freedom."[69] Because it is elemental, art is primarily something to be encountered, not explained. Art is a communication of the artist that invites participation and imagination before interpretation.

Symbols are images or objects that evoke or are evoked by feelings.[70] Feelings are intentional responses to values. They can be repressed if we find them repugnant, or transient if the object by which they are evoked disappears, but there is also a feeling of the kind described above in terms of a dynamic state of being in love. Lonergan writes: "There are in full consciousness feelings so deep and strong, especially when deliberately reinforced, that they channel attention, shape one's horizon, direct one's life. Here the supreme illustration is loving."[71] Feelings then "are related to their subject: they are the mass and momentum and power of his affective capacities, dispositions, habits, the effective orientation of his being."[72] But feelings develop, and symbols that were once evocative may lose their power. What one once feared is now welcome; what one once welcomed one now finds abhorrent. Human beings undergo affective development as their speech develops. Unlike logic, the symbolic sphere holds conflicts in tension so that for Christians a Roman technique of punishment and

---

[68] Ibid., 61. Lonergan refers the reader to Susanne K. Langer, *Feeling and Form: A Theory of Art* (New York: Scribner, 1953).

[69] Lonergan, *Method in Theology*, 63. Lonergan notes in *Insight*, "Not only . . . is man capable of aesthetic liberation and artistic creativity, but his first work of art is his own living. The fair, the beautiful, the admirable is embodied by man in his own body and actions before it is given a still freer realization in painting and sculpture, in music and poetry. Style is the man before it appears in the artistic product" (p. 211).

[70] Ibid., 64.

[71] Ibid., 32.

[72] Ibid., 65.

torture, a symbol of imperial power, can be at the same time a symbol of the fullness of divine love.[73]

It is in language that meaning finds liberation. Through a system of conventional signs the human desire to understand and to communicate understanding finds a vehicle for its expression. For example, Helen Keller's breakthrough to language transformed the world of her experience. For most of us, language molds our conscious intentionality at the same time as it structures our world.[74] Ordinary language develops in specialized directions into technical and literary language, but ultimately and for the most part "the expression of feeling is symbolic and, if words owe a debt to logic, symbols follow the laws of image and affect. With Giambattista Vico, then, we hold for the priority of poetry."[75]

Poetry reaches its fulfillment in incarnate meaning, which combines all the carriers of meaning. For incarnate meaning "is the meaning of a person, of his way of life, of his words, or of his deeds. It may be his meaning for just one other person, or for a small group, or for a whole national, or social, or cultural, or religious tradition."[76] Each of us is incarnate meaning. Our living unfolds as meaning in the world, revealing to others who we are. Just as our living is an expression of meaning, the life, death, and resurrection of Christ is the incarnate meaning of a divine person by which the life of the Trinity is communicated to human persons in history.

---

[73] Symbols can operate not only at the level of feeling but also as compact and complex explanatory accounts in the world mediated by meaning. See John D. Dadosky, "Sacred Symbols as Explanatory: Geertz, Eliade, and Lonergan," *Fu Jen International Religious Studies* 4, no. 1 (Summer 2010): 137–58.

[74] Ibid., 71. Lonergan's reflections on language at this point parallel Chauvet's Heideggerian analysis in *Symbol and Sacrament*.

[75] *Method in Theology*, 73. Chauvet and Heidegger hold for the same prioritization of poetry over logic. The further question is whether poetry is adequate to meet the systematic exigence of the desire to know. Certainly, human wonder is expressed in its native orientation toward the whole of being in poetry. But that same wonder moves human intelligence toward knowing, toward conception and affirmation. That requires a shift into the world of theory.

[76] Ibid.

3.2. Elements of Meaning

In addition to the functions of meaning, Lonergan distinguishes sources, acts, and terms of meaning. The sources of meaning include all of our conscious acts of meaning, the semiconscious acts of meaning that make up our dream life, and the other acts of the four levels of waking consciousness. Transcendental sources are the questions for intelligence, reflection, and deliberation proper to the dynamism of consciousness. The answers to those questions, grounded in experiencing, understanding, judging, and deciding, provide the categorial sources.[77]

Acts of meaning can be potential, formal, full, constitutive or effective, and instrumental. Potential acts of meaning are elemental. A smile or a work of art is a potential act of meaning that awaits further interpretation for the meaning to become explicit. Potential acts of meaning raise the question, what does it mean? Similarly "acts of sensing and understanding have only potential meaning" that emerges through the activation of sense and intelligence.[78] A formal act of meaning occurs in the act of thinking, or in possibly relevant interpretations of elemental meaning awaiting further determination. Formal acts distinguish meaning from meant, but as initial acts of formulating and defining what is meant, they need to be verified; they may be wrong and rejected as possible interpretations of meaning. "A full act of meaning is an act of judging."[79] It judges whether a formal act refers to an object of thought, a mathematical entity, a real thing in the world of human experience, or a transcendent reality beyond that world. Constitutive or effective acts of meaning are judgments of value or decisions that are embodied in courses of action. Finally, instrumental acts encompass all the expressions that externalize or make explicit the potential, formal, full, and constitutive or effective acts of meaning of the subject.[80]

A term of meaning is what is discovered through potential, formal, and full acts of meaning, but again, terms of meaning can refer to different spheres of being or different worlds. For example, we can say that the definition of a circle exists, but it exists in a different way than a tree or the moon. A mathematical or geometric definition is a conceptual reality

---

[77] Ibid.
[78] Ibid., 74.
[79] Ibid.
[80] Ibid., 74–75.

but does not exist in the world of experience, so Lonergan distinguishes between a "sphere of real being and other restricted spheres such as the mathematical, the hypothetical, the logical, and so on."[81] The difference regards the conditions to be fulfilled in each sphere. One need not, indeed cannot, observe the mathematical definition of a circle because it is empirically given only approximately. Mathematical definitions, like all concepts, are not explicitly connected to particular empirical data and so are invariant. Concepts do not properly "exist" for that reason.[82] These definitions are instances of meanings that exist in restricted sphere of being. The tree outside my window, on the other hand, is verifiable by the fact that the conditions for its existence have been fulfilled. If tomorrow it is uprooted and taken away, the conditions for its being outside my window will no longer be fulfilled. The statement "there is a tree outside my window" would no longer be true. The tree exists in a sphere of real being.

Transcendent being has no conditions and so is absolute. While we know transcendent being as we know anything else—through a judgment of the virtually unconditioned—in itself, transcendent being is without conditions. This means that transcendent being is not contingent. At a point in the past the tree outside my window did not exist, and at a certain point in the future it will cease to exist. Its existing is conditioned. Transcendent being transcends precisely such conditions. This is Lonergan's way of explaining the kinds of judgments Thomas makes when he concludes that God is "being itself" or "goodness itself."[83] Such judgments are terms of meaning in the sphere of transcendent being.

3.3. Functions of Meaning

In addition to identifying the various elements of meaning, Lonergan explains the variety of ways in which meaning functions. At its most basic level, meaning is cognitive. It is what promotes us from the world of the infant, who neither speaks nor understands speech—a world of immediacy—

---

[81] Ibid., 75.

[82] This recalls the fundamental difference between Scotus and Aquinas on distinction between essence and existence. See Bernard Lonergan, *Verbum: Word and Idea in Aquinas*, CWBL 2, ed. Frederick E. Crowe and Robert M. Doran (Toronto: University of Toronto Press, 1997), 166.

[83] See *Summa Theologiae*, I, q. 4, a. 3, and q. 6.

into a larger world, mediated by meaning and motivated by values, that includes not only immediately sensible data but also the past, the present, the future, "not only what is factual but also the possible, the ideal, the normative."[84] All the meanings and values that make up this world are communicated. They are not just an individual's meanings and values but those of entire historical cultures left by them to posterity, which continue to shape history. However, besides this accumulated tradition, the world of meaning is a concretely emerging world-historical situation with its own intelligibility: "In this larger world we live out our lives. To it we refer when we speak of the real world. But because it is mediated by meaning, because meaning can go astray, because there is myth as well as science, fiction as well as fact, deceit as well as honesty, error as well as truth, that larger real world is insecure."[85] There is no necessity to this world, only a concrete and contingent intelligibility that is subject to change.[86] But there is no other world for humans to know. Our world is neither the all-at-once intelligibility experienced by angels nor the brute animal instincts and sensations of kittens and dogs. Without careful attention to that world mediated by meaning, our penchant for the immediate may cause us to slip into either the angelic or the brute animal perspective in thinking about the real.[87] Meaning is initially cognitive; eventually it is an accumulation of knowledge that results as we move from being toddlers through adolescence and on into adulthood and that provides a set of meanings and values and a language through which we develop our orientation toward the world and our way of being in it.

As we work out our way of being in the world, meaning becomes efficient by intending and projecting into history what Lonergan calls "man's making

---

[84] Lonergan, *Method in Theology*, 77.

[85] Ibid.

[86] Related to this way of thinking about the world mediated by meaning is Lonergan's distinction between a classical understanding of culture as a normative reality, and therefore statically conceived, and the shift in modern social sciences to a historically conscious notion of culture as concrete and therefore subject to change.

[87] By distinguishing between the world of immediacy and the world mediated by meaning Lonergan is transposing Thomas's distinction between animals and rational animals. As rational animals, humans occupy a unique place in the created order. We know reality through the mediation of the senses and the operations of the intellect. To this fundamental distinction Lonergan adds his critical insights into the human subject as historically and culturally formed and the polymorphism of human consciousness.

of man."[88] Making the human world takes us out of a purely natural setting and into the humanly made world that "is the cumulative, now planned, now chaotic, product of human acts of meaning."[89] Effective meaning builds a world through acts of meaning that command the actions of human beings. Effective meanings motivate us to sail across an ocean or traverse an unknown wilderness. As performative answers to questions, they embody our meaning and values in an effective history of which we are a part even while we build it. These effective meanings are enacted by individuals and groups and make up a world constituted by meaning.

Constitutive meanings shape horizons through culture, religion, philosophy, literature, and politics. These meanings and values not only shape identity but also constitute people. They are "intrinsic" to what a person or group is and is to be. These meanings change, and insofar as they change, the individual or the group moves beyond what they had been hitherto. Those changes can be conversions that yield not only a new horizon but a transformed subject in a new horizon. Constitutive meanings adapt to new situations, scientific discoveries, philosophical revolutions. For example, the subjects of a monarchy understand themselves and their reality differently from the citizens of a democratic republic. On the other hand, the term "democratic republic" can acquire radically different meanings over time, encompassing not only constitutional democracies and their bourgeois individualists but also the one-party collectivist rule of communist states. That shared meaning constitutes a new reality, but it is not known in the way that sensible things informed by intelligibility are verified through a reflective insight into the sufficiency of the sensible evidence. Rather, in the case of realities constituted by the human meaning that informs them, their reality is known by assenting to a truthful speaker and consenting to act in accord with that truth. Inasmuch as the speaker is truthful, the term is a reality constituted by meaning. When a lover says "I love you" in total truthfulness, the statement as true constitutes a new reality. When Christ, who as a divine person is the truth, and as a human nature without sin is also truthful, says of some bread "this is my body," then the true meaning of

---

[88] See Bernard Lonergan, "Theology in Its New Context," 55–68, in *Second Collection*, CWBL 13, ed. William F. J. Ryan and Bernard J. Tyrrell (Toronto: University of Toronto Press, 1996).

[89] Lonergan, *Method in Theology*, 78.

the statement constitutes a new reality for the one who believes the word of Christ. For Lonergan this is an instance of constitutive meaning. A further question is whether an ontology of meaning can account for such statements of fact as "this is my body" about a thing that metaphysical analysis affirms is bread. Answering that question moves us further into a world constituted by common meaning.

Meaning is communicative whenever individual meanings become common to the group and those common meanings have a life in and through the members of the group; they become the constitutive meaning of the group: "The conjunction of both the constitutive and communicative functions of meaning yield the three key notions of community, existence, and history."[90] For Lonergan a community is an achievement of common meaning, and because it is concrete it is continually emergent. Community is therefore potential, formal, and actual: potential insofar as meanings reside in common experiences; formal when there is a shared understanding of experiences; actual insofar as members affirm common judgments so that "all affirm and deny in the same manner."[91] Further, common meaning becomes real in history through the common decisions and actions of the group. Each of us is born into communities of meaning such as family, religious tradition, and nation. Within these communities we become ourselves either authentically or unauthentically within a dialectical tension as regards the authenticity or unauthenticity of the community.[92] Consequently, as Lonergan indicated, "What I am is one thing, what a genuine Christian or Buddhist is, is another, and I am unaware of the difference. My unawareness is unexpressed. I have no language to express what I am, so I use the language of the tradition I unauthentically appropriate, and I thereby devaluate, distort, water down, corrupt the language."[93] Rarely is unauthenticity an isolated phenomenon. Indeed, "it may occur on a more massive scale, and then the words are

---

[90] Ibid., 79.

[91] Ibid. Lonergan's reflections on common meaning hold tremendous resources for thinking about the church as a concretely emerging reality that is not simply equivalent to any historical form or institutional structure. See Joseph A. Komonchak, *Foundations in Ecclesiology*, supplementary issue of the *Lonergan Workshop Journal*, vol. 11, ed. Frederick G. Lawrence (Chestnut Hill, MA: Boston College, 1995).

[92] See Robert M. Doran, *Theology and the Dialectics of History* (Toronto: University of Toronto Press, 1990, 2001).

[93] Ibid., 80.

repeated, but the meaning is gone."[94] As a result, "the unauthenticity of individuals becomes the unauthenticity of tradition. Then in the measure a subject takes the tradition, as it exists, for his standard, in that measure he can do no more than authentically realize unauthenticity."[95] Certainly this dialectic can illumine the problems surrounding eucharistic doctrines discussed in the Introduction. Moreover, the underlying confusions are related to a failure to distinguish between the different acts of meaning and the various functions of meaning, and to affirm the ontology of meaning.

3.4. Meaning and Ontology

Later in *Method in Theology*, while outlining the functional specialty communications, Lonergan explains the ontological aspect of meaning. Each of the functions of meaning, he says, has an ontological aspect: "In so far as meaning is cognitive, what is meant is real. In so far as it is constitutive, it constitutes part of the reality of the one that means: his horizon, his assimilative powers, his knowledge, his values, his character. In so far as it is communicative, it induces in the hearer some share in the cognitive, constitutive, or effective meaning of the speaker. In so far as it is effective, it persuades or commands others or it directs man's control over nature."[96] The ontological aspects of meaning "are found . . . in all the diverse stages of meaning, in all the diverse cultural traditions, in any of the differentiations of consciousness, and in the presence and absence of intellectual, moral, and religious conversion."[97] The ontological aspect of meaning is verifiable in human history.[98] The ontology of meaning in history affirms that human beings cocreate the world of proportionate being that is the object of metaphysical analysis. So religious traditions include among their constitutive meanings not only myths but plain matters of factual, historical occurrence. For example, that there was a historical occurrence of the man Jesus of Nazareth is the condition for the possibility of Christian faith. Similarly, that this Jesus died is both a matter of historical fact and a tenet of

---

[94] Ibid.
[95] Ibid.
[96] Ibid., 356.
[97] Ibid.
[98] See Doran, *Theology and the Dialectics of History*, 592–629.

the Christian creed. That this man was a divine person is a common meaning, a belief held in faith that is constitutive of the church as a historical reality. That this Jesus was raised from the dead is clearly a statement of faith, but the statement has consequences related to concrete judgments of historical fact, namely, that the bodily remains of Jesus are not waiting to be discovered in a tomb outside Jerusalem. Contingent matters of historical occurrence are implicated in a world constituted by human meaning, and yet that world goes beyond historical facts to speak about future hopes that condition present action.

To further clarify his ontology of meaning, Lonergan distinguishes three worlds: (1) a world of immediacy that is "the world of immediate experience, of the given as given, of image and affect without any perceptible intrusion from insight or concept, reflection or judgment, deliberation or choice";[99] (2) a world mediated by meaning that is initially only an extension of the world of immediacy into a larger world of pictures, speech, stories, but "gradually leads to the discovery of the difference between fact and fiction, between what is just a story and what really and truly is so";[100] (3) a world constituted by meaning, which includes the previous worlds but adds to them the properly human acts of intellect and will that make up entire cultures. The world mediated by meaning is "a universe of being, that is known not just by experience but by the conjunction of experience, understanding, and judgment."[101] Lonergan explains:

> Human acts occur in sociocultural contexts; there is not only the action but also the human setup, the family and mores, the state and religion, the economy and technology, the law and education. None of these are mere products of nature: they have a determination from meaning; to change the meaning is to change the concrete setup. Hence there is a radical difference between the data of natural science and the data of human science. The physicist, chemist, biologist verifies his hypothesis in what is given just as it is given. The human scientist can verify only in data that besides being given have a meaning. Physicists, chemists, engineers might enter a court of law, but after making all their

---

[99] Lonergan, "*Existenz* and *Aggiornamento*," 240–51, in *Collection*, CWBL 4, ed. Frederick E. Crowe and Robert M. Doran (Toronto: University of Toronto Press, 1993), at 225.
[100] Ibid.
[101] Ibid.

measurements and calculations they could not declare that it was a court of law.[102]

The human sciences include the painstaking process of interpreting human meanings in a world not only mediated by but also constituted by those meanings. For example, what makes a particular arrangement of space a court of law is not something that can be verified by physical or chemical analysis of a building or some furniture. Rather, to understand what makes a courtroom what it is, one must observe the legal proceedings it hosts. This raises the further question of what contribution meaning makes to the ontological status of the things that make up a courtroom related to their metaphysical constitution.[103]

According to Lonergan's metaphysics as articulated above, things are known according to central and conjugate potency, form, and act, which are isomorphic with the first three levels of consciousness: experiencing, understanding, judging. Among the things rational intelligence experiences, understands, and judges in the universe of proportionate being are human acts of meaning.[104] Included among those acts of meaning are the words and deeds of the man Jesus, which faith holds are the incarnate acts of meaning of a divine person. But we are getting ahead of ourselves. The point here is to suggest that there is a metaphysics of meaning that can be developed by attending to the operations of intelligence in the world constituted by meaning.

The temptation when using the term "metaphysical" is to imagine that it describes an essence underlying appearances: for example, that there is an essence of a tree that lies at a deeper level than the sensible appearances of the tree. For Lonergan this is a basic counterposition that equates knowing with looking. What distinguishes the metaphysical from the physical is a matter of method. If a metaphysician wants to explain what a tree is, he suspends his metaphysical investigations and begins doing botany. On the other hand, if the botanist wants to understand *how* she understands what

[102] Ibid., 225–26.

[103] This question was helpfully posed to the author by Charles Hefling.

[104] See Doran, *Theology and the Dialectics of History*, 612: "For potential, formal, and full acts and terms of meaning are not metaphysical elements, but intelligible items in the universe of proportionate being, and so they call for explanation in terms of the metaphysical elements that characterize all such intelligible items."

a tree is she sets aside her botany and begins to do metaphysics. Lonergan explains: "If one wants to know just what forms are, the proper procedure is to give up metaphysics and turn to the sciences; for forms become known inasmuch as the sciences approximate towards their ideal of complete explanation; and there is no method apart from scientific method by which one can reach such explanation."[105] Metaphysics deals with the integral heuristic structure of proportionate being. It does not offer an alternative explanation of reality but a higher viewpoint on the whole, "in which one grasps the relations between experience, understanding, and judgment, and the isomorphism of these activities with the constituents of what is to be known."[106] What is known, in terms of formal content, is the same for the metaphysician or the botanist: the *unity-identity-whole* that the tree is. The metaphysician has no special access to "tree-ness" or a metaphysical substance lying underneath the appearances of the tree. Frequently theologians have mistakenly employed the category of substance in this way to understand eucharistic doctrines. But this is simply another version of what Lonergan has identified as the *already-out-there-now-real*. For Lonergan this is the mythical "look" of philosophical intuition that is the fundamental mistake of both Kantian analysis and the uncritical realist Thomistic metaphysics of Etienne Gilson.[107] For the critical realist the metaphysical substance is the physical substance.[108] The formal contents of things are known by the specialized departments of science, not by metaphysicians doing metaphysics. Rather, the metaphysician gives the specialized departments of science the heuristic categories within which the formal contents of science are found, namely, central and conjugate potency, form, and act. Substance is one such heuristic category that Lonergan identifies with his

---

[105] Lonergan, *Insight*, 521.

[106] Ibid., 521–22.

[107] Raymond Moloney, "Lonergan on Substance and Transubstantiation," *Irish Theological Quarterly* 75, no. 2 (May 2010): 131–43, at 138. See Lonergan, "Metaphysics as Horizon," 188–204, in *Collection*, CWBL 4, at 196–97; and Lonergan, "Analogy of Meaning," 183–213, in *Philosophical and Theological Papers 1958–1964*, CWBL 6, ed. Frederick E. Crowe, Robert C. Croken, and Robert M. Doran (Toronto: University of Toronto Press, 1996), at 199. See also Giovanni B. Sala, *Lonergan and Kant: Five Essays on Human Knowledge*, trans. Joseph Spoerl, ed. Robert M. Doran (Toronto: University of Toronto Press, 1994).

[108] Raymond Moloney, "Lonergan and Eucharistic Theology," *Irish Theological Quarterly* 62 (1996/97): 17–28, at 23.

"central form." This is what he means when he employs the simple term "thing" to identify a *unity-identity-whole* in data.

The question we are presently attempting to answer asks whether the world constituted by meaning impacts the metaphysical constitution of things: whether, for example, the constitutive act of meaning expressed in the words "this is my body" about some bread in fact changes the thing that the bread is, its substance. To affirm that it does is to affirm the meaning of the doctrine of transubstantiation. But Lonergan says there are no things within things. There is not an agglomeration of substances in bread, as some argue, for this would be substance understood as *already-out-there-now-real*.[109] When we are talking about a thing we are talking only about one thing, a *unity-identity-whole*, which is not an aggregate of things but the relationship between all the data that pertain to one thing. To follow the courtroom analogy, we would say that a courtroom is an order among things, an order that pertains to use of this room for legal proceedings. In this case the meaning does not change the metaphysical constitution of individual constituent elements which remain things. The chairs, tables, lights, etc., are not different things because they are used in a trial.[110] But the Eucharist is one thing. According to dogma, it is the *unity-identity-whole* that is Jesus Christ: body, blood, soul, and divinity. What makes the eucharistic bread the body of Christ is the full act of meaning in the utterance "this is my body." Although this instrumental act of meaning is communicated in human terms through words, the object (the body, blood, soul, and divinity of Christ) is a transcendent reality. Because it is expressed in human terms, this statement of a divine person can be subject to a hermeneutics, as are the other sayings of Jesus recorded in the gospels. But because it is on the level of statement or affirmation, interpreting it is not properly a matter of understanding but of judging. We do not ask "what is it?" about the statement "this is my body . . . this is my blood"; rather, we ask "is it so?"

---

[109] See Karl Rahner, "The Presence of Christ in the Sacrament of the Lord's Supper," 287–311, in *Theological Investigations IV*, trans. Kevin Smyth (Baltimore: Helicon, 1966), at 307–8.

[110] The fact that these things are artifacts further complicates their status as things. They are things, but part of their being things includes their being made by human beings through acts of effective meaning, or planning. Trees are different from chairs even though some of them may share certain data. We will have to think more about this difference when we consider the status of bread as a thing in the human world.

To answer that question "yes" is to affirm the meaning of the doctrine of transubstantiation. By implication, when the faithful ask "what is it?" about the consecrated bread and wine, the dogmatic answer is "the body, blood, soul, and divinity of Christ." The affirmation of Christ is a third-level operation, a judgment that affirms the reality of what is to be known on the second level. We'll have more to say on that below, but our interpretation will be helped by distinguishing different realms of meaning.

3.5. *Realms of Meaning*

In the previous section I argued that the kinds of utterances communicated in eucharistic liturgy pertain to a world constituted by meaning but also include basic cognitive meanings. Now we also need to attend to the different realms of meaning to which meanings refer. For Lonergan the three basic realms of meaning have to do with common sense, theory, and interiority. Attending to the different realms of meaning helps clarify the hermeneutics of ritual language.

Realms of meaning are distinguished by the different inner exigencies that move conscious operations toward different objects. The realm of common sense identifies things in the world mediated by meaning that are related to us.[111] Recalling the distinction between understanding either what is *first for us* and what is *first in itself,* we find that the same distinctions apply in the world mediated by meaning. What is "first for us" are the most prevalent aspects of our daily living: family, friends, acquaintances, community, nation, world. We describe and discuss these things in everyday language in order to make our attitudes toward these realities understood by others and to render our actions meaningful. For example, accumulated folk wisdom can cultivate individuals who are respectful and compassionate toward others, not out of any theoretical reflection on the dignity of the person or moral duty but because the elders acted toward and spoke about others in the same way. But even laudable behavior can be accompanied by prejudice toward other ethnic groups, or by suspicion, or even malice, toward members of other political parties. Other ethnic groups can be reduced to animals or opposed political parties characterized as traitors. A further exigence may bring greater clarity and precision.

---

[111] Lonergan, *Method in Theology,* 81.

The systematic exigence seeks a comprehensive understanding characteristic of the realm of theory.[112] For example, in the context of theory one does not inquire "who counts as person for me?" or "who deserves my respect?" but "what is a person?" and "why is a person worthy of respect?" One attains answers to such questions only by considering the broader context of humanity generally. Explanations attained by theory may challenge us to act in ways that live up to the discoveries of the systematic exigence. The technical languages that pertain to the realm of theory recontextualize questions that emerge in commonsense conversation but quickly go beyond the ability of common sense to answer. The reasons behind a recession will be discovered not by dinner-table discussions but by sound theoretical analyses of monetary functions, market mechanisms, and the economics of production. Similarly, it is one thing to ask of a religious text, "what does it mean to me?" but another to ask about the meaning it may have had in its original context. The perfectly legitimate question "what does it mean to me?" will be answered in accord with the myriad perspectives of those asking it, but an even greater illumination or challenge for religious experience may come from grasping the differences between our immediate concerns and those of the author in relation to his or her *Sitz im Leben*. Religion, after all is anything but a radically private affair. But beyond the *ad hoc* contexts of devotion and scholarship, questions arise about the truth of the reality believed in among the shifting skein of historical contexts. What does it mean that we are saved by the work of Christ? Why is this event eschatologically decisive? What is needed is a shift from descriptive, metaphorical discourse to explanatory analogies gained by achieving a theoretical understanding of appropriate finite, terrestrial relationships as related among themselves.

The shift to theory motivated by a systematic exigence will call forth a critical exigence to critically assess possibly relevant interpretations and appraise possibly relevant analogies. The critical exigence reveals the need to appropriate the realm of interiority by asking "what am I doing when I am knowing? why is doing that knowing?" and "what do I know when I do it?" That realm is the focus of this book's survey of Lonergan's cognitional theory, epistemology, and metaphysics. The critical exigence of the realm of interiority "is a heightening of intentional consciousness, an attending

---

[112] Ibid., 82.

not merely to objects but also to the intending subject and his acts."[113] But Lonergan is quick to point out that the withdrawal into interiority is "not an end in itself,"[114] because the withdrawal is for the sake of a return to the realms of common sense and theory in order to reintegrate them methodically through transcendental method illumined by being in love with God and faith as the eyes of being in love. The objectification of conscious intentionality as transformed by grace in the realm of interiority calls forth a further exigence.

Reflection on one's questioning leads to the basic insight that one's intending is infinite. That unrestricted desire to know is an immanent source of self-transcendence that moves one toward higher viewpoints. The enactment of the systematic and critical exigencies can usher in a transcendent exigence that demands absolutely transcendent and even supernatural fulfillment. By grace, the transcendent exigence desires not only the natural fulfillment of answers to an infinite series of questions for knowing but also the supernatural fulfillment of the gifted desire of God's love flooding the heart.[115]

Differentiation of the several realms is not only descriptive but pushes toward an explanatory account of the different kinds of human inquiry and their relations to each other. The failure to distinguish these realms in theological reflection leads to the confusion of commonsense meanings with more theoretical explanations, abetted by a much-needed but inadequate concern for human subjectivity. As a result, systematic theology falls short of its goal of shedding some light on the mystery through a fruitful analogical understanding. To be sure, the differentiation of consciousness is no mean feat: "It is only by knowledge making its bloody entrance that one can move out of the realm of ordinary languages into the realm of theory and the totally different scientific apprehension of reality. It is only through the long and confused twilight of philosophic initiation that one can find one's way into interiority and achieve through self-appropriation a basis, a foundation, that is distinct from common sense and theory, that acknowledges their disparateness, that accounts for both and critically grounds them both."[116]

---

[113] Ibid., 83.
[114] Ibid.
[115] Ibid., 115. See Romans 5:5.
[116] Ibid., 85.

4. Conclusion

Bearing in mind our ontology of meaning in terms of the differentiations of consciousness, in the next chapter we turn to the doctrinal tradition whose statements regard the true meaning of realities articulated in propositions that arise from a theoretical understanding in theology. Because those propositions are articulated on the level of statement, or judgment, they do not explain themselves but are accepted in faith. Those statements are, of course, articulated in metaphysical terms that had a particular meaning in a particular context but may no longer be meaningful to the faithful. Herein lies the current problem in sacramental theology. As Lonergan explains:

As believers, we accept statements; and we accept statements not as acceptable modes of speech or obligatory modes of speech but as having a meaning. When a philosophy eliminates the possible meaning of fundamental elements in our statements, it can eliminate fundamental elements from our faith. And the elimination of, or the objection against, objective thinking, against metaphysical thinking, if taken seriously, eliminates dogma, eliminates Christian doctrine, for the simple reason that Christian doctrine is doctrine; it is a message.[117]

Transposing doctrines stated in metaphysical categories into categories of meaning will allow us to retain the truth of statements while developing a fruitful analogical understanding of their meaning, the ultimate purpose of which is a lived Christian witness to those truths.

---

[117] Lonergan, "Theology as Christian Phenomenon," 244–72, in *Philosophical and Theological Papers 1958–1964*, CWBL 6, at 266–67.

Chapter Five

The Eucharistic Presence of Christ
Metaphysics and Meaning

Having identified the categories of meaning in which eucharistic doctrines might be helpfully transposed, we have the remaining task of executing the transposition. Although I indicated briefly how the categories apply as part of a hermeneutics of the sacramental acts of meaning, I still have to offer an interpretation of those acts. In order to apply the categories of meaning to sacramental theology we will have to first survey what the doctrinal tradition has had to say specifically in regard to the Eucharist and then propose an analogical understanding of those doctrines in terms of meaning.

1. Doctrines

Doctrines, as I indicated earlier, are simply answers to questions.[1] Nevertheless, they raise many more questions, and in many cases problems. These problems emerge when the cultural contexts in which doctrines were articulated no longer exist. Theology, in its role as a mediator between a religion and a culture, faces these problems by proposing a fruitful, analogical understanding of the mysteries. Lonergan explains:

> Man's response to transcendent mystery is adoration. But adoration does not exclude words. Least of all, does it do so when men come together to worship. But the words, in turn, have their meaning within

---

[1] See Charles Hefling, *Why Doctrines?* (Chestnut Hill, MA: The Lonergan Institute, 2000).

some cultural context. Contexts can be ongoing. One ongoing context can be derived from another. Two ongoing contexts can interact. Accordingly, while mystery is very different from the problems of common sense, of science, of scholarship, of much philosophy, still the worship of God and, more generally, the religions of mankind stand within a social, cultural, historical context and, by that involvement, generate the problems with which theologians attempt to deal.[2]

The problems emerge at the intersection of the mysteries of revealed religion and the social, cultural, and historical context of their interpretation. Lonergan's historical study of the theological developments on the way to Nicaea demonstrates how the development of doctrine is animated by questions that gradually call forth a systematic expression of the faith that goes beyond scriptural vocabulary.[3] Doctrine is mediated by explanatory propositional statements that reformulate the truth of Scripture while answering questions the Bible neither asks nor answers. Questions emerge historically in response to experience. What was a question for the ancient Israelites may no longer be a relevant question for contemporary people.[4] While human speech about God is carried out in social, cultural, and historical contexts shaped by symbols, often enough the global and compact nature of those symbols is opaque when it comes to answering more differentiated questions about the mystery of God. Lonergan offers the example of the anthropomorphisms of the Hebrew Bible, which can be easily misunderstood by commonsense ways of thinking. To describe God as a divine warrior made sense in the context of ancient Babylonian cultures,[5] but it leaves a number of theoretical questions about what God is unanswered. And so symbols

---

[2] Bernard Lonergan, *Method in Theology* (New York: Herder & Herder, 1972), 344. It is hard to imagine that Lonergan would not have had Catholic sacramental doctrines in mind when he composed these words. It is around this same time that he suggested a broadening out of the notion of instrumental causality in sacramental theology.

[3] See Bernard Lonergan, *The Triune God: Doctrines,* CWBL 11 (Toronto: University of Toronto Press, 2009).

[4] An obvious example is the question of creation. If the creation accounts in Genesis attempted to answer the question of cosmogony for their time, they no longer answer that specific question within a scientific horizon. They may, however, provide answers for other kinds of theological questions.

[5] See Bernhard Lang, *The Hebrew God: Portrait of an Ancient Deity* (New Haven, CT: Yale University Press, 2002).

change in order that "undesired meanings are excluded and desired meanings are elucidated."[6] One of the ways theologians have done this through the generations is to invent terms or to employ existing terms in new ways to indicate a new possibility for a doctrinal clarification of meaning in the form of a statement. For example, the terms *"homoousios,"* or *"prosopon,"* or even *"transubstantiation"* all emerge as explanatory answers to questions about the meanings expressed in the narrative and symbolic language of Scripture.

Lonergan's study of the development of doctrine reveals that doctrinal development is *not* a matter of overlaying a preexisting set of philosophical categories or concepts on biblical narratives in order to illuminate their meaning. The history of Christian theology is not simply a series of baptisms of pagan philosophy. What Augustine referred to as "plundering the Egyptians" involves the use of techniques and terms already existing within a culture to work out a more differentiated account of the meaning of what is revealed in Scripture and held as true in faith, in order to meet issues raised by theological questions. Frequently the terms used in doctrinal statements have a heuristic character, not providing final answers themselves but naming the unknown more clearly. For example, Augustine does not use the term "person" or *prosopon* to designate a person according to modern philosophical understandings of individuals as bearers of rights, nor does he mean the mask of the Greek theater from which the term was originally borrowed. He simply uses "person" to answer the question regarding what there are three of in the Trinity.[7] It is a technical term that specifies what is given in faith as a mystery. Similarly, the terms "substance" and "transubstantiation" provide heuristic responses to the questions "what changes in the Eucharist?" or "in what manner is Christ present in the Eucharist?" or "what kind of change occurs in the Eucharist?" each of which is a further determination of the question "what does Christ mean when he says 'this is my body'?" the answer to which is given primarily in the experience of eucharistic faith.

---

[6] Lonergan, *Method in Theology*, 344.

[7] For Saint Augustine the answer to this question could also be "three substances." See Bernard Lonergan, *The Triune God: Systematics*, CWBL 12 (Toronto: University of Toronto Press, 2007), 308f.

1.1. The Language of Doctrine

Put very simply then, the theological purpose of the doctrines on the Eucharist from the Council of Trent is to stress that when Jesus spoke the words, "This is my body" over bread and "This is the cup of my blood" over a cup of wine, he meant what he said.[8] These doctrinal clarifications have a long history dating back to the eleventh-century controversy over the teaching of Berengar of Tours, through the definitive theological treatment of the relevant questions in the *Summa Theologiae* of Thomas Aquinas, to their authoritative doctrinal statement in the decrees of Trent in response to the Reformation controversy.[9] The problem is that the meanings of these conciliar statements can be difficult to retrieve today. Lonergan once remarked in a discussion of theological method:

> The Council of Trent says that transubstantiation is an excellent way to express the truth about the Eucharist; but there are difficulties about "substance" at the present time that did not exist at the Council of Trent. Solving those difficulties in a convenient way, and so on, is one thing; but deserting what was meant at the Council of Trent is another. What was meant at the Council of Trent was not terrifically difficult: this is my body; my body is not bread; this is not bread.[10]

The point of Lonergan's informal response is simply that transubstantiation is a technical but merely heuristic explanation of the conversion of the substance of the bread that is *aptissime conveniens* in contrast to theories of

---

[8] See Karl Rahner, "Christ in the Sacrament of the Lord's Supper," in his *Theological Investigations IV*, trans. Kevin Smyth (Baltimore, Helicon Press, 1966), 287–311. Rahner argues that "the dogma of transubstantiation (insofar as it is really strict dogma) is a logical and not an ontic explanation of the word of Christ taken literally" (p. 302). This does not mean that the words do not refer to some objective reality but that the words of the doctrine say no more than do the words of Christ when they are taken seriously (ibid.).

[9] The reader interested in the history of the Eucharist leading up to Trent is urged to consult the masterful historical study of Edward Kilmartin, *The Eucharist in the West: History and Theology*, ed. Robert J. Daly (Collegeville, MN: Liturgical Press, 1998). See also Joseph M. Powers, *Eucharistic Theology* (New York: Herder and Herder, 1967); Gary Macy, *Treasures from the Storeroom: Medieval Religion and the Eucharist* (Collegeville, MN: Liturgical Press, 1999); Enrico Mazza, *The Celebration of the Eucharist: The Origin of the Rite and the Development of Its Interpretation* (Collegeville, MN: Liturgical Press, 1999).

[10] Lonergan, "1969 Institute on Method Lecture 4B," http://www.bernardlonergan .com/pdf/52200DTE060.pdf (accessed December 2, 2013), 28.

annihilation, consubstantiation, or impanation.[11] To say that it is *aptissime conveniens* does not mean, as some have argued, that it is merely one among other possible ways of explaining the whole conversion of the bread and wine into the body and blood.[12] The doctrine answers the question, "What are the conditions to be fulfilled for it to be true that Christ is present to the faithful in a unique way through the eucharistic elements?" The doctrine expresses the belief that Christ's words uttered over bread and wine in our contemporary eucharistic rituals are no less true for us than they were for his disciples.[13] Because doctrines employ terms used in the philosophical

[11] Lonergan goes on to answer the question, "Is the notion of substance at Trent a heuristic notion?" by saying, "You can say it is a heuristic notion with respect to what is not species, it is something distinct from species, and I don't think you can say it is more determinate than that. Remember, there were nominalists, Scotists, and Thomists, and so on, at the Council of Trent, and they made it perfectly plain that they were not condemning themselves or any one of themselves." See previous note. The critical point is that Trent does not embrace a particular metaphysics; it simply affirms that transubstantiation is the most appropriate way to talk about the whole conversion of the bread and wine into the body and blood. Raymond Moloney clarifies this exchange in "Lonergan on Substance and Transubstantiation," *Irish Theological Quarterly* 75, no. 2 (May 2010): 131–43, at 141. Cf. Joseph M. Powers, *Eucharistic Theology*, 127–28.

[12] This fairly standard interpretation of the language of the decree can be found in Edward Schillebeeckx, Louis-Marie Chauvet, Herbert McCabe, Karl Rahner, and others. Lonergan's comment in the previous note indicates a different way of thinking about the openness of the term. To say that it is *aptissime conveniens* does not mean that other terms, such as "transignification" or "transfinalization," cannot be found to take its place, but that transubstantiation is open enough and precise enough to clarify the core belief in Christ's eucharistic presence. On the other hand, *Dei Filius* clarifies that with respect to the permanence of doctrine it is the meaning that is not open for discussion. It may be that the term used to communicate the meaning changes, so that transubstantiation might be stated in other equivalent terms that communicate the conversion of the whole substances of bread and wine into the whole substances of the body and blood of Christ, which is what is affirmed by the term "transubstantiation." For example, based on our reading of Lonergan's notion of things we might properly and adequately refer to the change in question as "transthingification." But that too is bound to be misunderstood outside of the context of its formulation.

[13] There has been much debate within liturgical studies over the status of the so-called words of institution. For a historical study, see Joachim Jeremias, *The Eucharistic Words of Jesus* (London: SCM Press, 1966). For a helpful survey of New Testament research on the Last Supper, see Jerome Kodell, *The Eucharist in the New Testament* (Collegeville, MN: Liturgical Press, 1991). For purposes of understanding doctrinal statements, I take the words of institution as true; their accuracy as historical reportage is not relevant to

milieu of the time, understanding the doctrines and the mysteries of faith they seek to articulate will benefit from a transposition into terms with less historical baggage than "substance" and "species."[14] That will be the task of the next section of this chapter. Before doing this, allow me to make two preliminary points on theological understanding.

First, it will be noted that our attempt to rediscover the meanings of the doctrines ranging from the composition of the Last Supper narratives to the medieval debates over metaphysical terms involves a tremendous amount of historical work. This is certainly true, but systematic theology, in the functionally specialized sense, departs from doctrines as articulated. Most of the historical work is the proper domain of the functional specialties research, interpretation, and history. Systematic theology, far from neglecting the historical development of doctrine, requires that we lean heavily on the historical work of others in understanding the meaning of doctrinal statements in their context. Important historical investigations have highlighted the influence of Thomas Aquinas on eucharistic theology in the West.[15] If we recapture the insights from Thomas in our interpretation of the doctrines we can transpose their meaning into our new context. In proposing an understanding of a doctrine we remain open to further relevant questions that may lead to doctrinal development. If there are such questions we may have to return to the specialties of the mediating phase in order to locate potential resources in the tradition for such development.[16]

---

understanding the belief stated in the doctrines the church holds in faith. What is clear from St. Paul's account of the liturgical celebration in 1 Cor 11:23-29 is that Christ's words were included in the earliest stages of the church's liturgical practice, and they remain constitutive of the church's collective memory.

[14] These terms have a complicated history before the Tridentine formula. Many suggest that their inclusion in the doctrinal statements reveals an overwhelming Aristotelian influence in Catholic theology during the Middle Ages. This critique is insufficiently nuanced and has been criticized in turn by others who have carefully researched the development of the scholastic terminology. For a helpful historical survey of the terminology, see Gary Macy, *Treasures from the Storeroom*, 81–120.

[15] See Kilmartin, *Eucharist in the West*; Powers, *Eucharistic Theology*; David N. Power, *The Sacrifice We Offer: The Tridentine Dogma and Its Reinterpretation* (New York: Crossroad, 1987).

[16] For example, Lonergan's suggestion that the category of instrumental causality be broadened may lead in the direction of doctrinal development. It raises a relevant question that does not have a doctrinally defined answer, namely, "how do sacraments work?" That the sacraments confer grace is affirmed in conciliar decrees (*DS* 1606) and through

Second, as for the permanence of dogma and doctrinal development, if the systematic theologian interprets the doctrines as they are stated, it frequently occurs that articulating the meaning of those doctrines in a new historical context involves restating them in terms prevalent in the theologian's culture. Because the doctrines in question are formulated in technical terms that require clarification, we must confront the question of whether the permanence of dogma attaches to the *meaning* of a doctrine or its *manner of expression*.

In "Theology and Understanding" Lonergan distinguishes two ways of knowing through an analysis of theological understanding in light of the first Vatican Council's claim that a most fruitful understanding of the faith can be attained in this life.[17] Theology is not principally reflection on the articles of faith; rather, according to Thomas, *"Deus est subiectum huius scientiae."*[18] The challenge is that in this life the subject of the science of theology, God, cannot be known by any natural powers.[19] However, revealed

---

the regular teaching office of the church (*CCC* 1131), but the manner of the change in the subject, how it occurs, is not defined. Chauvet offers an important account of that aspect of sacramental grace in terms of symbolic mediation, which may ultimately lead to doctrinal development. Lonergan refers to the first four functional specialties—research, interpretation, history, dialectic—as the "mediating phase." These specialties operate *in ordo inventionis*, or in the way of discovery. Here, I am working in the *ordo disciplinae*, or order of teaching, in which one attempts to understand the statement of the tradition (See *Method*, 133f.).

[17] Bernard Lonergan, "Theology and Understanding," 114–32, in *Collection*, CWBL 4, at 116. He notes that in making this claim in *Dei Filius*, the council was in fact reacting to those who understood theology's task as a demonstration of the necessity of the truths of faith: "Such a notion the Council wished not merely to repudiate but also to replace, and so it affirmed an *intelligentia mysteriorum* that remained obscure and imperfect in this mortal life, yet nonetheless was a positive and most fruitful enlightenment. Its obscurity and imperfection imply that one does not understand the mysteries in their internal content or substance. Its element of positive enlightenment lies in a grasp of relations that stand in an analogy of proportion with naturally known truths and link the mysteries to one another and to man's last end." See *DS* 3016.

[18] *ST* I, q. 1, a. 7c, cited in Lonergan, "Theology and Understanding," 117n7. J. Michael Stebbins examines Lonergan's idea of theological understanding in some detail in *The Divine Initiative: Grace, World-Order, and Human Freedom in the Early Writings of Bernard Lonergan* (Toronto: University of Toronto Press, 1995), 3–35.

[19] While *Dei Filius* holds as an article of faith that the existence of God can be demonstrated through the things that are made, the only understanding of God that can be had on that account is purely negative, simply a "refutation of objections or a grasp of

truths can be understood in some positive fashion, precisely by human intelligence operating in the presence of religious conversion, or in the light of reason illumined by faith. Here, Lonergan introduces three ways in which "one may express the possibility of understanding the revelation of a reality that itself is not understood."[20] The first is by way of sanctifying grace or a *donum intellectus*, the gift of understanding attributed to the Holy Spirit. The second is in the way indicated in the council's decree, by a fruitful yet essentially imperfect analogical understanding of revelation. The third is the function of theology as a subaltern science.[21] As such a science, theology seeks an understanding of what God reveals of God's self. What is revealed is the truth of faith. The revelation of God in Scripture, especially as it is proclaimed in the worship of the church, constitutes a horizon within which theological reflection takes place, a horizon of faith within which theology can operate in the manner of Aristotle's logical ideal of science.[22]

---

the absence of inner contradiction" (Lonergan, "Theology and Understanding," 119). In the beatific vision, theology reaches its fulfillment when "we know as we are known." See Lonergan's essay, "Natural Knowledge of God," 117–34, in *A Second Collection* (Toronto: University of Toronto Press, 1996). See also Denys Turner, *Faith, Reason and the Existence of God* (New York: Cambridge University Press, 2004).

[20] Lonergan, "Theology and Understanding," 119.

[21] Lonergan elaborates on the phrase "subaltern science" in Thomas: "By a single technical phrase one conveys (1) that the subject of theology is not a set of propositions or a set of truths but a reality, (2) that theology itself is an understanding, for a science is a process towards a terminal understanding, (3) that this understanding is not of God himself, for then the science would be not subalternated but subalternating, and (4) that an understanding of the revelation cannot be adequate, for the revelation is about God and God himself is not understood" (Lonergan, "Theology and Understanding," 119). See also Lonergan, *Verbum: Word and Idea in Aquinas*, CWBL 2, ed. Frederick E. Crowe and Robert M. Doran (Toronto: University of Toronto Press, 1997): "The ideal of theology as science is the subalternated and so limited, analogical, and so imperfect understanding of *quid sit Deus*, which, though incomparable with the vision of God, far surpasses what can be grasped by the unaided light of natural reason" (p. 219).

[22] This is the basis of Thomas's introductory question of the *ST*, "Whether sacred doctrine is a science?" (*ST* I, q. 1, a. 2). Thomas argues that God is the object of sacred doctrine as a science and that the mysteries of faith are treated in theology as a science "so far as they have reference to God" (*ST* I, q. 1, a. 7, c.). Related to this claim is Thomas's argument that being is the proper object of the intellect, not as the being of particular beings (something like substances), but being itself insofar as all human knowing aims toward knowledge of the whole of being, toward God. See Lonergan, "Theology and Understanding," 118 and n. 10: "precisely because understanding is *quo est omnia fieri*,

Theology, then, is reason operating within the horizon of faith, or faith seeking fruitful analogical understanding of the divine wisdom that God is. But faith is already a gift of God's grace, the gift by which the Holy Spirit illumines intellect. Therefore "[j]ust as grace is beyond nature yet perfects nature, so faith is beyond reason yet perfects reason."[23] In theological inquiry we begin from the doctrines, the deposit of faith, which reason formed by faith explores in order to understand through fruitful, if imperfect, analogies. The *meanings* of doctrines, not the specific terms in which they are expressed, are the matter to be understood, for "the meaning of the dogma is not apart from a verbal formulation, for it is a meaning declared by the church. However, the permanence attaches to the meaning and not to the formula. To retain the same formula and give it a new meaning is precisely what the third canon [of *Dei Filius*] excludes."[24] The doctrinal language is a carrier of meaning, certainly, but of itself is not equivalent with what is meant by divine revelation.[25]

In addition, the issue concerns the permanence rather than the immutability of doctrine. The latter would pit the council against itself inasmuch as *Dei Filius* also proposes the possibility of "growth and advance in understanding, knowledge, wisdom with respect to the same dogma and the same meaning,"[26] not to mention the simple historical fact of doctrinal pluralism in the tradition. Therefore the meaning a decree had in its original context is held as true and not subject to further development "on the pretext of

---

its object is not any restricted genus of being but being itself" (with footnote reference to *ST* I, q. 79, a. 7, c.).

[23] "Theology and Understanding," 124. The relation between faith and reason is, of course, a subject of great debate among theologians. There are those who argue that faith cannot but run contrary to reason, that it is ultimately a stumbling block to reason, because reason is a secular *modus operandi*. This interpretation drives much of the project of "radical orthodoxy." See John Milbank, *Theology and Social Theory: Beyond Secular Reason* (Cambridge, MA: Wiley-Blackwell, 1993). Lonergan offers a substantial critique of this kind of position in "The Dehellenization of Dogma," 11–32, in *Second Collection*.

[24] Lonergan, "Doctrinal Pluralism," 70–106, in *Philosophical and Theological Papers 1965–1980*, CWBL 17, ed. Robert C. Croken and Robert M. Doran (Toronto: University of Toronto Press, 2004), at 92, citing *DS* 3043.

[25] This is probably what critics of the term "transubstantiation" mean when they say that it is not the only way of expressing the kind of change that occurs in the Eucharist. It is the term that is problematic, not necessarily the revealed truth it expresses.

[26] Lonergan, "Doctrinal Pluralism," 92, citing *DS* 3020.

some profounder understanding." The key to understanding the meaning of a dogma is grasping the context of its statement, for the "meaning of a dogma is the meaning of a declaration made by the church at a particular place and time and within the context of that occasion. Only through the historical study of that occasion and the exegetical study of that declaration can one arrive at the proper meaning of the dogma."[27] Lonergan explains that the "meaning of the dogmas is permanent because that meaning is not a datum but a truth, and that truth is not human but divine."[28]

1.2. The Eucharistic Doctrines

The eucharistic doctrines of the Catholic Church answer questions regarding the church's faith in Christ's presence and work in the liturgy. They address (a) Christ's presence in the eucharistic liturgy of the church,[29] (b) the liturgy as a participation in the sacrifice of Christ, and (c) the effect on the faithful of participation in liturgy. We will propose a systematic treatment of each of these doctrines in the following section, but not in isolation from each other. The temptation to treat the doctrines separately, for example beginning with transubstantiation and then moving to sacrifice, tends to create confusion, because each of the doctrines informs the others. To speak of Christ's presence in isolation from the acts of meaning communicated in his self-sacrificing suffering, death, and resurrection would be to treat that presence as a brute fact lacking in meaning, precisely the kind of reified static presence Chauvet has rightly opposed.[30]

Regarding Christ's presence in the Eucharist, the Council of Trent states that (1) Christ is truly, really, and substantially present in the Eucharist[31] and

---

[27] Ibid., 97.

[28] Ibid., 95. Lonergan echoes John Henry Newman, *An Essay on the Development of Doctrine.*

[29] Crucially, the doctrinal tradition does not restrict Christ's presence to the elements, as popular understanding tends to. Both *Sacrosanctum Concilium* and *Mysterium Fidei* emphasize the multiple presences of Christ in the liturgy. See Michael Witzcak, "The Manifold Presence of Christ in the Eucharist," *Theological Studies* 59 (1998): 680–702.

[30] Historically, the doctrines were articulated in isolation because of the fifteen years that elapsed between Trent's consideration of eucharistic presence and its discussion of eucharistic sacrifice.

[31] *DS* 1651: Can. 1. "*Si quis negaverit, in sanctissimae Eucharistiae sacramento contineri vere, realiter, et substantialiter, corpus et sanguinem una cum anima et divinitate*

(2) his presence in the bread and wine is the result of a whole conversion fittingly called transubstantiation.[32] Refusal to affirm these doctrinal statements is condemned: "*anathema sit.*" Again, these formulations developed partly out of the eleventh-century Berengarian controversy, leading initially to the Fourth Lateran Council (1215), where the Latin term *transubstantiatio* was authoritatively introduced, to be followed by Thomas's exposition of eucharistic theology and Reformation-era debates.[33] The Tridentine decrees were reaffirmed by recent papal magisterium in *Mediator Dei* (1943), *Mysterium Fidei* (1968), and *Ecclesia de Eucharistia* (2003). These restatements raise the question whether the meaning the doctrines conveyed in their original context is retained in contemporary statements.

In the recent authoritative writings we find both an increasing awareness of the multiple presences of Christ in the liturgy that expand our notion of the divine presence in liturgy (especially in *Sacrosanctum Concilium* 7 and *Mysterium Fidei* 35–39) and expressions of eucharistic doctrine that can be taken to entail naïve realist ways of understanding Christ's presence in the Eucharist. An enhanced awareness of diverse modes of presence appears prominently in *Mysterium Fidei*, where Pope Paul writes:

> All of us realize that there is more than one way in which Christ is present in His Church. . . . Christ is present in His Church when she prays, since He is the one who "prays for us and prays in us and to

---

Domini nostri Iesu Christi ac proinde totum Christum; sed dixerit, tantummodo esse in eo ut in signo vel figura, aut virtute: anathema sit."

[32] *DS* 1652: "*Si quis dixerit, in sacrosancto Eucharistiae sacramento remanere substantiam panis et vini una cum corpora et sanguine Domini nostri Iesu Christi, negaveritque mirabilem illam et singularem conversionem totius substantiae panis in corpus et totius substantiae vini in sanguinem, manentibus dumtaxat speciebus panis et vini, quam quidem conversionem catholica Ecclesia aptissime transsubstantiationem appellat: anathema sit."*

[33] See Lee Palmer Wandel, *The Eucharist in the Reformation: Incarnation and Liturgy* (New York: Cambridge University Press, 2006). The polemics of the era were not simply about Christ's presence or a lack thereof, because, of course, all Christians affirmed that Christ was present in the world in many ways. The decisive question was "in what manner is Christ present in the Eucharist?" Ultimately, the differences between the reformers, Luther and Calvin, and the Council of Trent are primarily philosophical and secondarily theological. All affirm that Christ is "really" present in the Eucharist, but each explains that presence in different ways corresponding to distinct philosophical horizons. On this question, then, philosophical clarification is the foundation for ecumenical agreement.

whom we pray: He prays for us as our priest, He prays in us as our head, He is prayed to by us as our God"; and He is the one who has promised, "Where two or three are gathered together in my name, I am there in the midst of them." He is present in the Church as she performs her works of mercy, not just because whatever good we do to one of His least brethren we do to Christ Himself, but also because Christ is the one who performs these works through the Church and who continually helps men with His divine love. He is present in the Church as she moves along on her pilgrimage with a longing to reach the portals of eternal life, for He is the one who dwells in our hearts through faith, and who instills charity in them through the Holy Spirit whom He gives to us.[34]

Adverting to the multiple presences of Christ in the church helps resist the temptation to render the presence of Christ in the Eucharist in a simplistic way. Indications of a naïve realist understanding of eucharistic presence may be evident, however, in *Ecclesia de Eucharistia* 15, where Pope John Paul II quotes Paul VI as saying, "Every theological explanation which seeks some understanding of this mystery, in order to be in accord with Catholic faith, must firmly maintain *that in objective reality, independently of our mind*, the bread and wine have ceased to exist after the consecration, so that the adorable body and blood of the Lord Jesus from that moment on are really before us under the sacramental species of bread and wine."[35] The formulation *"in objective reality, independently of our mind"* can easily be taken in a counterpositional way insofar as it suggests that objectivity is something that can be attained without minds. The Latin speaks less misleadingly: *"ut in ipsa rerum natura, a nostro scilicet spiritu distincta."* To say that there is a distinction between the very nature of things and our intellect is not equivalent to stating, as the translation does, that there is an objective reality independent of our minds. In the translation the relationship between

[34] Paul VI, *Mysterium Fidei*, 35.

[35] John Paul II, *Ecclesia de Eucharistia* (2003), emphasis added. The passage is quoting the homily of Paul VI for June 30, 1968. The Latin reads: *"Quaevis porro theologorum interpretatio, quae huiusmodi mysterio aliquatenus intellegendo studet, ut cum catholica fide congruat, id sartum tectum praestare debet, ut in ipsa rerum natura, a nostro scilicet spiritu distincta, panis et vinum, facta consecratione, adesse desierint, ita ut adorandum Corpus et Sanguinis Domini Iesu post ipsam vere coram nobis ad sint sub sacramentalibus panis et vini."*

reality and human intelligence apparently rests on a naïve realist notion of objectivity, one that gets along without minds. Such an *already-out-there-now-real* construal of objectivity is as available to a mouse or a dog as to a human.[36] A further ambiguity emerges in the claim that the bread and wine "cease to exist" which sounds similar to annihilation, a position rejected by Thomas.[37] These ambiguities highlight the challenges eucharistic doctrines present to contemporary Christians who do not share a common philosophical foundation, and they raise important questions. What did the doctrinal decrees of Trent mean? Can Catholics affirm these doctrinal formulas today?

Paul VI argued that the traditional formulas "express concepts that are not tied to a certain specific form of human culture, or to a certain level of scientific progress, or to one or another theological school. Instead they set forth what the human mind grasps of reality through necessary and universal experience and what it expresses in apt and exact words, whether it be in ordinary or more refined language. For this reason, these formulas are adapted to all men of all times and all places."[38] The claim that the formulas are "adapted to all men of all times and all places" or that the human mind grasps reality through "necessary and universal experience" seems exaggerated. This is because the pope speaks from within a horizon informed by a classicist notion of culture. Paul VI could have secured his point by simply indicating the coherence of the doctrines as stated with his own position instead of claiming abstract universality.

---

[36] The reader of English is given to believe that faith in the reality of the eucharistic presence of Christ has nothing to do with human apprehension and judgment by the light of faith and is only about an ill-defined "objective reality." Of course, the human mind is not the criterion of reality. Insofar as things exist, they do so without relying on human intelligence. Things exist independently of human experiencing, understanding, and judging, because the efficient cause of their being is divine causative knowledge; they exist because of God's understanding, affirming, and willing them to be. So in the case of the Eucharist, the church affirms that Christ is present in the manner articulated in the dominical words of institution as the word of a divine person. But speaking about the presence of Christ in the Eucharist without relating it to human minds illumined by faith, for whom that presence is a communication of divine love oriented toward communion, is simply begging the question.

[37] See *ST*, III, q. 75, a. 3. What secures the presence of Christ in the Eucharist is not that the bread and wine "cease to exist" but that they are wholly converted into the body and blood of Christ.

[38] *Mysterium Fidei*, 24.

Furthermore, as a matter of simple historical fact the doctrinal formulas *are* tied to a certain specific form of human culture, and their terms belong to a particular period of scientific development, but this does not mean that they are not true or even universal. As we noted above, their truth depends on a divinely revealed meaning. On the other hand, recognizing that there is room for greater understanding and clarification, Pope Paul writes:

> They can, it is true, be made clearer and more obvious; and doing this is of great benefit. But it must always be done in such a way that they retain the meaning in which they have been used, so that with the advance of an understanding of the faith, the truth of faith will remain unchanged. For it is the teaching of the First Vatican Council that "the meaning that Holy Mother the Church has once declared, is to be retained forever, and no pretext of deeper understanding ever justifies any deviation from that meaning."[39]

The key here is that any "deeper" meaning is not to deviate from the original meaning. That it can be made clearer with the benefit of advances in understanding while retaining its original meaning seems clear enough. But is the meaning of the eucharistic doctrines effectively communicated when we speak in phrases like "universal and necessary experience" or of "objective reality independently of our minds"? If the eucharistic doctrines of the Catholic Church are to be considered more than sectarian eccentricities that frequently obscure the mystery of sacramental communion with Christ, the true meaning of the doctrines will have to be reappropriated and restated. We cannot rewrite doctrinal statements according to our own designs, but by drawing on new philosophical tools we can preserve their meaning for a new audience.[40]

---

[39] *Mysterium Fidei*, 25.

[40] In "Dimensions of Meaning" (p. 243), Lonergan notes the challenge facing doctrines and theologians in the contemporary climate of opinion:

> [Doctrines] exist, but they no longer enjoy the splendid isolation that compels their acceptance. We know their histories, the moment of their births, the course of their development, their interweaving, their moments of high synthesis, their periods of stagnation, decline, dissolution. We know the kind of subject to which they appeal and the kind they repel: Tell me what you think and I'll tell you why you think that way. But such endlessly erudite and subtle penetration generates detachment, relativism, scepticism. The spiritual atmosphere becomes too thin to support the life of man.

1.3. Summary

Jean-Luc Marion has suggested that to "explain" the Eucharist is a "decisive moment of theological thought."[41] The Eucharist stands as a test for theologians who are attempting to speak to our culture about revealed realities. Marion clarifies that the Eucharist is a gift "and this one above all, does not require first that one explain it, but indeed that one receive it."[42] But in receiving this gift, this mystery, questions arise. Answering those questions does not mean explaining (away) what is ultimately entirely gift; rather, it involves us in a central aspect of theological reflection famously articulated by Augustine:

> Heaven forbid, after all, that God should hate in us that by which he made us more excellent than the other animals. Heaven forbid, I say, that we should believe in such a way that we do not accept or seek a rational account, since we could not even believe if we did not have rational souls. In certain matters, therefore, pertaining to the teaching of salvation, which we cannot yet grasp by reason, but which we will be able to at some point, faith precedes reason so that the heart may be purified in order that it may receive and sustain the light of the great reason, which is, of course, a demand of reason! And so, the prophet stated quite reasonably, *Unless you believe, you will not understand* (Is 7:9 LXX). There he undoubtedly distinguished these two and gave the counsel that we should believe first in order that we may be able to understand what we believe.[43]

Believing to understand is essential not only in the case of the Eucharist but also in all sacramental performance. The oft-cited dictum of liturgical theology, *lex orandi, lex credendi,* "the law of prayer is the law of belief," is altogether pertinent here. One's practice of prayer shapes one's belief, and one's belief enables theological understanding. A fruitful analogical under-

---

Shall we turn to authority? But even authorities are historical entities. It is easy enough to repeat what they said. It is a more complex task to say what they meant.

[41] Jean-Luc Marion, *God without Being* (Chicago: University of Chicago Press, 1991), 161. Marion writes: "To explain the Eucharist—a multiform, inevitable, and instructive naïveté. In another sense, a decisive moment for theological thought."

[42] Ibid., 162.

[43] Augustine, "Letter 120," 100–155, in *Letters: Volume* 2, ed. John E. Rotelle and Boniface Ramsay (New York: New City Press, 2002), at 131.

standing of the doctrines will therefore be grounded in eucharistic worship and belief and will inquire into their intelligibility in order to appropriate their meaning more fully into a lived imitation of Christ. As statements about the meaning of the Eucharist these doctrines have their foundations not in abstract first principles but in the concrete, lived faith of those who encounter Christ in the Eucharist and live as his friends. The doctrines may find further explanation in a systematic understanding of the truths they contain, and the argument of the present work is that systematic understanding of doctrine can illumine faith and practice.

It is important to emphasize before moving forward that when a systematic explanation of eucharistic doctrines is grounded in a theoretical differentiation of consciousness it will not attempt to explain the meaning of the Eucharist in purely theoretical terms alone. That meaning, as with all theological meaning, is also always practical, elemental, and experiential. As human beings, however, we ask questions about our experiences that intend adequate understanding, however incomplete. The better that understanding, the more fruitful it can be. I have argued that Lonergan's overall contribution to theology can bear fruit in the area of eucharistic theology. This is so despite the fact that sacramental performance of its very nature pertains most directly to the aesthetic and dramatic differentiations of consciousness. In the sacraments we find both a need for the development of aesthetic and dramatic categories of "symbol" and "embodiment" advanced by Chauvet and the clarification of meaning attainable through a critical-realist metaphysics in systematic theology. The result might be a critical sacramental realism that recaptures key distinctions in Thomas and transposes them into our new context.

2. Systematics:
Toward a Fruitful Analogical Understanding of Eucharistic Doctrine

The effort to transpose classical understandings of doctrines in order to appropriate their meaning more adequately is nothing new, especially in the area of eucharistic theology. As noted in the introduction, much of twentieth-century reflection on the Eucharist has attempted to reinterpret the Tridentine formulae with the aid of insights from contemporary philosophy. I am convinced that Lonergan's thorough analysis of human knowing, his epistemology, and his critical-realist metaphysics enable us to make sense of the doctrines in categories of meaning that eliminate false problems of objectivity lurking in the writings of Paul VI and John Paul II and implicit in so much liturgical practice. These problems can easily obscure the true mystery of eucharistic communion. To begin resolving problems I will consider the objective presence of Christ in the Eucharist in terms of the notion of objectivity sketched in chapter 4.

The kind of objective reality that exists independently of minds, to which Paul VI refers, disappears in a coherent understanding of the human world mediated by meaning in which the sacramental celebration of the Eucharist actually takes place. On the other hand, the decree of Trent explicitly focuses on objectivity by saying that "in the most holy Eucharist are contained *really, truly, and substantially* the body and blood, along with the soul and divinity of our Lord Jesus Christ, and thus the whole Christ."[44] Whatever is meant here by "really, truly, and substantially," it cannot mean that the presence is held as objective according to any serious comparison of knowing with looking, inasmuch as one cannot see the soul or divinity of Christ. The objectivity in question is therefore very much a matter of human minds, not operating according to the canons of empirical method but working in accord with the eyes of faith, which are attuned to their proper object by the already active presence of the Holy Spirit in the subject. Let me explain.

2.1. Eucharist in the World of Meaning

In the Eucharist, objectivity pertains to an act of meaning whose intelligibility is irreducible to sensible data. The words of consecration, the words of Christ, uttered by the priest acting in the person of Christ by uttering these words, are a constitutive act of meaning. The words communicate a meaning as well as a statement of fact, though not in the empirical order. Clearly, Christ's body is not bread, either at the Last Supper or in any subsequent eucharistic celebration. On the other hand, that bread can become Christ's body is simply a matter of belief in a God who uses matter to communicate divine meanings to human intelligence, meanings and values mediated into history by God's word incarnate. But why should bread become Christ's body and wine Christ's blood? What is the purpose of the presence of the

---

[44] *DS* 1651: "*in sanctissimae Eucharistiae sacramento contineri vere, realiter, et substantialiter, corpus et sanguinem una cum anima et divinitate Domini nostri Iesu Christi ac proinde totum Christum.*" See *ST* III, q. 76, a. 1, ad 1m.

body and blood of Christ? And why is the sacramental encounter with the body and blood of Christ carried out by eating it? To answer these questions we need a fruitful analogical understanding of the mysteries preserved in the doctrinal decrees regarding eucharistic worship, which we develop by using Lonergan's categories of meaning as integral to the ontology of meaning compatible with his critical-realist metaphysics.

2.2. *Thomas Aquinas: Eating and Meaning*

Our transposition of eucharistic doctrines *from* dogmatic-realist metaphysics *into* categories derived from Lonergan's ontology of meaning will borrow an important distinction Thomas makes between different kinds of "eating" or ways of receiving the sacrament:

> There are two things to be considered in the receiving of this sacrament, namely, the sacrament itself, and its fruits. . . . The perfect way, then, of receiving this sacrament is when *one partakes of its effect.* Now . . . it sometimes happens that a man is hindered from receiving the effect of this sacrament; and such a receiving of this sacrament is an imperfect one. Therefore, as the perfect is divided against the imperfect, so sacramental eating, whereby the sacrament only is received without its effect, is divided against spiritual eating, by which one receives the spiritual effect of this sacrament, whereby a man is spiritually united with Christ through faith and charity.[45]

Thomas notes that, unlike the other sacraments in which "the receiving of the sacrament is the actual perfection of the sacrament," in the Eucharist this is *not* the case because "this sacrament is accomplished in the consecration."[46] Physically consuming the consecrated bread and wine is a

---

[45] *ST* III, q. 80, a. 1, c (emphasis added).

[46] Ibid., ad 1m. The point here, often missed by interpreters of Thomas who focus attention on the recipient, is that in the Eucharist the action is completed in the communication of a meaning, not in the application of the matter of the sacrament. Hence Thomas emphasizes the form of the Eucharist in the words of institution, the act of meaning that brings the Eucharist to act. See *ST* III, q. 78, a. 1, c:

> And because the form should suit the thing, therefore the form of this sacrament differs from the forms of the other sacraments in two respects. First, because the form of the other sacraments implies the use of the matter, as for instance, baptizing, or signing; but the form of this sacrament implies merely the consecration of the matter,

secondary and potentially imperfect act, while the primary act is a matter of desiring the effect of the Eucharist. Consequently, even the desire to receive this sacrament can secure its effect. On the other hand, Thomas affirms that the "actual receiving of the sacrament produces *more fully* the effect of the sacrament than does the desire thereof."[47] The effect of the sacraments belongs to the intentional order, that is, to the desires of the recipient. According to Thomas, then, the effect of the sacrament is had through desire, not rites alone, no matter how ornate or simple, though some symbols might elicit the desire for communion more fully, especially insofar as they invite active participation. By distinguishing between spiritual and sacramental eating, Thomas clarifies that the heart of the eucharistic presence of Christ belongs to the intentional order, or to the world mediated by meaning, not the world of immediacy of the senses.

Thomas clarifies the meaning of sacramental eating by considering the unjust recipient of the sacrament. He raises the objection, "It would seem that none but the just man eats Christ sacramentally."[48] To meet the objection he distinguishes between spiritual and sacramental eating. If it falls to the just alone to eat sacramentally, then some additional miracle would need to occur to prevent the reception of the sacrament by the unjust, for example, that the unjust would experience vomiting were the consecrated bread and wine to touch their tongue. Instead, Thomas invokes Paul's argument in 1 Corinthians that

---

which consists in transubstantiation, as when it is said, "This is My body," or, "This is the chalice of My blood." Secondly, because the forms of the other sacraments are pronounced in the person of the minister, whether by way of exercising an act, as when it is said, "I baptize thee," or "I confirm thee," etc.; or by way of command, as when it is said in the sacrament of order, "Take the power," etc.; or by way of entreaty, as when in the sacrament of Extreme Unction it is said, "By this anointing and our intercession," etc. But the form of this sacrament is pronounced as if Christ were speaking in person, so that it is given to be understood that the minister does nothing in perfecting this sacrament, except to pronounce the words of Christ.

[47] *ST* III, q. 80, a. 1, c. Emphasis added. Eucharist is unique among the sacraments in that, as food, it fully enters into our bodies where the material signs of other sacraments remain physically outside. Like food, the Eucharist transforms from the inside out. The increased emphasis on participation in the Eucharist in the twentieth century from Pius X to Vatican II to John Paul II highlights this fundamental insight into the sacramental mediation of food as something whose full symbolic power is actualized in eating. The emphasis here on spiritual eating responds to a countervailing tendency toward mindless eating, which is increasingly common in a culture where eating is regularly detached from meaningful communion with others.

[48] *ST* III, q. 80, a. 3, ob. 1.

those who eat or drink without discerning the body "eat and drink judgment unto themselves."[49] Those who eat spiritually, on the other hand, receive what they desire, union with Christ. The unjust eat Christ sacramentally insofar as they have been present for the acts of meaning that bring about the presence, they have heard and understood grammatically the words uttered over the bread and wine, they have ingested the sacramental species in which Christ is present, but they have not affirmed the meaning of those words spoken about bread as true or consented to live in accord with that meaning. They eat sacramentally because they do in fact consume the consecrated species, which they understand to have been consecrated, but they do not do so fruitfully because they do not affirm the meaning of the consecration and consent to its practical implications because they do not desire the effect.[50]

Thomas clarifies the distinction by raising a common question at the time: "What does the mouse eat?" Although this question is likely to embarrass contemporary Christians, Thomas takes it seriously as a way of clarifying that the Eucharist is primarily meaning. He distinguishes between animal intelligence and human intelligence in order to underline the importance of understanding the meaning of eucharistic presence and to situate sacraments in the human world, where reality is constituted by acts of meaning that communicate to rational animals. The question is worth entertaining.

When we toss crumbs to pigeons or squirrels we know nothing of the animal's experience of bread. Bread as it exists in the human world is not the bread animals eat. To the mouse, bread is simply edible, as opposed to inedible, stuff within a sheerly biologically extroverted pattern of experience. But when a rational animal, a human being, participates in the production, distribution, and consumption of bread, the effective function of meaning shapes a new reality.[51] About the world of the mouse we know very little; it

---

[49] 1 Cor 11:29.

[50] *ST* III, q. 80, a. 1, m 2: "Sacramental eating which does not secure the effect, is divided in contrast with spiritual eating; just as the imperfect, which does not attain the perfection of its species, is divided in contrast with the perfect." Relating these modes of eating to Lonergan's levels of consciousness, we can say that sacramental eating pertains to the second level of consciousness while spiritual eating pertains to the third and fourth. Spiritual eating brings the recipient to act, at which moment the presence of Christ in the Eucharist is affirmed as real and consented to as the truth of one's existence.

[51] Thomas argues that in fact bread and wine are not human creations but natural potencies of wheat and grapes and therefore not artifacts. This is critical because, for

is a world of immediacy, a mass of sensible data related to the biologically extroverted behavior of animals, wherein questions about "substance" or meaning do not occur. But once we move to the level of human understanding we have gone beyond the world of pure sensation proper to the infant or the nonrational animal. The world of pure sensation is constituted at the level of mere accidents; it is ignorant of substances, intelligibilities, and signs, let alone sacramental signs which find meaning in matter.

Thomas contrasts the animal's world of immediacy to the world in which the Eucharist is received sacramentally or spiritually. However, even while he allows that the bread can be consumed accidentally, he affirms that Christ does not cease to be present under the species of the bread and wine:

> Even though a mouse or a dog were to eat the consecrated host, the substance of Christ's body would not cease to be under the species, so long as those species remain, and that is, so long as the substance of bread would have remained; just as if it were to be cast into the mire. Nor does this turn to any indignity regarding Christ's body, since He willed to be crucified by sinners without detracting from His dignity; especially since the mouse or dog does not touch Christ's body in its proper species, but only as to its sacramental species. Some, however, have said that Christ's body would cease to be there, directly were it touched by a mouse or a dog; but this again detracts from the truth of the sacrament. . . . Nonetheless it must not be said that the irrational animal eats the body of Christ sacramentally; since it is incapable of using it as a sacrament. Hence it eats Christ's body "accidentally," and not sacramentally, just as if anyone not knowing a host to be consecrated were to consume it.[52]

As regards Thomas's first point, we can suppose that his position that the substance of Christ's body does not cease to be "under" the bread even

---

Thomas, artifacts are not substances and are not in potency to transubstantiation. See Christopher M. Brown, "Artifacts, Substances, and Transubstantiation: Solving a Puzzle for Aquinas' Views," *The Thomist* 71 (2007): 89–112. Chauvet's emphasis on the analogy of manna is quite to the point in considering the eucharistic bread as pure gift, not something we create *ex nihilo*, even if we cooperate with nature in bringing it to the altar. These aspects of the givenness of the sacramental bread and wine and human cooperation are maintained in the Eucharistic Prayer ("earth has given and human hands have made . . . fruit of the vine and work of human hands").

[52] *ST* 3, q. 80, a. 3 ad 3m (emphasis added).

when consumed by a dog may be the result of taking seriously the truth constituted by the act of meaning through which the bread has been changed. This is ritualized bread that has had certain words spoken over it that have changed its meaning in the human world and therefore it remains a sacramental sign in the human world until the accidents cease to exist. The data on this bread include certain predicates that do not pertain to other kinds of bread. Unlike a human being, a dog is utterly unaware of this fact. Thus Thomas argues the truth of the presence of Christ's body even under the species of the partially eaten host left by a mouse. But Thomas compares the dog or mouse to a human who eats a consecrated piece of bread without being aware of its having been consecrated and so does not eat sacramentally, for example, a thief who knows nothing of Christian faith but who eats the consecrated hosts from inside a stolen golden ciborium. Because he eats the bread purely for the sustenance of his organism, his experience of the bread's meaning is restricted to what Lonergan identifies as a biological pattern of experience that concerns only the sugars, protein, etc., that his body needs: "I need food. This is food." Bread can mean only physical nourishment, in which case it is eaten accidentally.

While dogs and mice, and possibly humans, can eat the eucharistic bread accidentally, such eating is confined to the biological pattern and approximates the experience of the world as immediately available to the senses. Once acts of meaning, which identify a form in matter, are involved, we have moved into a world mediated by meaning wherein even the unbeliever as a rational animal can experience, understand, and judge that *this* bread has had *these* words spoken over it in *this* ritual. Certain predicates have been added to this bread. This bread is sacramental; it is meaningful bread: endowed with a certain meaning, capable of being a sacrament or a sign of sacred reality. Affirming the meaning of the words spoken over the bread in the context of the ritual constitutes "spiritual eating," by which one assents and consents to the words of Christ that transform ordinary bread into an effective sign of communion.

Criticisms of a "metaphysics of meaning" in eucharistic theology, aimed primarily at the Dutch school, are not equipped to account for the distinction between animals and rational animals.[53] To encounter, understand, affirm,

---

[53] See, for example, Roch Kereszty, *The Wedding Feast of the Lamb: Eucharistic Theology from a Biblical, Historical and Systematic Perspective* (Chicago: Liturgy Training

and consent to meanings are conscious acts of rational animals. For example, there may be something about the red portion of the light spectrum that indicates "danger" to an animal, but the use of red in the human world of meaning enables the actual functioning of stoplights, and so the ordering of an entire transit system and an economy that depends on it. This transformation of a natural potency into an effective meaning is the action of a rational animal, or of the human being as a symbolic or language-using animal. These signs are conventional, of course, but because they are part of a human world mediated by meaning they have a cognitive, effective, constitutive, and communicative meaning. Theologies of transignification emphasize that bread already has a meaning related to the nourishment and fellowship of a meal and already functions as a sign before being transignified through a meaningful act of ritual consecration.[54] In terms of Lonergan's framework, one can grant that a transignification would involve a change of constitutive and communicative meaning through the understanding, assent, and consent of the church. In the Eucharist, however, the constitutive and communicative functions of meaning that must also be taken into account transcend the meaning that humans give ritual bread. Christ's words, his acts of constitutive and communicative meaning, *acts of a divine person*, transform and elevate the meaning of the Eucharist. That the words of consecration are Christ's acts of meaning means that in this case transignification is transubstantiation.[55]

Publications, 2004), 213: "If a human change of meaning cannot change the reality of things, the theory of transignification falls short of upholding what the dogma affirms, an ontological change of the objective reality of bread and wine into the body and blood of Christ." Kereszty fails to recognize that changes of meaning are of the ontological order because he imagines reality in terms of the *already-out-there-now-real*. In the book he repeatedly refers to "material reality" as a way of securing the ontological weight without recognizing that such a "material reality" would be as available to a mouse or a dog as to a human. Rational animals inhabit a different world.

[54] See Edward Schillebeeckx, *The Eucharist*, trans. N. D. Smith (New York: Sheed and Ward, 1968), 134–36.

[55] See Neil Ormerod, "The Four-Point Hypothesis: Transpositions and Complications," *Irish Theological Quarterly* 77, no. 2 (2012): 127–40. Ormerod plays out the ramifications of understanding Christ's eucharistic presence in terms of created participations in Trinitarian relations identified in Lonergan's "four-point hypothesis," especially the relation of paternity: "This expression of divine meaning constitutes a substantial change in the reality of the sacramental species. The *transsignification* is a genuine *transubstantiation*, a fundamental change in the reality of the bread and wine through its participation in

3. Eucharist as Constitutive Meaning

The Eucharist is indeed part of the human world; it is therefore a meaningful reality. On this point we can agree with Chauvet's emphasis on the symbol as essential to the human being as a being in the world of meaning, and his employing Heidegger's *ad-esse* to talk about the eucharistic bread as a "being for" humans. Chauvet's mistake is to separate symbol from metaphysics, witnessed by his need to add the preposition. This is because Chauvet is primarily operating in a descriptive rather than an explanatory mode. Metaphysics, understood as the integral heuristic structure of proportionate being, includes within it all those meanings and values that are humanly communicated intelligibilities in the human world. The world mediated by meaning, the world that Lonergan repeatedly affirms is the *real* world,[56] can therefore be analyzed in terms of the integral heuristic structure of proportionate being, or metaphysics. Sacraments operate within the world mediated by meaning, and so within proportionate being. As signs, they are communications of meaning. As sacred signs they are communications of divine meaning, or mysteries that transcend the bounds of proportionate being and depend on the cooperation of the Holy Spirit in the recipient for their fruitful reception. As effective signs that "make human beings holy," they mediate human sharing in the inner life of the Trinity.

The point of sacraments is that they are *for* human beings as human, living in a world mediated by meanings and motivated by values that is the real world of rational animals. Indeed, Thomas Aquinas insists on the human finality of the sacraments and the exclusively human ability to receive the sacrament in faith as an effective sign. Human intelligence uses signs and symbols in order to understand, both in the universe of proportionate being and in the realm of transcendent being. Therefore talk about the sacraments that prescinds from their human context assumes a version of the counterposition that the real is what is known by looking, the myth of

---

the expression of divine meaning. . . . Meaning is constitutive of human existence and God's entry into human history is the entry of divine meaning. Such meaning in human history has ontological ramifications and in fact can only properly be accounted for by a properly developed ontology of meaning" (138).

[56] Cf. Lonergan, "Is It Real?" 119–39, in *Philosophical and Theological Essays 1965–1980*; Lonergan, "The Analogy of Meaning," 183–213, in *Philosophical and Theological Papers 1958–1964*, CWBL 6, ed. Robert C. Croken, Frederick E. Crowe, and Robert Doran (Toronto: University of Toronto Press, 1996).

the *already-out-there-now-real* identified above. Thinking of sacraments in this way goes together with considering the consecrated species in isolation as objectively present independently of our minds. In general, approaching the Eucharist as an *already-out-there-now-real* engenders idols of our own making. The consecration cannot occur independently of a rational animal's intelligence as capable of articulating human meaning. So at least one intelligence is required for the very fact of consecration, i.e., originally Christ's in his own person and thereafter a priest's acting *in persona Christi*. By mediating meanings through signs, sacraments are suitable for communicating neither to angels nor to brute animals, but to rational animals, to human intelligence.[57] As signs, sacraments both communicate to human beings and "make" human beings holy in virtue of that very communication

[57] *ST* III, q. 60, a. 2, c.: "Signs are given to men, to whom it is proper to discover the unknown by means of the known. Consequently a sacrament properly so called is that which is the sign of some sacred thing pertaining to man; so that properly speaking a sacrament, as considered by us now, is defined as being the 'sign of a holy thing so far as it makes men holy.'" See also *ST* II–II, q. 81, a. 7, c.: "Wherefore in the Divine worship it is necessary to make use of corporeal things, that man's mind may be aroused thereby, as by signs, to the spiritual acts by means of which he is united to God. Therefore the internal acts of religion take precedence of the others and belong to religion essentially, while its external acts are secondary, and subordinate to the internal acts." According to Thomas, angels eat Christ spiritually but in his proper species, his glorified body in heaven. See *ST* III, q. 80, a. 2, c:

> Christ Himself is contained in this sacrament, not under His proper species, but under the sacramental species. Consequently there are two ways of eating spiritually. First, as Christ Himself exists under His proper species, and in this way the angels eat Christ spiritually inasmuch as they are united with Him in the enjoyment of perfect charity, and in clear vision (and this is the bread we hope for in heaven), and not by faith, as we are united with Him here. In another way one may eat Christ spiritually, as He is under the sacramental species, inasmuch as a man believes in Christ, while desiring to receive this sacrament; and this is not merely to eat Christ spiritually, but likewise to eat this sacrament; which does not fall to the lot of the angels. And therefore although the angels feed on Christ spiritually, yet it does not belong to them to eat this sacrament spiritually.

Angels receive the meaning of Christ immediately without a sacramental mediation. But human intelligence is activated through the mediation of the senses and exists in a world mediated by meanings expressed in words, signs, and symbols, some of which are sacramental, or signs of sacred realities. Our experience of Christ is of a historical human being who revealed divine meanings to human beings in his own incarnate meaning, through touching, healing, preaching, sharing food, innocently suffering, and dying. That incarnate meaning is offered to human intelligence.

of meaning. If this is the case, it is the meaning of the sign that sanctifies—not the sign itself, but that to which it refers, its meaning. These meanings are not comprehended outside the horizon of faith, because they are tran-scendent and so disproportionate to the realm of proportionate being. Only the eye of faith that is a gift of the Holy Spirit allows their meaning to be affirmed. Faith, which illumines human intelligence with its supernatural light, precedes understanding, especially in the case of the Eucharist, in which Christ's word gives the constitutive meaning, so that faith in Christ and in the veracity of Christ's word is essential to the experience of Christ's presence in the Eucharist.[58] But Christ's word is spoken to human beings and received by human intelligence as enabled to receive meaning by the gift of the Holy Spirit.

In the Eucharist a meaning is given by a divine person. Like all the words and actions of Christ that are intended to convey divine love for human be-ings, it communicates a divine meaning in human words and signs. Unlike the conventional aspect of a stoplight, which functions by the community's consent, the meaning of the Eucharist is a constitutively incarnate mean-ing that requires only the intention of the one communicating the meaning. When Christ says "this is my body" about a piece of bread he is not making a statement of brute fact about "material reality," because to be bread is one thing and to be Christ's body is another.[59] Rather, Christ is giving a new

[58] Aquinas clarifies this point at *ST* III, q. 78, a. 5, s.c.: "These words are pronounced in the person of Christ, Who says of Himself (John 14:6): 'I am the truth.'" Thomas goes on in the corpus to clarify the significance of Christ's words by distinguishing between possible positions, concluding: "This sentence possesses the power of effecting the conversion of the bread into the body of Christ. And therefore it is compared to other sentences, which have power only of signifying and not of producing, as the concept of the practical intellect, which is productive of the thing, is compared to the concept of our speculative intellect which is drawn from things, because 'words are signs of concepts,' as the Philosopher says (*Peri Herm.* i). And therefore as the concept of the practical intellect does not presuppose the thing understood, but makes it, so the truth of this expression does not presuppose the thing signified, but makes it; for such is the relation of God's word to the things made by the Word." Thomas's emphasis on the words of Christ as the form of the sacrament indicates their productive power, which Lonergan speaks of in terms of the constitutive and effective functions of meaning, in which a meaning changes reality or makes it exist.

[59] See *ST* III, q. 75, a. 2, c.: "This position is contrary to the form of this sacrament, in which it is said: 'This is My body,' which would not be true if the substance of the bread were to remain there; for the substance of bread never is the body of Christ. Rather

meaning to this bread and by his word effects a new reality. Consequently, it is no longer bread.[60] No longer does this bread only offer sustenance for the physical organism; rather, it is ordered to the sustenance of the spirit. Even further, Thomas emphasizes that, unlike bread, which is assimilated to the body through the process of digestion,[61] the presence of Christ in the Eucharist is not assimilated by the faithful, but the faithful are assimilated to Christ.[62] This assimilation occurs through eating and drinking as acts of meaning that can be explained in terms of elemental meaning and mutual self-mediation.

With these clarifications of the importance of meaning in sacramental theology in mind we can simply state: Christ is present in the Eucharist by a constitutive act of meaning when he proclaims, "This is my body . . . This is my blood . . ." and to affirm the presence of Christ in the Eucharist is to share that meaning and consent to a mutual self-mediation wherein

---

should one say in that case: 'Here is My body.'" Christ's body does not become bread, but bread becomes the body.

[60] See Michael Stebbins, "The Eucharistic Presence of Christ: Mystery and Meaning," *Worship* 64 (1990): 225–36. Stebbins clarifies the point about the bread no longer being bread through an analysis of Lonergan's understanding of things, in which the central claim is that there are no things within things. A thing is a *unity-identity-whole*, not an agglomeration of substances but a single substance. Hence, in the context of the Eucharist, the change of meaning is transubstantiation. There is no need for an additional change to the accidents of bread. There is simply no need to hold, as Schillebeeckx does, for transignification as distinct from but related to transubstantiation. When properly understood, they are equivalent statements. Schillebeeckx was not fully cognizant of the world mediated by meaning when articulating his position. His dependence on Kant prevented him from saying anything about the ontological dimension entailed in a change of meaning. If he were equipped with the ontology of meaning that emerges in a critical-realist metaphysics he could push his claim more consistently without reserving space for a misunderstood doctrine of transubstantiation alongside transignification. See Giovanni Sala, "Transubstantiation oder Transignifikation: Gedenken zu einem Dilemma," *Zeitschrift für Katholische Theologie* 92 (1970): 1–34.

[61] The accidents of the bread are assimilated to the body through the normal processes of digestion, absorption, and excretion. Therefore the bread still has the ability to nourish (*ST* III 3, q. 77, a. 6, c.) since nourishment of the human organism occurs through the accidents of matter. Consecrated bread maintains what Lonergan would call "conjugates," which, as it regards explanatory conjugates, in the case of bread are the sugars and proteins that can sustain the human organism.

[62] See *ST* III, q. 77, a. 6, ad 1m: "Christ's very body can be called bread, since it is the mystical bread 'coming down from heaven.' Consequently, Ambrose uses the word 'bread' in this second meaning, when he says that 'this bread does not pass into the body,' because, to wit, Christ's body is not changed into man's body, but nourishes his soul."

Christ's words become our own through the power of the Holy Spirit as we join ourselves to his incarnate meaning, i.e., his loving self-sacrifice for sinful humanity prefigured in the elemental acts of meaning of the Last Supper and fully revealed on the cross. Let us explicate these claims.

3.1. Eucharistic Sacrifice: Redemption in the Liturgy

To treat the presence of Christ in the Eucharist in categories of meaning requires that we suspend any inclination to deal with that presence as *already-out-there-now-real*. In accord with the ontology of meaning of the human world, we cannot separate Christ's presence from the way that presence is enacted. The presence of Christ in the Eucharist is *real* as a dynamic and complex mediation of divine meaning, which is revealed in the institution narrative itself: "this is my Body, / which will be given up for you . . . this is the chalice of my Blood, / the Blood of the new and eternal covenant, / which will be poured out for you and for many / for the forgiveness of sins."[63] The meaning Christ gives to his actions in the narrative reveals that the presence is a sacrificial presence. What is made present is not brute materiality, cells, DNA, and the like, all of which are accidents, but Christ's *body as offered*, that is, the incarnate meaning of the cross, by which Christ fully reveals his mission of redeeming sins and overcoming evil through love.[64] Therefore discerning the presence of Christ in the Eucharist begins with a consideration of the sacrifice of the cross.

[63] This is the English translation of the Third Typical Edition of the Roman Missal (2010). For a thorough analysis of translation method behind the new translations, see Peter Jeffery, *Translating Tradition: A Chant Historian Reads* Liturgiam Authenticam (Collegeville, MN: Liturgical Press, 2005). The critical point here is not the particular translation but the biblical witness that Christ offers his body for others and his blood as a covenant (1 Cor 11:24-25). For a historical survey of the various prayers of the Eucharist, including variations in the institution narrative, see R. C. D. Jasper and G. J. Cuming, *Prayers of the Eucharist: Early and Reformed* (Collegeville, MN: Liturgical Press, 1990).

[64] The Lutheran theologian Oswald Bayer captures this insight when he says, "We receive his sacrifice" (Oswald Bayer, "Worship and Theology," 148–61, in *Worship and Ethics: Lutherans and Anglicans in Dialogue*, ed. Oswald Bayer and Alan M. Suggate (Berlin and New York: de Gruyter, 1996). Bayer emphasizes the important point that we do not offer Christ in sacrifice; rather, we *receive* Christ's sacrifice. Bayer criticizes the cooperative dimension of eucharistic sacrifice inasmuch as classical Roman Catholic interpretations tended to reduce the ethical dimension to the ritual act. Ritual self-offering in liturgical sacrifice is not a replacement for self-sacrificing loving in the form of Christian discipleship in the world. The major achievement of Chauvet's theory of

The category of sacrifice, despite its ambiguity, holds a fundamental place in the history of Christian theology and worship. The theological tradition has employed the category since the apostolic period to understand the works of Christ and the application of those works in the present through sacraments.[65] Lonergan proposed a general articulation of the notion of sacrifice while teaching in Montreal in the early 1940s. As part of a course in sacramental theology he composed the scholion *De Notione Sacrificii*.[66] There, he defines sacrifice as "a proper symbol of a sacrificial attitude."[67] This definition provides a general notion of sacrifice that pertains to any sacrificial act but emphasizes the intentionality of the one offering sacrifice. Sacrifice is what it is because it communicates externally an interior act of meaning. Focusing too intently on the external expression at the expense of the intended meaning can reduce sacrifice to a mechanistic and ultimately meaningless and brutal affair. The meaning has to do with the symbolic nature of the expression of the sacrificial attitude. The manifold character of a symbol allows the sacrificial attitude to continually elicit affective responses in a way that a sign, because of its univocal character, does not.[68]

---

symbolic gift exchange is to move definitively beyond any interpretation of liturgical sacrifice as fulfilling the ethical dimension. Chauvet helpfully draws out the ethical dimension of the return gift in terms of the "liturgy of the neighbor"—a phrase borrowed from Emmanuel Levinas (Louis-Marie Chauvet, *Symbol and Sacrament: A Sacramental Reinterpretation of Christian Existence* [= *SS*], trans. Patrick Madigan and Madeleine Beaumont [Collegeville, MN: Liturgical Press, 1995], 238). See also Timothy Brunk, *Liturgy and Life: The Unity of Sacrament and Ethics in the Theology of Louis-Marie Chauvet* (New York: Peter Lang, 2007).

[65] The place of sacrifice in the theology of the Eucharist and the properly Christian understanding of sacrifice are subjects of ongoing debate. See, *inter alia*, Robert J. Daly, *Sacrifice Unveiled: The True Meaning of Christian Sacrifice* (New York: Continuum, 2009); Erin Lothes-Biviano, *The Paradox of Christian Sacrifice: The Loss of Self, the Gift of Self* (New York: Crossroad, 2007); Matthew Levering, *Sacrifice and Community: Jewish Offering and Christian Eucharist* (Malden, MA: Blackwell, 2005); Michael McGuckian, *The Holy Sacrifice of the Mass: A Search for an Acceptable Notion of Sacrifice* (Chicago: Liturgy Training Publications, 2005).

[66] The text of the scholion was translated and published as Bernard Lonergan, "The Notion of Sacrifice," *Method: Journal of Lonergan Studies* 19 (2001): 3–34, repr. with the original Latin in *Early Latin Theology*, CWBL 19, ed. Frederick E. Crowe and Robert M. Doran (Toronto: University of Toronto Press, 2011) 3–51.

[67] Ibid., 3.

[68] For example, while a stop sign communicates a single meaning, a crucifix evokes a torrent of feelings.

Lonergan begins working out a notion of the symbol in his notes on sacrifice; that notion finds a new context in *Method in Theology*. In "The Notion of Sacrifice," Lonergan defines a symbol as "an objective manifestation that is perceptible and is social in itself."[69] Further he explains: "Symbols have a twofold function in human nature. One is their foundation in man's sentient and corporeal nature; hence the need to express outwardly in a perceptible and bodily way what one thinks and feels interiorly. The other is their foundation in man's social nature; hence the need that individuals have of gathering together to communicate to their community or group what they are thinking and feeling interiorly."[70] In *Method in Theology*, Lonergan develops this notion of the symbol by relating it directly to feeling: "A symbol is an image of a real or imaginary object that evokes a feeling or is evoked by a feeling."[71] The key relation is between feelings and symbols. It is through the mutual interplay of symbols and feelings that we are incorporated ever more into a world mediated by meaning and motivated by values. In that context our living becomes the dramatic artistry of symbolic living, so that our being human is by and large a symbolic evocation of our feelings, "the mass and momentum and power of [our] conscious living."[72]

For Lonergan, feelings are complex. They relate us to objects, for example, in the way we desire food, fear pain, or enjoy music.[73] They are related to one another through changes in the object, as when one desires the absent good, hopes for a good that is sought, or enjoys a present good.[74] Feelings are also related to one another through personal relationships: "So love, gentleness, tenderness, intimacy, union go together; similarly, alienation, hatred, harshness, violence, cruelty form a group," etc.[75] Although feelings

---

[69] Lonergan, "The Notion of Sacrifice," 3.

[70] Ibid., 4.

[71] Lonergan, *Method in Theology*, 64. Lonergan's understanding of symbols in this work is informed by studies of the role of symbol in the functioning of the human psyche (pp. 65–69). Here, symbols are understood as operators in the affective development of the psyche. One responds differently to images at different stages of development. These elements of Lonergan's exploration of the human world of meaning are unpacked and developed in Robert M. Doran, *Subject and Psyche* (Milwaukee, WI: Marquette University Press, 1994).

[72] Lonergan, *Method in Theology*, 65.

[73] Ibid., 64.

[74] Ibid.

[75] Ibid.

may conflict, they may still come together so that "one may desire despite fear, hope against hope, mix joy with sadness, love with hate," etc.[76] Finally, then, feelings are related to the subject: "They are the mass and momentum and power of his conscious living, the actuation of his affective capacities, dispositions, habits, the effective orientation of his being."[77] Just as affective capacities, dispositions, and habits develop, so the symbols that move the subject change over time: "Affective development, or aberration, involves a transvaluation and transformation of symbols. What before was moving no longer moves; what before did not move now is moving. So the symbols themselves change to express the new affective capacities and dispositions."[78] Within the dialectic of development and decline we come to understand the complex nature of the symbolic.

Symbols do not function logically. Rather, they carry a multitude of meanings and are related to each other in complex ways through the coincidence of opposites and the convergence of images. A symbol can reveal both love and hate, as in the way the cross reveals to a Christian both loving forgiveness of sins and the hatefulness of sin. Because of this ability to deal with internal tensions in human experience, symbols meet the need for internal communication that human beings experience as they seek to construct a world of meaning. Lonergan emphasizes that symbols have the ability to meet this need in a way that the refinements of logic and dialectic cannot.[79] He argues that "our apprehensions of values occur in intentional responses, in feelings," and that those intentional responses are mediated by symbols through which "mind and body, mind and heart, heart and body communicate."[80] Symbolic meaning is elemental. It is prior to any objectification and analysis; it remains, like art, in the experiential pattern.[81] Because

---

[76] Ibid., 65.

[77] Ibid.

[78] Ibid., 66.

[79] Ibid.

[80] Ibid., 67.

[81] Lonergan's emphasis on the sacrificial attitude symbolized by the cross reminds us that the cross, although it is a communication of meaning, is a mystery, and therefore is not to be understood primarily through objectification and analysis, but through participation. Similarly, the Eucharist as the preeminent symbol of the mystery of the cross invites our participation before it can be analyzed in any fruitful way. The task of the theologian operating in the functional specialty of systematics is to throw some light on the mystery, but within the context of participation in it on the level of feeling.

it is a symbol, the Eucharist invites, indeed *allows,* participation in a way that the mere proximity of material reality or the intellectual apprehension of concepts do not.[82]

What Lonergan speaks of as "attitude" in "The Notion of Sacrifice" can be articulated in terms of the categories of meaning outlined in *Method in Theology.* The former focuses on sacrifice as a symbol of a sacrificial attitude. The attitude is sacrificial in that the intended meaning is complex, including latreutic, propitiatory, eucharistic, and impetratory aspects: "'Sacrificial attitude' designates the proper stance of one's mind and heart towards God (1) as God (hence it is latreutic), (2) as offended by sin (hence it is propitiatory), as the source of all good gifts both past and future (and hence it is eucharistic and impetratory). As such, 'sacrificial attitude' denotes a compendious synthesis of the virtue of religion which regulates the relationship of one's mind and heart towards God."[83] Lonergan speaks of the same sacrificial attitude in a brief exhortation written for a popular journal in 1947: "To merely human judgment the passion and death of Our Lord is the symbol of human suffering caused by human wrong; it is the drama of human vice and the consummation of human virtue. But to faith it is the chief act of religious worship, the act of sacrifice. Common to all sacrifices is that they are outward signs, acts more charged with meaning than the outward acts themselves possess. Behind the sacrifice, effecting it, giving it its excess of meaning, there is a sacrificial spirit."[84] In terms of the

---

[82] Think, for example, of the religious icon. What is present is not merely matter but meaning. Without the meaning, to worship the icon is simply idolatry. This point is emphasized repeatedly by Saint John of Damascus in *On the Divine Images: Three Apologies against Those Who Attack the Divine Images,* trans. David Anderson (Crestwood, NY: St. Vladimir's Seminary Press, 2002). As we noted above, Thomas Aquinas uses the same reasoning for sacramental worship. The distinction between physical and spiritual does not involve a divorce of symbol and reality, but their union, as we will see below.

[83] "The Notion of Sacrifice," 3. Lonergan refers to Aquinas's articulation of the virtue of religion at *ST* II-II, q. 81, a. 7, particularly Thomas's citation of Augustine (*City of God,* 10, 5), viz., "the visible sacrifice is the sacrament or sacred sign of the invisible sacrifice" (ad 2m), and to Thomas's formulation of the interior sacrifice at *ST* II-II, q. 85, a. 2 c.: "a sacrifice is offered for the purpose of signifying something; the sacrifice that is offered outwardly is a sign of that inward spiritual sacrifice in which the soul offers herself to God" (cited in Lonergan, "The Notion of Sacrifice," 5).

[84] Bernard Lonergan, "The Mass and Man," *Canadian Messenger of the Sacred Heart* 57 (1947): 345–50; repr. in *Shorter Papers,* CWBL 20, ed. Robert C. Croken, Robert M. Doran, and H. Daniel Monsour (Toronto: University of Toronto Press, 2007), 95.

categories of meaning a sacrificial attitude or spirit is an incarnate meaning: "the meaning of a person, of his way of life, of his words, or of his deeds."[85] An incarnate meaning is the objective manifestation of meanings and values in the dramatic artistry of one's living; it epitomizes a symbol evoked by feelings, and it pertains to Lonergan's functions of meaning: cognitive, effective, constitutive, and communicative. Lonergan writes: "An objective manifestation is made in order to reproduce or express a higher perfection in a lower order of being. Just as God manifests his infinite perfection in the finite order by creating, so humans represent spiritual perfection in the social order of sense perception by symbolizing."[86] This manifestation is based on an analogical proportion between higher and lower, so that the objective manifestation of a spiritual perfection is communicated in a way that is accessible to human knowing, mediated through the senses. Lonergan notes that the *convenientia*—fittingness or beauty—of the symbol increases in the measure that a real connection is established between the manifesting symbol and the spiritual perfection to be manifested. This connection reaches its perfection in Christ, whose bodily expression itself is a proper symbol of the spiritual perfection objectively manifest on the altar of the cross.[87] The sacrifice of Christ on the cross is the perfect sacrifice, and the proper symbol of the perfectly sacrificial attitude of Christ described in the letter to the Philippians in terms of *kenosis*.[88] As a symbol it evokes and is evoked by Christ's feelings of detestation of and sorrow over sin. Indeed, the sacrificial attitude of Christ is the cause of redemption.

---

[85] Lonergan, *Method in Theology*, 73.

[86] Lonergan, "The Notion of Sacrifice," 5.

[87] Ibid., 7, where Lonergan explains: "The closest connection between the spiritual and the sensible order is that which exists between the soul and the body of one and the same person."

[88] Lonergan's emphasis on Christ's sacrificial attitude will make some uneasy. Indeed, trying to intuit Christ's feelings in the passion is a slippery exercise. However, either the cross is an act of meaning that is willingly undertaken in order to offer an objective manifestation of Christ's spiritual perfection ("obedience unto death" in Philippians' terminology) or it is a meaningless act of human sinfulness. Lonergan reads the passion as the definitive act of divine self-communication and a revelation of divine meaning in sensible human acts. As a meaningful act, the passion is a communication of meaning that invites attentive, intelligent, reasonable, and responsible response as much as it does awe and worship.

❧

Lonergan on Christ's Redemptive Sacrifice

Lonergan interprets the passion in terms of vicarious satisfaction through an analogy with the sacrament of penance. In his Latin textbook, *De Verbo Incarnato*, composed for students at the Gregorian University in Rome, Lonergan interprets the work of Christ in two key theses that will help us to understand the attitude or feelings to which Lonergan refers in his discussion of the sacrificial attitude of Christ in "The Notion of Sacrifice." First, we will look at thesis 16, which deals with redemption as satisfaction. Then we will explore thesis 17, which offers Lonergan's understanding of the mystery of Christ's redemptive death in terms of the "Law of the Cross."

a. Satisfaction

In his lecture "The Redemption," Lonergan emphasizes that the redemption is a communication: "The incarnation and the redemption are the supreme instance of God communicating to us in this life. . . . And it is not only God communicating with us, it is God giving himself to us. The Gospels repeatedly affirm that the motive of Christ's coming was love."[89] How does the redemption communicate divine love? Through the suffering and death of Christ. Is there an intelligibility communicated in the passion? Lonergan thinks there is. It is a dynamic and incarnate intelligibility; it is concrete and so complex, a manifold intelligibility.

Following Thomas, Lonergan interprets the passion in terms of sacrifice, redemption, vicarious satisfaction, merit, and efficiency.[90] Each indicates an aspect of a complex intelligibility. Ultimately the redemption expresses a mystery or "secret counsel," the divine plan that Christ identifies as the kingdom of God and that the church incarnates as the body of Christ. It is a divine solution to the problem of evil that is revealed in the person and works of Christ.[91] But how exactly does Christ satisfy for sins? And how can we participate ritually in his satisfaction through eucharistic sacrifice?

---

[89] Lonergan, "The Redemption," 3–28, in *Philosophical and Theological Papers, 1958–1964*, CWBL 6, at 6.

[90] In proposing a multiple intelligibility Lonergan echoes Aquinas, *ST* III, q. 48, a. 1–5.

[91] See Bernard J. Lonergan, *Insight: A Study of Human Understanding*, CWBL 3, ed. Frederick E. Crowe and Robert M. Doran (Toronto: University of Toronto Press, 1992), 750–51.

Lonergan consistently interprets the redemption in terms of personal relations. He interprets the cross through an analogy with the sacrament of penance rather than through the more familiar legal analogy of Anselm. That the cross removes sins is a doctrine Christians affirm, but *how* it removes sins has been interpreted in different, even conflicting, ways. Lonergan proposes that Christ's passion satisfies for sins through an act of meaning leading to reconciliation. Commenting on this interpretation, Charles Hefling notes that retributive justice extracts a penalty against the will of the one paying and so does not effect any reconciliation of the parties involved, for example, a thief who is forced to pay restitution is not thereby reconciled to his victims. On the other hand, as Hefling explains, satisfaction not only considers the just payment of the penalty; "it also involves the seeking and granting of pardon, where pardon is understood as the remission of offense, as reconciliation, which is not to be confused with remission of punishment." Lonergan uses "satisfaction" to indicate "a willing acceptance or taking-on of punishment so that pardon may be granted."[92] Because Christ's passion is a divine expression of "utmost detestation for all sins and utmost sorrow over every offense against God," it satisfies for all sins.[93] More important, the intelligibility of satisfaction is based on the personal relations of the parties involved, and so emphasizes reconciliation.

The reconciliation of God and human beings wrought by Christ in the passion occurs because of his detestation of and sorrow over sins grounded in his judgment that God is love and is to be loved. That is to say, Christ's feelings are expressed in the symbol of the cross, and this is the heart of the incarnate intelligibility of the redemption; neither logic nor necessity are relevant to this interpretation, but rather a recurring sequence of feelings.[94] Lonergan indicates the sequence of feelings in his discussion of feeling in *Method in Theology*, which contrasts the sequence that pertains to retributive justice (offense, contumacy, judgment, punishment) with that pertaining to satisfaction/reconciliation (offense, repentance, apology, forgiveness).[95] Because these feelings are related to one another through

---

[92] Charles C. Hefling Jr., "A Perhaps Permanently Valid Achievement: Lonergan on Christ's Satisfaction," *Method: Journal of Lonergan Studies* 10 (1992): 63.

[93] Ibid., 69, quoting Bernard Lonergan, *De Verbo Incarnatio*, 3rd ed. (Rome: Gregorian University *ad usus auditorium*, 1964), 486; unpublished translation of Charles Helfing to appear as *The Incarnate Word*, CWBL 8.

[94] Ibid., 64.

[95] Ibid., 64n19, citing Lonergan, *Method in Theology*, 65.

personal relationships, satisfaction is a matter of "intentional responses to value and of incarnate meaning."[96] The work of the passion is a *vicarious* satisfaction because Christ is not satisfying for his own sins, but for those of others. Christ, as a friend, makes satisfaction for his friends by showing utmost detestation of and sorrow over their sins.[97] However, in contrast to natural friendship, Christ's friendship with human beings is grounded in the virtue of charity and is therefore properly a supernatural love that acts to bring about similar love in the offender. Christ's death "not only sets the seal on his friendship with sinners but produces such friendship by giving its proper object to the supernatural love poured into their hearts by the mission of the Spirit. And it is as a result of this friendship that Christ's friends are enabled to bear one another's burdens in charity. What Christ does by making vicarious satisfaction he does as Head, and what his friends do by participating in his satisfaction they do as members, of one Body."[98]

The Body of Christ, the church, participates in the saving work of Christ by continuing to offer satisfaction for sins, animated by the supernatural virtue of charity. Through charity the faithful reach the same judgments of value expressed in Christ's detestation of sin inasmuch as sins are offenses against a loving God. Sorrow over those offenses is also animated by charity insofar as love for God elicits sorrow over any offense against God, one's own and those of others alike. Through its detestation and sorrow over sins the church participates in the saving work of Christ. But because these acts are interior, they seek a proper symbolic expression. In the same way that the cross as a symbol reveals Christ's sacrificial attitude, his detestation of and sorrow over sin, so the Eucharist as the church's participation in the incarnate meaning of the cross is the proper symbol of the Mystical Body's own detestation of and sorrow over sin. This is why the remembrance of Christ's suffering in the Eucharist is a dangerous memory: it continually brings to our attention the manifold personal and structural sins that we should rightly detest and feel sorrow over, but often enough tolerate as the "way things are," or perhaps even embrace as pleasurable or profitable.[99] At

[96] Hefling, "A Perhaps Permanently Valid Achievement," 64.
[97] John 15:13.
[98] Hefling, "A Perhaps Permanently Valid Achievement," 67.
[99] See Bruce Morrill, *Anamnesis as Dangerous Memory: Political and Liturgical Theology in Dialogue* (Collegeville, MN: Liturgical Press, 2000).

the same time, the Eucharist is an expression of gratitude, a thanksgiving, for the gift of a divine solution to the problem of evil by love, without which sin and evil would not be overcome.

b. The Law of the Cross

Lonergan expresses the complex intelligibility of the divine solution to the problem of evil as a law of historical causality, which he calls the "Law of the Cross." Thus the work of Christ communicates a single intelligibility that can be understood in the manner of a universal law. He formulates his position in thesis 17 of *De Verbo Incarnato*: "The Son of God became man, suffered, died, and was raised again: because divine wisdom has ordained and divine goodness has willed, not to do away with the evils of the human race through power, but to convert those evils into a supreme good according to the just and mysterious Law of the Cross."[100] The Law of the Cross is the intrinsic intelligibility of the redemption revealed by the saving work of Christ.

The Law of the Cross is conceived as a general law that pertains to the actual order of the universe. Because fallen humanity suffers the problem of moral impotence and the consequent longer cycle of decline brought about by the distortions of bias, God provides a divine solution that is a "harmonious continuation of the actual order of the universe."[101] As a supernatural solution to a human problem it stands beyond the natural range of human knowing. But with the mission of the second person of the Trinity the Law of the Cross is made known to sinful humanity. Lonergan points out that, because this is a universal law, Christ too had to learn and make the Law of the Cross his own through the passion, in which he consents to obey the Law of the Cross rather than to triumph over sin in power.[102] In his divinity Christ knows the Law of the Cross as it is known to the Trinity, and Scripture reveals that in his humanity he had to learn it in human terms in order to communicate it to us. To make this law his own, Christ conformed his actions to a divine intelligibility, a divine meaning, which he had to discover gradually in human terms, to incarnate it on the cross and to rise again that

---

[100] Lonergan, *De Verbo Incarnato*, 552.
[101] Lonergan, *Insight*, 719.
[102] Cf. Matt 26:51-54.

we might also choose it.[103] The cross of Christ is thus a symbolic communication of the Law of the Cross, the divine solution to the problem of evil through which evil is turned to the good revealed proleptically in Christ's resurrection from the dead.[104] The church continues to manifest the Law of the Cross both in sacramental symbols, preeminently in the Eucharist, and also in every instance in which evil is turned to good or that suffering willingly accepted produces a good. The Law of the Cross shapes an ethic that is embodied in sacramental worship, through which Christians are called to make this law their own by incarnating it in their lives.

❦

3.2. Lonergan on Eucharistic Sacrifice: The Symbol of the Cross

In "The Notion of Sacrifice," Lonergan extends the analysis of the symbolic expression of the sacrificial attitude to the ritual sacrifice of the Eucharist. The eucharistic sacrifice is a proper symbol of the sacrificial attitude of the Mystical Body of Christ. In the Eucharist the bloody sacrifice of the cross is represented in a way that is proportionate to the Mystical Body; however, "the natural aptitude these objects have is not for representing the sacrifice of the cross but rather for *participating in this sacrifice* by way of a sacrificial meal."[105] It is by eating and drinking that Christians proclaim the death of the Lord until He comes.[106] There is not some other way of remembering Christ's incarnate meaning equivalent to the sacrificial meal. No artistic representation of the cross or dramatic passion play can so adequately communicate the meaning of Christ's death; rather, "[s]o complete is the identity between the sacrifice of the cross and the Eucharist that, as Trent declares, only the manner of offering is different."[107] The identity of the cross and the Eucharist in Roman Catholic doctrine, and the potential confusions to which that teaching can lead, provoked Martin Luther's

---

[103] See Charles C. Hefling Jr., "Lonergan's *Cur Deus Homo*: Revisiting the 'Law of the Cross,'" 145–66, in *Meaning and History in Systematic Theology: Essays in Honor of Robert M. Doran, SJ*, ed. John D. Dadosky (Milwaukee, WI: Marquette University Press, 2009).

[104] Rom 12:14-21. See Mark T. Miller, "Why the Passion? Bernard Lonergan on the Cross as Communication" (PhD diss., Boston College, 2008).

[105] Lonergan, "The Notion of Sacrifice," 9.

[106] 1 Cor 11:26.

[107] Lonergan, "The Notion of Sacrifice," 9–10 (citing *DS* 1743).

criticism of Catholic interpretations that suggest each Mass is a new sacrifice of Christ.[108] Indeed, Luther raises a crucial question about the relationship between the altar and the cross.

In a 1975 article drawing heavily on Lonergan's works, Brian McNamara noted the challenge theologians face in attempting to intelligently articulate the intelligibility of Christ's suffering and death and the sacrifice of the altar. He asks:

> In the Mass are we in the presence of Christ dead on the cross, or Christ dying, Christ glorified or Christ being glorified, Calvary itself or a living commemoration of an event that occurred over nineteen centuries ago, and if the latter, what exactly do we mean by 'living' commemoration? How is it possible to bridge the gap of centuries and be present at Golgotha? If we ultimately appeal to the theology of signs and symbolism, how far does that lead us?[109]

McNamara refers to the potential solutions to the problem offered by Dom Odo Casel's "mystery-presence" thesis and Abbot Anscar Vonier's emphasis on the Mass as a symbol of the heavenly liturgy.[110] McNamara's different approach is grounded in Lonergan's critical metaphysics: "It must be said

---

[108] See Kilmartin, *The Eucharist in the West*, 172. Cf. Robert C. Croken, *Luther's First Front: The Eucharist as Sacrifice* (Ottawa: University of Ottawa Press, 1990).

[109] Brian McNamara, *"Christus Patiens* in Mass and Sacraments: Higher Perspectives," *Irish Theological Quarterly* 42 (1975): 17–35, at 17. McNamara's resolution of these questions relies on Lonergan's metaphysics. Despite the fact that McNamara's analysis plays a pivotal role in Edward Kilmartin's systematic treatment of eucharistic theology in *The Eucharist in the West*, the editor of that volume only briefly refers the reader to Lonergan's work in his introduction. Kilmartin considers McNamara's contribution to the problem of *Mysteriengegenwart* significant because it "introduces into the discussion considerations that frequently have been overlooked in the literature on this subject" (p. 312). Those considerations are found in Lonergan's clarifications of the distinction between time and eternity, of secondary causality, and of presence understood within a critical-realist metaphysics. See also R. Gabriel Pivarnik, *Toward a Trinitarian Theology of Liturgical Participation* (Collegeville, MN: Liturgical Press, 2012). Strangely, Pivarnik describes Kilmartin's reliance on McNamara as a "weakness" (p. 193). The present work is an effort to demonstrate why McNamara and others found Lonergan so helpful for solving problems in sacramental theology.

[110] See Odo Casel, *The Mystery of Christian Worship*, trans. Burkhard Neunheuser, Milestones in Catholic Theology (New York: Crossroad, 1999); Anscar Vonier, *A Key to the Doctrine of the Eucharist* (Westminster, MD: Newman Press, 1956).

that at the root of many of the arguments offered for and against the actual presence of the mysteries lie ideas on causality and presence which cannot be substantiated in a realist metaphysics."[111] McNamara depends on key insights from Lonergan's work to articulate the critical-realist position on the relation between the cross and the altar. The first insight relates the cross and the altar, and the second resolves the issue of sacramental causality by attending to the general category of secondary causality.

3.3. Higher Viewpoints: Relating Cross and Altar

First, the speculative theologian attempting to deal with the relationship between the cross and the altar must attain a higher viewpoint that includes both simultaneously: namely, the divine viewpoint, in which all historical events are placed within a single view of contemporaneity that is revealed by God to human beings through salvation history. As events accumulate they reveal a divine plan for human history that points toward an eschatological goal disclosed in the Law of the Cross. From this higher viewpoint distinctions between different times fall away. Unless theology adopts this perspective it is plagued by an anthropomorphic image of God, imagining God to be always in potency toward acquiring further knowledge. As a result, the mission of the Word is interpreted as a divine afterthought, God the Father reacting to earthly events by sending the Son. Operating in terms of a higher viewpoint, theology affirms that there is an identity between divine being, knowing, willing, and acting, so that there is no temporal succession in God. Because God is pure act, just as there are no divine afterthoughts neither is there divine foreknowledge in the sense that a course of events is planned out ahead and simply implemented afterward, thus making God temporal. These imaginatively generated scenarios follow from basic misunderstandings of the difference between time and eternity—an issue of which theological reflection and preaching today tend to be oblivious.

Often when Christians use the word "eternal" they have in mind a very, very, very long time. But the distinction between time and eternity is between

---

[111] McNamara, "*Christus Patiens* in Mass and Sacraments," 19. The "realist metaphysics" to which McNamara refers is Lonergan's. McNamara, Raymond Moloney, and Phil McShane all studied sacramental theology with John Hyde, SJ. McShane describes Hyde being "deeply into Lonergan way back in the time of the 1940s articles" (Phil McShane, e-mail to the author, August 20, 2013).

temporal succession and its absence. Eternity means no time. From this perspective any solution to the mystery-presence problem in eucharistic theology that eternalizes the sacrifice of the cross fails to grasp the distinction between eternity and time. According to that distinction no temporal event can become eternal; rather, its intelligibility is to be found in its historical concreteness. On the other hand, intelligibility can be abstracted from the spatio-temporal residue that does not pertain directly to the intelligibility, so that the intelligible pattern can be present in many places at many times, depending on the probability of other conditions being fulfilled. As we have seen, the cross communicates an intelligible pattern Lonergan calls the Law of the Cross, a pattern that was realized and communicated in human history in the particular context of first-century Roman-occupied Palestine. In *Insight*, Lonergan explains that the empirical residue of particular places and times does not affect the core of meaning or intelligibility of an occurrence; therefore "Christ's death on Calvary is intimately and irrevocably linked with the circumstances of that first Good Friday. The basic meaning of what occurred on that afternoon, though as meaning it is independent of those circumstances, nevertheless cannot be separated from them and characterized as timeless without devaluing the historical features of the Incarnation."[112] The meanings communicated by Christ in his human historical life are communicated in a particular context. The actions and sufferings of Christ are related to particular places and times that situate the revelation of divine meaning in space and time. But the meaning revealed is not reducible in its meaning to those particular places and times; otherwise the meaning would have to be revealed repeatedly and differently at every moment and place in order to be understood over different times and in different places.

We have here a basic principle of cognitional theory that helps to solve a theological problem and brings us back to the issue of the presence of Christ in the Eucharist. Lonergan's distinction between the empirically residual and the intelligible allows us to understand the meaning of the mission of the second person of the Trinity in the divine plan. From the higher viewpoint the empirically residual is distinct from the meaning, so from the perspective of the divine plan that unfolds in history, the particular places and times of its revelation are not what give it its meaning; its intelligibility is indepen-

---

[112] McNamara, "*Christus Patiens* in Mass and Sacraments," 24. See Lonergan, *Insight*, 50–56.

dent of the spatial and temporal succession of its unfolding. The sacrifice of the cross is a historical event shaped by the confluence of particular actions and circumstances, but the Law of the Cross, which it symbolizes, is a historical intelligibility that transcends particular places and times. For it to be revealed in the present, therefore, does not require that the entirety of salvation history be revealed in each instant or that the meaning be placed in some eternal realm we reenact liturgically.

In the Eucharist the incarnate meaning of Christ is revealed in the symbol of a sacrificial meal. The meal offers human beings a participation in the sacrificial attitude of Christ, of which the cross is the proper symbol. The meaning of the cross and the meaning of the Eucharist are the same. Though they differ in the manner of their offering and in the degree of their perfection, they both reveal the incarnate meaning of Christ, in accord with the word of Christ. "The numerically same sacrificial attitude of Christ at his death is represented immediately on the cross and mediately in the Eucharist. For the Eucharist is a proper symbol of the sacrificial attitude of Christ at his death by the very fact that [it is] a proper symbol of the sacrifice of the cross."[113] Therefore in the Eucharist the incarnate meaning of Christ is really present in a sacramental sign. Christ is bodily present in his sacramental species, his incarnate meaning is "really, truly, and substantially" present. It is a bodily mediation of meaning in the form of nourishment and the sharing of a meal. As I will explain below, our encounter with Christ can be fruitfully understood as a mutual self-mediation in which Christ's incarnate meaning becomes our own. First, I turn to the question of presence.

Eucharistic theology begins with a consideration of the meaning of the Eucharist that tells us what kind of presence we are dealing with. Otherwise we are likely to be looking for another kind of presence. The meaning is not explained by simply equating the Eucharist with Christ's body according to a descriptive account of that presence, but by answering the further question "what kind of presence?" Lonergan argues, against Christologies of personal presence, "the fact is that the presence of Christ to us is not

---

[113] "The Notion of Sacrifice," 25. See *ST* III, q. 62, a. 5, c.: "Wherefore it is manifest that the sacraments of the Church derive their power especially from Christ's Passion, the virtue of which is in a manner united to us by our receiving the sacraments. It was in sign of this that from the side of Christ hanging on the Cross there flowed water and blood, the former of which belongs to Baptism, the latter to the Eucharist, which are the principal sacraments."

presence in the world of immediacy: 'Happy are they who never saw me and yet have found faith' (John 20:29). The fact is that divine revelation comes to us through meaning."[114] The sacrificial presence of Christ in the Eucharist is a revelation of his sacrificial attitude, his feelings of detestation of and sorrow over sin, his overcoming of evil by love, his incarnate meaning that communicates a divine mystery in human terms. This is why the doctrinal tradition refers to his presence in the Eucharist as body, blood, soul, and divinity. The divine meanings Christ revealed in his living, bodily intending and acting are not revealed by mere spatial proximity proper to the world of immediacy.[115] It is an act of meaning that constitutes the Eucharist, makes it to be what it is, i.e., the bodily presence of Christ. Taken in this way, the presence of Christ is not a spatial, *already-out-there-now-real* presence in the world of immediacy (which reduces Christ's presence to spatial predicates, especially quantity, a position Thomas explicitly rejects),[116] but a dynamic, concrete, complex intelligibility mediated by the conscious human acts of the living Christ, which are made present to human beings in an effective sign or sacrament.

But to affirm that Christ's presence is a mediation of meaning raises a question: why affirm transubstantiation, especially if the doctrine can be interpreted as meaning that the divine presence enters the world of immediacy? Is there something about this mediated presence of Christ that makes

---

[114] Bernard Lonergan, "Christology Today: Methodological Reflections," 74–99, in *A Third Collection*, ed. Frederick E. Crowe (New York: Paulist Press, 1985), at 79.

[115] See Michael Stebbins, "The Eucharistic Presence of Christ: Mystery and Meaning," *Worship* 64 (1990): 225–36, at 230. Lonergan consistently makes a distinction between the subject as substance and the subject as subject. The former is ascribed to the human being whether asleep or awake, conscious or unconscious, and so refers primarily to the biological functioning of the human organism. The latter takes into account the acts of meaning of a conscious subject. When Thomas Aquinas speaks of the substance of Christ being in the Eucharist he is not making this distinction. Thomas's use of "soul" indicates the conscious element. The soul of a rational animal is different from that of a brute animal because it has the light of intellect, which is a participated likeness in the divine light. Where Thomas employs a metaphysical category we can employ Lonergan's subject as subject, or subject as meaning, incarnate meaning, to point to that aspect of eucharistic presence that is irreducible to the biological level. Other theologians working on eucharistic presence have moved in this direction by speaking in terms of a "personal" presence, but in a more descriptive manner. See Piet Schoonenberg, "The Real Presence in Contemporary Discussion," *Theology Digest* 15 (Spring 1967): 3–11.

[116] See *ST* III, q. 76, a. 4, 5.

it different from all other sacramentally mediated presences of Christ, for example, those affirmed in *Mysterium Fidei*? Pope Paul suggests that the presence of Christ in the Eucharist "is called 'real' not to exclude the idea that the others are 'real' too, but rather to indicate presence par excellence, because it is substantial and through it Christ becomes present whole and entire, God and man."[117] The justification circles back on the meaning of a "substantial" presence. To illuminate his meaning the pope cites Thomas Aquinas's explanation that the Eucharist is "a kind of consummation of the spiritual life, and in a sense the goal of all the sacraments."[118] Thomas elaborates: "The reception of Baptism is necessary for starting the spiritual life, while the receiving of the Eucharist is requisite for its consummation; by partaking not indeed actually, but in desire, as an end is possessed in desire and intention."[119] The Eucharist is the consummation of the spiritual life and the goal of all the sacraments because it is an encounter with Christ and the fulfillment of Christian desire, but a certain kind of encounter, i.e., a sacramental one.

A key distinction that clarifies the character of this encounter is between what Thomas calls "proper species" and "sacramental species."[120] If we have identified the substance of Christ with his incarnate constitutive meanings, those meanings are mediated both by his physical organism in his human, historical life or his "proper species" and in the church in his twofold "sacramental species": (1) in the Mystical Body of the church as a sacrament that gives visible witness to Christ's incarnate and constitutive meanings, preeminently in acts of repentance and martyrdom that embody the Law of the Cross by transforming evil into good,[121] and (2) in the consecrated

---

[117] Paul VI, *Mysterium Fidei*, 39.

[118] Ibid., 38.

[119] *ST* III, q. 73, a. 3, c.

[120] See *ST* III, q. 76, a. 7, c.

[121] Note that this is not the church understood as a juridical structure, but an emergent reality of those who embody Christ's constitutive meanings in their lives. Ultimately Chauvet's emphasis on divine absence in *Symbol and Sacrament* can be understood as an ecclesiological goad. By emphasizing the divine absence Chauvet is challenging Christians to resist the temptation to point to a presence of Christ "out there" that lets them off the hook of embodying divine meanings and values in history. Chauvet identifies this as the time of the church in which Christ is "absent as 'the same'; he is no longer present except as 'the Other.' . . . From now on, it is in the witness of the Church that he takes flesh" (*SS*, 170). In explanatory terms we would say that Christ is no longer

bread and wine of the Eucharist. While Christ's meanings and values are transmitted in the Scriptures and embodied in the church and each of the sacraments, the tradition holds that they are present in a unique way in the consecrated bread and wine of the Eucharist. But what is the difference? If transubstantiation affirms that the whole substance of the bread and wine is converted into the whole substance of the body and blood of Christ, along with his soul and divinity, we are back to the meaning of substance. The substance of Christ, his constitutive incarnate meaning (central form), is the sacrificial attitude (recurring sequence of feelings and judgments) that is embodied (central act) in all his actions and passions, ultimately in the sacrifice of the cross. In the ritual action of the church that incarnate meaning of Christ is revealed on the level of elemental meaning, not merely as a linguistic or cognitive meaning to be understood but as a symbolic and dramatic action that invites participation. Lonergan explains: "Participating in the sacrifice of the cross by spiritual communion and especially by sacramental communion effects an intimate union between the Head and the members. The attitudes of the members are assimilated to those of the Head, including above all Christ's sacrificial attitude."[122] To participate in that meaning is to affirm and consent to Christ's words, "This is my body . . ." and to eat spiritually in order to enter into communion with Christ so that Christ's incarnate meaning becomes one's own. Christ is the principle of the sacrificial attitude as Head of the sacrificial attitude of the members of the Mystical Body. As principle, Christ acts by offering himself under the sacramental species of bread and wine as Head, to effect the sacrificial attitude in those who eat spiritually and who become the Mystical Body by embodying Christ's meanings and values in history. The sacramental species enable communion with Christ by eating, which could not be done if Christ were to remain in his proper species.[123] Because they offer fullness of communion and assimilation to the sacrificial attitude of Christ, the elements of bread and wine must be said to "contain" Christ's sacrificial attitude, his incarnate meaning, or Christ himself, body, blood, soul, and divinity,

---

visible in his proper species but only in his sacramental species, the reality of which is verified performatively in the lives of Christians. This is why sacraments are "the word of God at the mercy of the body." Chauvet is very helpful on these points. See *SS*, 161–78.

[122] Lonergan, "The Notion of Sacrifice," 13.

[123] See *ST* III, q. 75, a. 5, c.

i.e., they undergo a whole conversion, or "transubstantiation." We can affirm, therefore, that the constitutive incarnate meaning of Christ present in the Eucharist is the effective meaning and communicative meaning of the Mystical Body and is therefore a verifiable *real* presence. Sacramental communion and assimilation is accomplished by Christ's presence, which is not "out there" as an object of sense perception or even a "metaphysical" object/ substance of intellectual intuition but is verifiably present by its acting on and transforming the church into his body, his meaning.[124]

3.4. *Presence as Action*

The other insight from Lonergan employed by McNamara resolves problems surrounding the language of causality by relating presence to action as a real relation of dependence. Historically, in order to emphasize that the real presence was the necessary precondition for a real sacrifice, dogmatic treatments of the Eucharist began with a consideration of the presence of Christ in the bread and wine through a change of the bread and wine into the body and blood by the consecratory power of the words of institution.[125] We have mixed up the typical order to emphasize that in the Eucharist Christ is not *first* present and only *then* acting. This way of separating the presence

---

[124] See Augustine, *Confessions* 7.10, cited in *Summa Theologiae*, III, a. 73, q. 3, ad 2m.: "I am the food of the fully grown, grow and you will feed on me; but you will not change me into yourself as with the food of your flesh, rather you will be changed into me." Augustine elaborates elsewhere: "What can be seen has a bodily appearance, what is to be understood provides spiritual fruit. So if you want to understand the body of Christ, listen to the apostle telling the faithful, *You, though, are the body of Christ and its members* (1 Cor 12:27). So if it's you that are the body of Christ and its members, it's the mystery meaning you that has been placed on the Lord's table; what you receive is the mystery that means you. It is to what you are that you reply Amen, and by so replying you express your assent. What you hear, you see, is *The body of Christ*, and you answer, *Amen*. So be a member of the body of Christ, in order to make that *Amen* true. . . . Be what you can see, and receive what you are" (Saint Augustine, "Sermon 272: On the Day of Pentecost to the *Infantes*, On the Sacrament," in *Sermons 230–272B*, trans. Edmund Hill, *The Works of Saint Augustine: A Translation for the 21st Century*, part 3, vol. 7, ed. John E. Rotelle [New Rochelle, NY: New City Press, 1993], 300–301).

[125] See Kilmartin, *The Eucharist in the West*, 175–78. The obvious historical example of this ordering of the questions in the theology of the Eucharist is the Council of Trent. This is also in the background of Luther's criticism that the Mass seemed to sacrifice Christ again.

of Christ from the action automatically reduces it to the dimension of the *already-out-there-now-real*.[126] By considering the sacrificial aspect of Christ's presence first we can see that presence is, properly speaking, the action of the agent in the patient. This understanding of Christ's presence clarifies the meaning of sacramental causality while placing the encounter with Christ in the context of mutual self-mediation and interpersonal relations. It effectively rescues the instrumental causality of the sacraments from a narrow interpretation. The divine presence mediated in the sacraments is not an *already-out-there-now-real*, but the presence of the agent in act. The affirmation of the divine presence is simply the affirmation of an effect in the patient. We call the divine presence as experienced in the missions of the Trinity "grace," because it is grounded in the uncreated causing of created effects in the supernatural order. In the sacraments we do not experience God *plus* grace, or grace emanating from God, but the presence of the Trinitarian missions acting to sanctify the patient. So when Thomas says that sacraments "make human beings holy," this is what he means. He does not mean that people magically become saints through sacraments, because manifestly they do not, as Thomas knew well.

The *sanctificans homines*, making human beings holy, to which Thomas refers results from the total gift of divine love in the sacraments, each revealing an additional aspect of divine love for human beings, the Eucharist being the fullest revelation of God's loving self-giving in the person of Christ. Sacraments make divine love explicit in particular persons at particular places and times as mediators of the Trinitarian missions, thereby promoting and enabling human cooperation. But divine love is neither partial nor conditioned, for God is love. By revealed faith we know that divine love's self-understanding grounds the processions, relations, and persons of the Trinity, as well as the Father's sending of the Son and Spirit in the economy of saving and elevating grace. The gift of God's love given to human beings is a total self-donation enacted in human terms by the historical man Jesus, and by the Holy Spirit his incarnate meaning is remembered by the church and realized in the Eucharist. The Trinitarian dynamics of the eucharistic action are evident.

---

[126] Chauvet describes this version of presence without act vividly as a "necrotic temptation." Reifying Christ's presence as a static entity locates his bodily presence in terms of quantity and turns the tabernacle into a tomb.

The Eucharist, then, is the paradigmatic example of operative and co-operative grace from which the other sacraments flow. God's love operates on us and cooperates with us to bring our cooperative actions to perfection, making manifest our conversion to God. The cause of whatever holiness we manifest in our lives is God alone, and if a person who participates in the sacraments regularly embodies holiness we attribute it to the instrumental communication of divine love that person experiences, understands, affirms, and consents to in the sacraments. And because the affirmation of the presence of Christ in the Eucharist is made possible only by the presence of the Holy Spirit, through which one participates in divine knowing and loving, that affirmation is the fruit of a real relation of dependence in the one affirming. In other words, the presence of the Holy Spirit to the communicant is the condition of the possibility of spiritual eating. That sacraments make human beings holy, in Thomas's terms, does not amount to immediate and complete perfection as a kind of *fait accompli*, for surely regular reception of the sacraments is no guarantee of holiness. Thomas simply affirms a real relation of dependence of the one affirming on the reality affirmed, such that really both assenting and consenting to the presence of Christ in the Eucharist by the Holy Spirit yields a radical reorientation of one's living, a conversion known in its fruits.

Understanding causality as a real relation of dependence is *the* key to combating a productionist image of cause and effect in sacramental theology. Applying Lonergan's thought to sacramental causality a decade before McNamara, Philip McShane wrote: "The grace conferred by a sacrament is identically a real relation of dependence on the sacrament as sign, such a real relation being the necessary and sufficient condition for the truth of the traditional affirmation, *sacramenta causant significando*."[127] Defining a

---

[127] Philip McShane, "On the Causality of the Sacraments," *Theological Studies* 24, no. 3 (1963): 423–36, at 424–25. Mark Jordan criticizes McShane and Lonergan on this point as misreading Aquinas. See Mark Jordan, *Rewritten Theology: Aquinas after His Readers* (Malden, MA: Blackwell, 2006), 166–67. Jordan argues that interpreting causality exclusively in terms of the presence of the agent in the patient fails to give sufficient weight to the instrumental. Indeed, Thomas rejects the position that sacraments only cause grace by a certain coincidence (*ST* III, q. 62, a. 4 c.). He holds that sacraments have a real instrumental power for bringing about effects proportionate to the instrument. So the waters of baptism possess an instrumental power for producing the effect of spiritual cleansing. Lonergan's point is that instrumental power is attributed properly to the

thing necessarily involves an inquiry into the relations that make the thing to be what it is, but "sacramental grace is multiply related, to the divine Persons, to the humanity of Christ, to the members of the Church, to the sacrament and its ministers, etc., yet without absolute complexity. It is one and the same reality of grace which St. Thomas discusses in the *Secunda pars* as *forma animae* and in the *Tertia pars* as *beneficium salvatoris.*"[128] For Thomas, "making holy" needs to be understood in terms of a relation of dependence, meaning that, insofar as Christians are holy, that holiness is attributable to the sacraments. The sacraments are not independent actors but communications of grace, such that the recipient is transformed by the grace communicated. This is because the sacraments, like all instrumental causes, are instances of divine causative knowledge. McShane notes that "much of the discussion of sacramental causality has bogged down in the problem of the *virtus instrumentalis*. On the other hand, the thesis *scientia Dei est causa rerum* has found little place in such discussion."[129] Instrumental causality is part of the order of the universe God knows and loves into being.

The metaphysical element of act is the key to understanding the meaning of causality. Insofar as a thing exists it does so through divine causative knowledge. Lonergan explains that God's efficient causality is exercised as long as the universe exists. Consequently, the existence of anything is a case of efficient causality: "For the metaphysical condition of the truth of the proposition *A causes B* is the reality of a relation of dependence (*ut a quo*) in *B* with respect to *A*. It is not, as the counterpositions would have it, an imaginable 'influence' occupying space intermediate between *A* and *B*."[130] McShane explains that understanding sacramental causality as a real relation of dependence is grounded in the more basic affirmation that God's

principal mover, not the instrument acting on its own accord, a point Thomas makes in a subsequent article. Furthermore, Thomas attributes the spiritual power of a sacrament to the meaning of the words (ibid., ad 1m). But because the words combine with a sensible thing to form one instrument, they are not separable (ibid., ad 4m). Both the form and the matter of the sacrament act as a united instrument by which God communicates grace to rational animals for whom the sensible mediates the intelligible (see *ST* III, q. 62, a. 4, c).

[128] McShane, "Causality," 426.

[129] Ibid., 432.

[130] Lonergan, *Insight*, 686. It is this counterpositional rendering of causality that Chauvet has identified in his critique of a technico-productionist scheme of representation operating in some sacramental theologies. His desire to move out of that scheme and into the symbolic develops out of a significant insight into the kind of causality

knowing is the cause of things. He writes, "As God understands and wills the existence and occurrence of things in [the created] order, so things exist and occur. Hence, if God understands and wills sacramental grace to come to be in the recipient of a sacrament in dependence on a sign, then that sacramental grace does in fact come to be in dependence on a sign."[131] McShane employs the analogy of contingent predication to explain the occurrence of sacramental grace. By contingent predication Lonergan means that "whenever we make assertions about any matter of fact, all that is required for the truthfulness of the predication is that the conditions for the existence or occurrence of its referent be fulfilled . . . even though things might have been otherwise."[132] The analogy of contingent predication corresponds with Lonergan's derived metaphysics of proportionate being.

The analogy of contingent predication responds to contemporary criticisms of scholastic sacramental causality we find in Chauvet and others because it accepts the contingency of the created order, including the sacramental order. As Lonergan explains, "It is impossible for it to be true that God understands, affirms, wills, effects, anything to exist or occur without it being true that the thing exists or the event occurs exactly as God understands, affirms, or wills it. For one and the same metaphysical condition is needed for the truth of both propositions, namely, the relevant contingent existence or occurrence."[133] Things are the way they are because God understands, affirms, and wills them to be that way.[134] Inversely, "divine efficacy

---

God exercises in the universe. Chauvet plays out an alternative account in terms of symbolic mediation.

[131] McShane, "Causality," 427.

[132] Frederick G. Lawrence, "The Fragility of Consciousness: Lonergan and the Postmodern Concern for the Other," 173–211, in *Communication and Lonergan: Common Ground for Forging the New Age*, ed. Thomas J. Farrell and Paul A. Soukup (Kansas City, MO: Sheed and Ward, 1993), at 201. See Lonergan, *Insight*, 684–91.

[133] Lonergan, *Insight*, 685.

[134] This way of explaining divine causative knowledge will lead some to object that the claim implicates God in the evils of human history (Lonergan, *Insight*, 689–91). Lonergan, however, clarifies that, from this perspective, basic sin is the irrational (p. 690). In sin there is no intelligibility to be grasped and so no being, nothing that God understands, affirms, and wills. This is Lonergan's way of explaining Augustine's classic thesis that sin is nonbeing, i.e., it does not participate in divine causative knowledge but represents the failure of rational intelligence to act rationally. Therefore Lonergan calls sin a surd. Sin becomes a social, historical fact that Lonergan calls moral evil when the temptation to act irrationally is endorsed by rationalizations of irrational actions that

does not impose necessity upon its consequents."[135] According to Thomas's stock example, Socrates, as long as he is sitting, necessarily is sitting; nevertheless, the necessity is not absolute but conditioned.[136] All Socrates need do is stand up and walk away and the conditions for the truth of the statement "Socrates is sitting" are no longer fulfilled. The theological consequences of understanding the analogy are significant especially for understanding sacramental causality.[137] Sacraments need not, indeed often do not, make people holy. On the other hand, insofar as a person who receives the sacraments embodies holiness, the sacraments are verified as effective signs.[138] For example, if one is holy, the conditions for one's holiness have been fulfilled, among which conditions might be an experience of the sacraments as efficacious signs, moments of grace that enable one to act lovingly in a sinful world and to return good for evil. On the other hand, if the same person becomes vicious, the conditions for holiness are no longer fulfilled, including the possibility that the sacraments are no longer experienced as efficacious signs of grace. The verification of the efficaciousness of the sacraments is in the concrete performance of the particular Christian; thus there is an inherent connection between sacraments and ethics that is highlighted by attending to the analogy of contingent predication.

---

regularly occur within a given culture. Other things we experience as evil, such as disease or natural disaster, are simply part of a universal order characteristic of generalized emergent probability. See Brian Davies, *Thomas Aquinas on God and Evil* (New York: Oxford University Press, 2011).

[135] Lonergan, *Insight*, 685.

[136] See *ST* I, q. 19, a. 4.

[137] Frederick G. Lawrence ("The Fragility of Consciousness," 201–2) elaborates the broader theological significance of the analogy as follows:

> According to the analogy of contingent predication . . . the glorious thing about the created order of this universe is the fact that it does not have to exist at all, and does not have to be as it is. That is to say, once we make the breakthrough to an explanatory conception of divine transcendence as utterly beyond necessity and contingency and completely unconditioned by space and time, it is proper to analogically understand and affirm that the infinitely loving, creative power is a mystery of freedom who in knowing, willing, and bringing about the universe that exists is completely free. . . . What we do in the analogy of contingent predication, then, is to let God be a transcendent mystery. This means that God cannot function as a presence strictly comparable to any other presence in space and time, and that God cannot function as a center or fulcrum for managing the lives of people and things.

[138] See *ST* III, q. 62, a. 1, c.

The contingency of the effect of the sacraments does not deny the fact that they are efficient causes. "In a sacrament the sign leads beyond itself, not logically or naturally, but through the reasonable acceptance of revealed doctrine, through faith. God causes sacramental grace in man, not inhumanly, but only with reasonable co-operation and consent. Thus, the receipt of the grace is multiply conditioned: by the intention of the minister, by the adequate making of the sign and acknowledgment of the signification, by the dispositions of the recipient, etc."[139] The central act of a sacrament is the communication of divine love in an effective sign. To affirm the existence of that communication is to experience the presence of the one communicating, and to consent to the demands of that communication is to be transformed by divine love's effective communication. As God is the efficient cause of grace, so God's love communicated through effective signs is the efficient cause of sacramental grace.[140]

As in the case of "substance," the terminology has been so confused by subsequent usage that the basic meaning of causality can be lost. The impression most people have of causality is related to images derived from Newtonian mechanics: two bodies coming into contact and one acting on the other. This way of understanding sacraments would mean that there is something particular in the nature of sacraments, either their matter or their form, that allows them to communicate grace, so that coming into contact with the matter or the sound of the words would be sufficient for grace; for example, there is something in the nature of water that allows it to be the instrumental cause of baptismal grace. This would make all water baptismal water and every contact with water a baptism, but this is clearly not the case. Similarly, the mere sound of the words does not transmit grace. They are not spells. Thomas clarifies: "Sensible things considered in their own nature do not belong to the worship or kingdom of God: but considered

---

[139] McShane, "Causality," 435.

[140] See *ST* III, q. 62, a. 5, c.: "A sacrament in causing grace works after the manner of an instrument. Now an instrument is twofold; the one, separate, as a stick, for instance; the other, united, as a hand. Moreover, the separate instrument is moved by means of the united instrument, as a stick by the hand. Now the principal efficient cause of grace is God Himself, in comparison with Whom Christ's humanity is as a united instrument, whereas the sacrament is as a separate instrument. Consequently, the saving power must needs be derived by the sacraments from Christ's Godhead through His humanity."

only as signs of spiritual things in which the kingdom of God consists."[141] Therefore sacramental grace "is not physically dependent on the physical form of the matter and form of the sacrament."[142] Grace comes through a sacrament as an efficacious sign that communicates a particular meaning. McShane argues that "inadvertence to the thesis on divine causative knowledge leads to the neglect of the possibility of a higher type of mediate divine causality, not *per naturam* but *per signum*."[143] From the perspective of divine causative knowledge understood according to the analogy of contingent predication, the problem disappears. The key to sacramental theology, especially to understanding what is meant by instrumental causality in the sacraments, is adverting to the possibility of divine causative knowledge operative through signs. Signs mean things. The meaning of a sacrament is a divinely revealed meaning that transforms the matter and form of natural elements into signs of sacred things, or effective acts of meaning. Let us apply the analogy to the Eucharist.

3.5. Presence of Agent in Patient: Christ, Eucharist, and Communion.

As was noted previously, Christ is present under the species of bread and wine from the moment the words of consecration are uttered. At the same time we have proposed that these words pertain to a world mediated by meaning and so communicate a meaning that is meant insofar as it is intended by the priest uttering the words while intending to signify what the church means, what Christ means. The presence of Christ in the Eucharist rests on the truth of the statement of Christ. But the statement of Christ is the judgment of a divine person and so is true. This may not be satisfying for some. As Raymond Moloney explains, "The change of meaning in these judgments is, for ordinary purposes, a sufficient signal of the change of reality. If you are not a critical realist, however, you are going to have a gnawing dissatisfaction with such an approach, feeling that it is not real enough."[144] This brings us back once again to the basic problem that animated our treatment of Lonergan's metaphysics, namely, how we understand reality. If by reality we mean no more than what is available to the

---

[141] *ST* III, q. 60, a. 4, ad 2m.
[142] McShane, "Causality," 432.
[143] Ibid.
[144] Raymond Moloney, *The Eucharist* (Collegeville, MN: Liturgical Press, 1995), 224.

senses, then our theology of the Eucharist will be a grudging sacrifice of the intellect or a retreat to the dogmatic assertion of presence, because the experiential conjugates of the bread and wine do not change in the course of the liturgy. On the other hand, if reality is to be known by true judgment, or as central act, then our agreement with Christ's statement—our "Amen!"—is a real assent, including consent to a real presence with all it demands. This is because our assent and consent are not separate from Christ's presence but already acted upon and made possible by it.

Our thinking about presence is regularly dominated by images of things standing in proximity to each other. Accordingly, presence becomes a precondition for action; hence our image of causality derives from physical analogies such as billiard balls bumping into each other. In contrast, Lonergan agrees with Aristotle and Thomas Aquinas that action is the presence of the agent in the patient, not something performed by the *already-out-there-now* present agent. Brian McNamara elaborates the full ramifications of this affirmation:

> (a) Agent and effect are simultaneously present one to the other. This affirmation denies that the agent must be present before the effect of the action is realized; the empirical succession of agent, action and effect must be surmounted.
>
> (b) Action as intelligible is neither in the agent nor between the agent and the effect but is identical with the effect; this denies that action is some *sui generis* reality.
>
> (c) The power which experientially effects the action (*virtus*) is not a different reality from the action itself and is therefore also identifiable with the effect.
>
> (d) The instrument used by the agent is itself an agent acting, however, only insofar as it is used by the principal agent. This statement implies that the intelligibility of action is not to be sought within the instrument.
>
> (e) Efficient causality, therefore, is the relation of the effect to the cause and its reality is to be found in the effect as proceeding from the cause. The agent of efficient causality is not changed by acting notwithstanding the experiential distinction between acting and not acting, for the change *is* the effect.[145]

---

[145] McNamara, *"Christus Patiens* in Mass and Sacraments," 29.

Thesis (a) clarifies that our relationship to God is not to a being "out there," but that "God is present to man by acting on man."[146] God acts on human beings in two ways, immediately and mediately. God acts immediately by the gift of the Holy Spirit, which is the love of God poured into our hearts.[147] God acts mediately through instruments or instrumental causes. The entire order of the universe of proportionate being is an instrument for the revelation of the divine plan. God acts through the humanity of Christ as the instrument by which the divine plan is communicated to human beings in human terms by a divine person. Therefore the entire *transitus* of the Son to the Father, a divine intelligibility, is present in the sacraments as the incarnate meaning of Christ.[148] That action is continued in the sacraments, not merely because they are extensions of the humanity of Christ but because they are the continuation of God's revelation in human terms of the divine plan through signs. This affirmation need not come at the expense of a strong pneumatological dimension, as Chauvet fears. In fact, the presence of the Holy Spirit is the condition of the possibility of recognizing the incarnate meaning of Christ in the Eucharist. Indeed, the whole reality of the Trinity is communicated to us sacramentally. Because they are the revelation of the divine plan they are effective signs, or sacraments, through which the divine plan is incarnated in human history by the church.

To understand thesis (b) we begin by noting that the action of the sacraments is not something happening between God and human beings but something happening *in* human beings. Frequently theologians and faithful alike imagine the sacraments as mediations of divine presence in a way that places God at a distance only the sacraments bridge. This image is bound to an image of God as an object "out there." The temptation to imagine God as an object out there with which one comes into contact involves two significant errors. One is to imagine God as extended in space and time like a body available to sense perception; the other is to imagine God as part of this entitative order and so a being among others to be known as others are known.[149] Both presume that knowledge is a matter of confrontation, or look-

---

[146] Ibid.

[147] Rom 5:5.

[148] McNamara, "*Christus Patiens* in Mass and Sacraments," 29.

[149] This is the real danger of an onto-theology that reduces God to a being among other beings. However, this is not the position of Thomas Aquinas or Lonergan. Critics who have implied that Aquinas is representative of this way of thinking have had to

ing, and that God, insofar as God is knowable, will be known accordingly. A critical-realist metaphysics rejects this image as counterpositional. God, like all of reality, is to be known as a term in a process of knowing, a judgment. The Triune God, however, is not proportionate to human knowing, but is known in virtue of a gift of the Holy Spirit acting immediately in human intellect and enabling it to assent to divinely revealed truth.

Similarly, sacramental action is not a matter of bridging the gap between humans and God with the use of sacramental intermediaries. Sacramental action occurs in the recipient of the sacrament. This general principle is more complicated in the Eucharist because here, according to Thomas, the action reaches its term through the words of Christ, not in the material reception of the sacrament.[150] In the Eucharist we are present to the fulfillment of divine incarnate meaning as meant in the words of Christ that provide the form of the sacrament. As such the sacrament is primarily an act of meaning of a divine person that effects a whole conversion, a transubstantiation, of bread and wine into the body and blood of Christ, Christ's body in the fullness of its incarnate meaning.[151] Insofar as all of Christ's meanings and values are communicated in the Eucharist, "it follows that the entire *transitus* of Christ is present to the recipient of the sacraments, taking the effective form of configuration to him."[152] Consequently, the words of Christ effect not only a change of the substance of bread and wine into his body and blood but also a conversion of the one who receives those words spiritually in order to partake of their effect, which is communion with Christ and therefore a conversion of a sinful human being into an adopted son or daughter of the Father. This remains the case insofar as one continually eats spiritually and desires communion, so that Christ's incarnate meaning becomes one's own.[153]

---

refine their position. See, for example, Jean-Luc Marion, "Thomas Aquinas and Onto-theology," 38–74, in *Mystics: Presence and Aporia*, ed. Michael Kessler and Christian Sheppard (Chicago: University of Chicago Press, 2003); originally published as "Saint Thomas d'Aquin et l'onto-théologie," *Revue Thomiste* 95 (1995): 31–66.

[150] Other sacraments are completed by the application of the material. See *ST* III, q. 78, a. 1, c.

[151] See *ST* III, q. 76, a. 1.

[152] McNamara, "*Christus Patiens* in Mass and Sacraments," 29.

[153] The temptation lurking in an uncritical understanding of this dimension of eucharistic theology is a too easy assertion of one's own holiness. What the clarification of Christ's incarnate meaning in the Law of the Cross shows is that configuration to Christ, or divinization in the Christian sense, is not cheap grace but a real transvaluation of our

In regard to thesis (c), the power of God is revealed in the conversion of human beings. It is not "out there" moving entities (even against their will) as an external agent but transforms human wills and brings them to cooperative performance. Perhaps more typically, however, the power of God is pictured along the lines of imaginable physical entities moving through space and time, so that God applies Christ as an instrument in moving human beings through the medium of the passion and the sacraments (which derive their power from the passion). When divine cause and effect are understood to operate like a mechanism, mover and moved bear no relation; the knowledge and will of the mover are radically separated from the knowledge and will of the moved, so that cooperation is not possible. In the context of sacramental causality, this would entail that humans have no understanding of the meaning of the sacraments or any way of freely conserting to be configured to the divine will mediated by the sacraments.

The life of Christ *is* an instrument, as thesis (d) clarifies, not in a limiting sense but as an intelligible communication of the Father's love in history for sinful human beings. McNamara notes: "Traditional views on sacramental causality [have] taken the humanity of Christ statically rather than functionally."[154] But Christ's humanity expresses divine meaning in human terms. Understanding the divine plan is essential to sacramental causality. Insofar as that plan is revealed by the mission of the Son, an understanding of the mystery comes from attending to the works of the Son. This is why sacramental theology is so christocentric. Because the sacraments are prolongations of the work of the Christ, they communicate the intelligibility of what Lonergan calls the divine plan—the just and mysterious Law of the Cross. The configuration to Christ that occurs through the sacraments, especially the Eucharist, is a configuration to the divinely ordained solution to the problem of evil through human participation in the divine plan.

Finally, in thesis (e) it was noted that the sacraments do not effect a change in God. Another popular image implies that human beings are able

values into radical detestation of and sorrow over sins because of God's love through which friendly relations between God and human beings are restored. In this life the complexity of that experience means that holiness is the concurrence of thanksgiving and repentance (this coincidence of opposites is often reflected in the lives of saints and mystics, and communicated in symbols: the dark night of John of the Cross, the desert of Meister Eckhart, the excruciating love of Hadewijch's poetry); however, God promises complete joy in the beatific vision (Rev 21:4).

[154] McNamara, "*Christus Patiens* in Mass and Sacraments," 30.

to change the divine mind through the sacraments. One interpretation of the statement that a sacrament "makes human beings holy" understands the phrase as indicating a change in the recipient that precipitates a change in God. This commonsense interpretation of "making" imagines sacraments on the analogy of banknotes or chits of grace that we accrue in such a way that accumulated grace can be cashed in for salvation. In this interpretation, God's attitude toward us is contingent upon graces accrued, and so God's will can be changed by our participation in the sacraments. There is indeed a change in relationship between God and the human in the sacraments, but the change happens in the human person: "Every sacrament then is either the inauguration or the increase of interpersonal relations between the Father and man with the change in man rather than in God."[155] The dimension of interpersonal relations has not been sufficiently developed in sacramental theology generally and eucharistic theology specifically, but it frees sacramental theology from juridical, mechanical, or financial analogies and emphasizes that sacramental presence is properly understood as the presence of the agent in the recipient of the action, and therefore the presence of another subject rather than an object to us. We can develop a more sufficient treatment of interpersonal relations in the sacraments by broadening the category of causality in terms of mediation and by elaborating on the category of divine friendship.

4. From Causality to Mediation

I have spoken frequently of the "world mediated by meaning," but what precisely is mediation? Historically, mediation was associated with Aristotelian logic and the function of the middle term that connects subject and predicate; the middle term mediates between first principles or premises that are immediate and conclusions that are mediated.[156] From this, Lonergan derives a generalized understanding of mediation, and from Hegel, learns its universal application.[157] In any case of mediation there would be three aspects: a property, a source in which a given property is immediate, and

---

[155] Ibid., 30.

[156] Lonergan, "The Mediation of Christ in Prayer," 160–82, in CWBL 6, at 160.

[157] Ibid., 162. Lonergan emphasizes that his understanding of the universal character of mediation is distinct from that of Hegel, for whom mediation governs the relation between concepts in an idealist philosophy.

the mediated effect of that property in its manifestation.[158] If we apply them to the notion of sacrifice we can say that the sacrificial attitude of Christ is immediate in Christ's inner word and is mediated by his incarnate meaning, which is manifest in the symbol of the cross.

Mediation provides a general account of what is explained more narrowly by causality as a relation of intelligible dependence of one thing on another. It helps us to understand the relation between the inner and outer dimensions of human acts of meaning in a way that eliminates the mechanistic connotations of instrumentality. In *Method in Theology* Lonergan explains: "Once it was held that science was certain knowledge of things through their causes. Too often churchmen have presupposed that that definition was applicable to modern science. But modern science is not certain but probable. It attends to data rather than things. It speaks of causes but it means correlations and not end, agent, matter, form."[159] Similarly, the human sciences deal with meanings, and so, where classical writers would have applied the idea of causality to the human realm, a more capacious notion, less prone to reductionist misunderstandings, is desirable. Lonergan's account of the mediation of meaning provides an understanding and a new language to account for relationships between human beings. For example, the many connotations of "language as instrument," so objectionable to Chauvet and other postmodern thinkers, can be avoided by thinking in terms of mediation, while preserving the distinction between inner and outer words by which meaning is mediated. In terms of mediation, then, language both manifests what is innermost in a public way and at the same time, through the mediation of others, it mediates to persons what is innermost in them. To the linguistic aspect of human communication we can add the

---

[158] Lonergan elaborates on Aristotle's notion of the immediate and the mediated as follows: "We can say of any factor, quality, property, feature, aspect that has, on the one hand, a source, origin, ground, basis, and on the other hand, consequences, effects, derivatives, a field of influence, of radiation, of expansion, or that has an expression, manifestation, revelation, outcome—we can say that this factor, quality, property, feature, or aspect is immediate in the source, origin, ground, or basis, and on the other hand is mediated in the consequences, effects, derivatives, outcome, in the field of influence, radiation, expansion, in the expression, manifestation, revelation" (ibid., 162).

[159] Lonergan, *Method in Theology*, 315.

intersubjective, the incarnate, the symbolic, the artistic.[160] All of these are mediations of meaning in the human world which engage consciousness in a process of self-mediation. And because the human world includes one person's world in that of other people, it is a reality brought into being by ongoing mutual self-mediation.

4.1. Self-Mediation

Self-mediation pertains to living things that grow or change. Growth and change are processes of mediation whereby earlier stages mediate later stages so that "at any stage of its growth, the organism is alive at that stage and preparing later stages."[161] Self-mediation is future-oriented, in a process of becoming. In addition to being future-oriented, living things become something different through their interaction and combinations, so that a single-celled organism is incorporated as a part of a much larger, functioning whole. Lonergan describes this incorporation as a "displacement upwards."[162] In *Insight* such displacement is characteristic of vertical finality and may be understood in terms of his later notion of sublation. What is lower is sublated by the higher in such a way that it loses nothing of its own proper functioning but participates in a higher, more complex unity. For example, the millions of cells that together make a tree are not the tree itself, nor is the tree simply reducible to its individual cells. The functioning of those cells is displaced upward by the complex functioning of the living tree in the processes of photosynthesis and respiration. The further displacement that takes place in consciousness Lonergan describes as a "displacement inwards."[163] Through consciousness the animal mediates itself by its intending.

The intentional element of consciousness, Lonergan notes, includes three aspects: the act of intending, the intended object, and the intending subject.[164] In the act of intending, the intended object is made present to the intending

---

[160] This recalls Chauvet's articulation of the symbolic and his description of language as the "house of being" and the body as the "arch-symbol" of the human.

[161] Lonergan, "Mediation," 167.

[162] Ibid., 168.

[163] Ibid., 169.

[164] Ibid.

subject, while the subject is present to itself in the same act of intending.[165] Here, we have two distinct kinds of presence in which one is contingent on the other. Lonergan explains: "One can say that you are present to me. But for you to be present to me I have to be present to myself, and my being present to myself is a different sense of the word 'presence' from the sense employed when I say that you are present to me. . . . Consciousness is a presence of the subject to himself that is distinct from, but concomitant with, the presence of objects to the subject."[166] Without the presence of the subjects to themselves, the presence of the object would go unnoticed. Our discussion of consciousness in chapter 2 noted the difference between being awake and merely sensing but lacking enough attention to render one's looking more than empty gaping. Indeed, the presence to the self of the subject, the intentional element in consciousness, can differ both in quality and intensity.[167] Moreover, acts of intentional consciousness form a pattern of living within a larger pattern of situations, or a world, in which one's living unfolds within a group of other subjects, a "we" that performs the operations of living together.[168]

A further displacement away from organic self-mediation emerges in the self-consciousness proper to rational intelligence. Not only is rational intelligence present to itself in its intentional acts, it also assembles itself differently from an animal's consciousness. So, for instance, a drunk can understand that he has a problem and decide that what he needs is to sober up. In other words, rational intelligence adds the element of self-constitution or autonomy to consciousness, so that human development is a process of emerging autonomy that reaches "its climax, its critical and decisive phase, when one finds out for oneself what one can make of oneself, when one decides for oneself what one is to be, when one lives in fidelity to one's self-discovery and decision."[169] This is the existential moment when one decides either to be a drifter (thinking, saying, and doing what everyone else is thinking, saying, and doing) or understands oneself as an originating source of meaning and value and disposes of oneself autonomously through one's

---

[165] Ibid.
[166] Ibid., 169–70.
[167] Ibid., 170.
[168] Ibid.
[169] Ibid., 171.

existential commitments.[170] On the other hand, a person remains always "a piece of unfinished business."[171] Human commitments are never absolute, and recidivism is the norm. Still, there is a meaning one has for oneself and to which one returns when one recognizes that one has started drifting. Human autonomy, furthermore, does not pertain to an isolated, monadic self but unfolds in community. Lonergan speaks of the three fundamental communities in the mutual self-commitment of marriage to the family, in the overarching commitment to the nation or state, and in the eschatological commitment to the church, the body of Christ. Each of these communities is an intentional reality, constituted not merely by an experience of proximity or by simple recognition of the situation, but by decisions and commitments. Human self-mediation occurs within these communities with their histories of progress and decline, which form the human person as a social and historical being.[172] Psychological, social, and historical contexts are concretely constituted by the ongoing mutual self-mediation of human beings who are more or less authentic.

4.2. Mutual Self-Mediation

Our existential commitments unfold within communities that both inform our present decisions and develop or decline on account of our future decisions. Those commitments occur in a broad range of personal relationships. Such relationships are constituted by the sharing of meanings in trust and hope, for while "one's self-discovery and self-commitment is one's own secret . . . . [i]t is known by others if and when one chooses to reveal it, and revealing it is an act of confidence, of intimacy, of letting down one's defenses, of entrusting oneself to another. . . . We are open to the influence of others, and others are open to influence from us."[173] Mutual self-mediation is the truest sense of education as *paideia*, or formation, in which the incarnate meaning of the master influences the self-understanding of the pupil. Personal relations can effect a more radical transformation through the mutual self-mediation of love. The self in love is radically different

---

[170] See Lonergan, "Existenz and Aggiornamento," 222–31, in *Collection*, CWBL 4.
[171] Lonergan, "Mediation," 173.
[172] Ibid., 174. See Robert Doran, *Theology and the Dialectics of History* (Toronto: University of Toronto Press, 1990), especially 177–253.
[173] Ibid., 174–75.

from the self prior to falling in love because there has occurred a further displacement away from oneself toward the beloved; the beloved becomes a part of oneself and oneself a part of the beloved. The gift of God's love brings about a displacement of the beloved into the inner life of the Trinity.

4.3. Mediation of Christ in Worship

When Lonergan applies this notion of mediation to the mediation of Christ in prayer he pays special attention to the intersubjective mediation that occurs in mutual self-mediation. That mediation is also objective insofar as the mission of Christ mediates divine love to *all* human beings. The New Testament gives an account of that mediation, which the church continues to mediate in history in preaching, worship, and witness, in the way individual Christians reveal God's love to others. As Christ mediates between humans and the Father,[174] the Holy Spirit mediates between humans and Christ and his Father.[175] All of this pertains to the objective field of mediation, which is accessible as the data of revelation, preaching, and evangelization.

But the mediation of Christ in prayer is even more intimate. In the subjective dimension Christ is both immediate and mediator.[176] We are immediate to ourselves in our living prior to any reflecting on ourselves or our lives. Lonergan insists that "in that immediacy there are supernatural realities that do not pertain to our nature, that result from the communication to us of Christ's life."[177] These supernatural realities are the presence of the Trinitarian missions within us. They are immediate to us not as part of our natures but as a gift by which we are temples of the Holy Spirit, members of Christ, adopted children of God the Father.[178] Though this immediacy is not ours by nature, but by a gift, it is a concrete part of our reality, the concreteness of the life of grace. Lonergan suggests that the life of grace can function in the mode of our unconscious "vegetative" living insofar as it remains unappropriated, as perhaps in the holy innocent who lives the life of grace without ever reflecting on it. Growth in prayer, however, promotes the life of grace in us into our conscious, spontaneous, and deliberate liv-

---

174 1 Tim 2:5.
175 1 Cor 12:3.
176 Lonergan, "Mediation," 178.
177 Ibid.
178 Ibid., 179.

ing.[179] Just as self-appropriation of our consciousness's dynamic structure can be achieved by the spiritual exercises of philosophy, there can be an objectification and appropriation of the life of grace in us through prayer and sacramental worship. "What is immediate in us can be mediated by our acts, and gradually reveal to us in an ever fuller fashion, in a more conscious and more pressing fashion, the fundamental fact about us: the great gift and grace that Jesus Christ brought to us."[180] This mediation may take the form of praying without ceasing,[181] so that all our living, all our acting, becomes growth in the life of grace in response to "our *own* apprehension of [Christ] . . . in accord with our own capacities and individuality, in response to our own needs and failings."[182]

The life of grace may be conceived of as a self-mediation of what is immediate in us becoming manifest in our intentional acts but, more important, it is a mediation of oneself through another who is at the center of our self-mediation: "One is becoming oneself, not just by experiences, insights, judgments, by choices, decisions, conversion, not just freely and deliberately, not just deeply and strongly, but as one who is carried along. One is doing so not in isolation, but in reference to Christ."[183] Growing in the life of faith is personal development in relation to another and so an instance of mutual self-mediation. While it is not a mutual self-mediation of equals, it is a real mutual self-mediation that is similar to the way Christ himself developed in his human consciousness and thereby grew in knowledge, wisdom, and grace.[184] The self-mediation of Christ is at the same time a mediation of his incarnate meaning to other human beings. That meaning is revealed in the entire life of Christ and finds its perfect symbolic expression in the cross. "Christ chose and decided to perfect himself in the manner in which he did because of us. We think of the way of the cross primarily as the cross of Christ. But primarily the way of the cross is the way in which fallen nature acquires its perfection."[185] It is through that "just and mysterious" Law of the Cross discussed above that human beings reach their perfection. But

---

[179] Ibid.
[180] Ibid., 179–80.
[181] 1 Thess 5:17
[182] Lonergan, "Mediation," 180.
[183] Ibid.
[184] Ibid.
[185] Ibid., 181.

that law, which as an intelligibility in the universe, is explainable in abstract terms, is given flesh in the sacrifice of Christ, so that "instead of an abstract principle we have a mutual self-mediation."[186] Within the dynamic process of mutual self-mediation by which Christ symbolically mediates to us his sacrificial attitude (his incarnate meaning) we symbolically mediate our own sacrificial attitude, our own love for God and sorrow over sin (our graced incarnate meaning), to Christ as God in the Eucharist. Because the Eucharist is a proper symbol of the cross it makes participation in the cross possible. The reason why transubstantiation, or whole conversion, is a valid insight is that it affirms that Christ is made fully present for the sake of communion. Each of the other sacraments is preparatory for this communion, but it is fulfilled in the Eucharist.

In the Eucharist the mutual self-mediation of Christ and the faithful becomes bodily encounter with Christ's body in his sacramental species. Because Christ is really, truly, and substantially present in the Eucharist (which is to say that his meanings and values are present both bodily and spiritually), mediation happens as communion. Communion is symbolized in action in the Eucharist, in sacramental eating, but realized intentionally when Christ's meanings and values become one's own through spiritual eating. To share in communion with Christ is to have the mind of Christ.[187] This union of intentions, of hearts, of wills, of bodies, is being in love. It is to accept Christ's offer of friendship, to become Christ's beloved friend, to recognize in him the fulfillment of one's deepest longings. To have Christ as a beloved friend is to love the man Jesus, our friend, as a divine person—it is to worship him.

---

[186] Ibid.
[187] Phil 2:5.

Epilogue

1. The Trinitarian Missions in Worship

Lonergan has argued that the primary reason for the incarnation is the mediation of divine friendship.[1] That we can be friends of God is due to the gift of God's grace communicated in the missions of the Trinity. As I mentioned previously, the sacrifice of Christ both satisfies for sins by a perfect act of penance, of hatred of and sorrow over sin, and reveals the divine intelligibility of overcoming evil with good that Lonergan calls the Law of the Cross. That Christ satisfies for sins by his cross answers the question "what does the cross do?" That the cross reveals the universal intelligibility of the Law of the Cross answers the question "why a cross (suffering and death) and not some other form of redemption?" But a further question regarding the mission of the Second Person more generally asks "why a God-man?" It has long been held, especially in Western Christianity, that the reason for the Incarnation was sin. Anselm argued that sin makes the Incarnation necessary.[2] But Lonergan contends that the "the Son of God became man to

---

[1] In addition to his thesis on the Law of the Cross, Lonergan left an unfinished draft of a book on the redemption within which he places the Law of the Cross in the broader context of the mediation of divine friendship. The mediation of friendship is Lonergan's answer to the question "Cur Deus Homo?" See Charles C. Hefling Jr., "Lonergan's *Cur Deus Homo*: Revisiting the 'Law of the Cross,'" 145–66, in *Meaning and History in Systematic Theology: Essays in Honor of Robert M. Doran*, SJ, ed. John D. Dadosky (Milwaukee, WI: Marquette University Press, 2009). See also John Volk, "Lonergan on the Historical Causality of Christ: An Interpretation of "'The Redemption: A Supplement to *De Verbo Incarnato*'" (PhD diss., Marquette University, 2012).

[2] Anselm, "*Cur Deus Homo?*" 237–326, in *Anselm: Basic Writings*, ed. and trans. Thomas Williams (Indianapolis: Hackett Publishing, 2007), at 238. Thomas takes a more nuanced approach to necessity in the incarnation. See *ST* III, q. 1, a. 2 and 3. See also *ST* III, q. 46, a. 1.

communicate God's friendship to his enemies in due order."[3] The sinfulness of human beings would be the primary cause of the Incarnation only if the Incarnation were a divine afterthought. Charles Hefling explains: "What calls for God's Incarnation is not, in the first instance, the sinfulness of those whom God would befriend. In the first instance it is the self-diffusiveness of the divine friendship that God would share."[4] Human sinfulness, however, is a basic fact in the human world mediated by meaning. God's entry into that world, what Lonergan called God's participation in "man's making of man,"[5] must take that fact seriously, and God's communication of divine friendship to human beings includes a solution to the problem of evil.

Divine friendship is one way of understanding what the Trinity is. Lonergan explains: "Divine friendship is mutual benevolent love with respect to that which is good by its very essence. This friendship is proper to the divine persons alone, in which the Father and the Son and the Holy Spirit necessarily and eternally will divine good to the Father and the Son and the Holy Spirit."[6] Human participation in that divine friendship is understood according to a principle of extension by which a friend loves his friend's friends. Even while we are enemies of God, God sends a mediator, "a friendly go-between. . . a friend according to divine friendship and a friend also of men, so that because of him divine friendship may be extended to the rest of mankind."[7] By the principle of extension all human beings are invited to participate in the divine friendship by becoming friends of God through the friendship shown to human beings by the incarnate Word who lays down his life for them.[8] Christ loves God with perfect love and his fellow human beings for God's sake. Christ's love restores friendly relations between human beings and God the Father, who loves his friends' friends with a divine love. By that love with which God loves us first we are turned from enemies into

[3] Lonergan, *Cur Deus Homo?*, trans. Michael Shields, available from the Lonergan Center, Boston College, 237. See *ST* III, q. 1, a. 1.

[4] Hefling, "Lonergan's *Cur Deus Homo?*," 160.

[5] Bernard Lonergan, "Theology in Its New Context," in *Second Collection*, CWBL 13, ed. William F. J. Ryan and Bernard J. Tyrell (Toronto: University of Toronto Press, 1996), 62.

[6] Lonergan, *Cur Deus Homo?*, 237–38.

[7] Ibid., 240. Extending divine friendship would entail embodying the eschatological imagination of Christ in history. See James Alison, *Raising Abel: The Recovery of the Eschatological Imagination* (New York: Crossroad, 1996).

[8] John 15:13.

friends. It is not love as a reward for our good behavior, which would entail a change in God, but love for us even while we found ourselves unlovable.

There is a further ramification of the work of the intermediary. According to Lonergan, "This display of love and inducement to love in return is sufficient only to make men disposed to love. For it is one thing to love an incarnate divine person as man and another to love him as a divine person. For the former love, a human display of love and inducement to love will suffice; but for the latter there is an additional need for the supernatural gifts of grace."[9] The supernatural gifts of grace participate in the Trinitarian relations to which human beings are elevated and by which they are enlightened. By that elevation and enlightenment we are able to love Jesus Christ as a divine person. This is accomplished in human beings by the divine missions: the invisible mission of the Spirit and the visible mission of the Son who are sent to "establish and confirm new interpersonal relations" of friendship.[10] Hefling proposes that to love the man Jesus as divine would be to worship him. It is to find in the incarnate Word the mediated object of what is immediate in us, the love that is poured forth into our hearts by the Holy Spirit.[11] In that sense what is most immediate in us, the inner word that is the presence of the Holy Spirit moving us, finds its outer word or proper expression in the person and work of Jesus Christ.

The dynamic state of being in love with God, due to the presence of the Holy Spirit in us, or operative grace, enables us to cooperate with the incarnate meaning that is Christ Jesus. Hefling writes:

> Worship, as love for Jesus Christ as a divine person, could be conceived as an instance, perhaps in some sense the principal instance, of human cooperation with divine grace. In so far as it consists in loving God, worship depends on the unmediated gift of the Spirit. In so far as it has as its mediated object, directly or indirectly, the "expressive sign" who was Jesus Christ, it depends on the Incarnation of the Word. The cooperation may take the form of "sighs too deep for words"; it may take the form of crying, "Abba! Father!"; it may take the form of eucharistic *anamnesis* of the Lord's death "until he come."[12]

[9] Lonergan, *Cur Deus Homo?*, 244.
[10] Hefling, "Lonergan's *Cur Deus Homo?*," 164.
[11] Rom 5:5.
[12] Hefling, "Lonergan's *Cur Deus Homo?*," 165.

Such cooperation is communion with Christ symbolized in the sacrament of the Eucharist and realized in spiritual eating of a sacrificial meal, by which the movement of the Holy Spirit in us reaches its fulfillment. Thus Hefling offers the tantalizing suggestion:

> Christian worship is a kind of definitive microcosm of Christian living as supernatural. It involves the "ontic present" of God's love; it involves the "objective past in which God's revelation of his love . . . through Christ Jesus has been mediated . . . by the ongoing Christian community," and the result of cooperation between these "inner" and "outer" moments is an eschatological attitude and orientation that issues "from above downwards," in a transformation of existential ethics.[13]

While contemporary theologians may object to the term "supernatural," misunderstanding it as indicative of a metaphysical dualism, the supernatural life of grace in us is precisely what Christianity is about. It is not supernatural as opposed to what is natural, but as sublating and perfecting nature. It is the incorporation of the human being into the Trinitarian life that is ours not by nature but by the sheer gratuitousness, indeed lavishness,[14] of divine love.

By lavishing love on human beings God restores friendly relations with us through the Trinitarian missions. This lavishness of God's love in Christ made known by the gift of the Holy Spirit flooding our hearts is expressed in the church's worship. The liturgy is therefore a work of God wherein human beings are incorporated into the inner Trinitarian life through the mediation of effective signs or sacraments, and human desire is transformed into cooperation with the divine initiative. The love of God that is the unmediated gift of the Holy Spirit poured into our hearts is the dynamic state of being in love with God, but it precipitates acts. Lonergan explains: "The dynamic state of itself is operative grace, but the same state as principle of acts of love, hope, faith, repentance, and so on, is grace as cooperative."[15] We cooperate with the Spirit in acts of love, hope, faith, repentance, and thanksgiving that make up the worship of the church. We cooperate with the Son in making the Law of the Cross our own through eucharistic sacri-

---

[13] Ibid., 166
[14] See Lonergan, *Cur Deus Homo?*, 245.
[15] Bernard J. Lonergan, *Method in Theology* (New York: Herder & Herder, 1972), 107.

fice. By our cooperation in worship we are united with the body of Christ as brothers and sisters and give God a body in the world.[16]

Eating Christ spiritually, and partaking of the effect of the Eucharist, is intentional entry into the mystical body of Christ, the church. The affirmation that the body of Christ *is* the church is the heart of Christian ecclesiology.[17] The intentionality of the church is mediated through sacraments by which one grows in the life of grace, but the Eucharist is the source and summit of Christian living, and so it uniquely makes the church. The church, then, would be properly understood as the concretely emerging intentional reality composed of those who receive Christ in the Eucharist spiritually, for "the numerically same intentionality . . . which on the cross manifests Christ's sacrificial attitude is manifested in the Eucharist."[18] What does it mean concretely to eat Christ spiritually? Eating is receiving, but in eating Christ sacramentally, in bread and wine, we receive spiritual nourishment. Insofar as the spiritual nourishment of sacramental eating bears fruit it is a spiritual eating, for "by their fruits you will know them."[19] Through a transvaluation of our values in the mutual self-mediation of the eucharistic meal we become bearers of Christ's judgments of value in the world, because by feeding spiritually Christ's feelings and judgments become our feelings and judgments. We are nourished to bear Christ's incarnate meaning in the world—indeed, to bear the cross in the world by our intentional detestation of sin and love for God in a life of sorrowful penitence and joyful thanksgiving beautifully reflected in the symbols and rhythm of the liturgy. The repentant joy of the forgiven sinner who enters into communion with Christ

---

[16] See Louis-Marie Chauvet, *Symbol and Sacrament: A Sacramental Reinterpretation of Christian Existence*, trans. Patrick Madigan and Madeleine Beaumont (Collegeville, MN: Liturgical Press, 1995), 428.

[17] See Jean-Marie Tillard, *Flesh of the Church, Flesh of Christ: At the Source of the Ecclesiology of Communion*, trans. Madeleine Beaumont (Collegeville, MN: Liturgical Press, 2001).

[18] Lonergan, "The Notion of Sacrifice," 26. This ecclesiology takes the church out of the mythical realm in which it resides in more conceptualist ecclesiologies. To work out the ramifications of this way of understanding church would be to effect the "broadening out" Lonergan called for in ecclesiology as well as in instrumental causality in the sacraments. See also Laurence Paul Hemming, "Transubstantiating Our Selves," *Heythrop Journal* 44 (2003): 418–39, at 425.

[19] Matt 7:16.

in the Eucharist is authenticated in an existential ethics that bears the Law of the Cross into the world by returning good for evil in eschatological hope.

2. Conclusion

To talk about the mediation of Christ in worship is to talk about something that is admittedly intensely personal. Indeed, to talk about it at all is to objectify what is primarily experiential and so to talk about it in ways that go beyond experience. One can only say so much. Nevertheless, one does so with some trepidation but in hope. Much of what has been said here is provisional and experimental and responds to my own questions. Certainly not all readers will share my questions, but for those who do, I hope the preceding chapters have been a source of insights leading deeper into the saving mystery at the heart of Christian worship.

The preeminent symbol under which Christian worship is carried out, and around which worshipers gather, is the cross. Christian worship, then, is sacrificial in its basic meaning: it is latreutic, propitiatory, eucharistic, and impetratory. It is a participation in the sacrifice of the cross, in Christ's incarnate meaning mediated to the worshiper in the sacramental symbols of bread and wine. By articulating a verifiable ontology of meaning we have affirmed that Christ is really present in bread and wine in the totality of his meanings, body, blood, soul, and divinity. The whole conversion of the bread and wine into the body and blood of Christ makes those meanings available to us again in an incarnate, bodily way without which their meaning would be more exclusively cognitive and communicative, but in neglect of their affective component and so less accessible for our participation. Because Christ is really present in his incarnate meaning we are able to participate in that meaning through a process of mutual self-mediation in the symbol of a meal. In the Eucharist Christ is our food. But mutual self-mediation depends on the prior presence of the gift of the Holy Spirit, our created participation in God's love for God, without which Christ's own receive him not.[20]

This is what the doctrines state in the form of propositions, and often in the terms of a medieval metaphysics possibly compatible with critical real-

---

[20] See Bernard Lonergan, "Mission and the Spirit," 23–34, in *A Third Collection* (New York: Paulist Press, 1985).

ism, but not necessarily. The transition to be made in eucharistic theology today has to do with adverting to the historical and developmental aspects of the human world of meaning and discerning the performative elements that cannot be accounted for in the metaphysical terms of universal and necessary causes. The breakthrough to history, far from negating what was true in the medieval context, can help us understand it more adequately. That transition of historical retrieval allows us to maintain the meaning of the doctrines and challenges us to restate them in new terms and relations. Whereas we are *capable* of using the categories of instrumentality, causality, substance, and accidents to speak of them, with Lonergan's help we are enabled to speak of them in terms of meaning and mediations of meaning. These new terms and relations make possible a *fruitful* analogical understanding of the mysteries articulated in the doctrines. That understanding does nothing to exhaust the mystery that Christians experience in the Eucharist, namely, the elemental meaning of God's entry into the human world in Christ Jesus and of God's love sent into our hearts through the Holy Spirit he has given us. The hope is, rather, that a transposition into Lonergan's categories of meaning can enable a critical retrieval of the meaning of dogmas that, although they may be embarrassing at the present time, take us to the core of Christian faith where heart speaks to heart in a feast of love.

Bibliography

Works by Bernard J. F. Lonergan, SJ

Bernard J. F. Lonergan. *Collection, Collected Works of Bernard Lonergan* 4. Edited by Frederick E. Crowe and Robert M. Doran. Toronto: University of Toronto Press, 1988.

———. *De Verbo Incarnato.* 3rd ed. Rome: Pontifical Gregorian University, 1964.

———. *Early Latin Theology, Collected Works of Bernard Lonergan* 19. Edited by Frederick E. Crowe and Robert M. Doran. Toronto: University of Toronto Press, 2011.

———. *Grace and Freedom: Operative Grace in the Thought of St. Thomas Aquinas, Collected Works of Bernard Lonergan* 1. Edited by Frederick E. Crowe and Robert M. Doran. Toronto: University of Toronto Press, 2000.

———. *Insight: A Study of Human Understanding, Collected Works of Bernard Lonergan* 3. Edited by Frederick E. Crowe and Robert M. Doran. Toronto: University of Toronto Press, 1992.

———. *Method in Theology.* Toronto: University of Toronto Press, 1990.

———. *The Ontological and Psychological Constitution of Christ, Collected Works of Bernard Lonergan* 7. Edited by Frederick E. Crowe and Robert M. Doran. Translated by Michael Shields. Toronto: University of Toronto Press, 2002.

———. *Philosophical and Theological Papers, 1958–1964, Collected Works of Bernard Lonergan* 6. Edited by Robert C. Croken, Frederick E. Crowe, and Robert M. Doran. Toronto: University of Toronto Press, 1996.

———. *Philosophical and Theological Papers, 1965–1980, Collected Works of Bernard Lonergan* 17. Edited by Robert C. Croken and Robert M. Doran. Toronto: University of Toronto Press, 2004.

———. *A Second Collection.* Edited by Bernard J. Tyrrell and William F. Ryan. Toronto: University of Toronto Press, 1975.

———. *Shorter Papers, Collected Works of Bernard Lonergan* 20. Edited by Robert C. Croken, Robert M. Doran, and Daniel Monsour. Toronto: University of Toronto Press, 2007.

———. *A Third Collection: Papers by Bernard J. F. Lonergan.* Edited by Frederick E. Crowe. New York: Paulist Press, 1985.

———. *Topics in Education: The Cincinnati Lectures of 1959 on the Philosophy of Education, Collected Works of Bernard Lonergan* 10. Edited by Robert M. Doran and Frederick E. Crowe. Toronto: University of Toronto Press, 1993.

———. *The Triune God: Doctrines, Collected Works of Bernard Lonergan* 11. Edited by Robert M. Doran and H. Daniel Monsour. Translated by Michael Shields. Toronto: University of Toronto Press, 2009.

———. *The Triune God: Systematics, Collected Works of Bernard Lonergan* 12. Edited by Robert M. Doran and H. Daniel Monsour. Translated by Michael Shields. Toronto: University of Toronto Press, 2007.

———. *Understanding and Being: The Halifax Lectures on Insight, Collected Works of Bernard Lonergan* 5. Edited by Elizabeth A. Morelli and Mark D. Morelli. Toronto: University of Toronto Press, 1990.

———. *Verbum: Word and Idea in Aquinas, Collected Works of Bernard Lonergan* 2. Edited by Frederick E. Crowe and Robert M. Doran. Toronto: University of Toronto Press, 1997.

Other Sources

Ambrose, Glenn P. *The Theology of Louis-Marie Chauvet: Overcoming Onto-Theology with the Sacramental Tradition.* Burlington, VT: Ashgate, 2012.

Augustine. *Augustine: Earlier Writings.* Edited by John H. S. Burleigh. Philadelphia: Westminster Press, 1953.

———. *Sermons 230–272B, The Works of Saint Augustine: A Translation for the 21st Century,* vol. 7, part 3. Edited by John E. Rotelle. Translated by Edmund Hill. New Rochelle, NY: New City Press, 1993.

Austin, John L. *How to Do Things with Words.* Oxford: Clarendon Press, 1962.

Baldovin, John. *Reforming the Liturgy: A Response to the Critics.* Collegeville, MN: Liturgical Press, 2008.

Bayer, Oswald. "Worship and Theology." In *Worship and Ethics: Lutherans and Anglicans in Dialogue,* edited by Oswald Bayer and Alan M. Suggate, 148–61. New York: de Gruyter, 1996.

Beer, Peter. "Trent's Eucharist Today." In *Australian Lonergan Workshop II,* edited by Matthew Ogilvie and William Danaher, 75–91. Sidney: Novum Organum Press, 2000.

———. "G. B. Sala and E. Schillebeeckx on the Eucharistic Presence: A Critique." *Science et Esprit* 38 (1986): 31–48.

Bell, Ian. "An Elaboration of the Worshipful Pattern of Experience in the Work of Bernard Lonergan." *Worship* 81, no. 6 (November 2007): 521–39.

Blankenhorn, Bernard. "Instrumental Causality in the Sacraments: Thomas Aquinas and Louis-Marie Chauvet." *Nova et Vetera*, English Edition, 4, no. 2 (2006): 255–94.

Blaylock, Joy Harrell. "Ghislain Lafont and Contemporary Sacramental Theology." *Theological Studies* 66 (2005): 841–61.

Boeve, Leiven, and Lambert Leijssen, eds. *Sacramental Presence in a Postmodern Context.* Belgium: Peeters Press, 2001.

Bordeyne, Philippe, and Bruce Morrill, eds. *The Sacraments: Revelation of the Humanity of God; Engaging the Fundamental Theology of Louis-Marie Chauvet.* Collegeville, MN: Liturgical Press, 2008.

Brock, Stephen. "St. Thomas and Eucharistic Conversion." *The Thomist* 38 (1974): 734–46.

Brown, Christopher M. "Artifacts, Substances, and Transubstantiation: Solving a Puzzle for Aquinas' Views." *The Thomist* 71 (2007): 89–112.

Brunk, Timothy. "Consumer Culture and the Body: Chauvet's Perspective." *Worship* 82, no. 4 (July 2008): 290–310.

———. "A Critical Assessment of Sacrament and Ethics in the Thought of Louis-Marie Chauvet." PhD dissertation, Marquette University, 2006.

Caputo, John D. *Heidegger and Thomas: An Essay on Overcoming Metaphysics.* New York: Fordham University Press, 1982.

Casel, Odo. *The Mystery of Christian Worship.* Translated by Burkhard Neunheuser. New York: Crossroad, 1999.

Chauvet, Louis-Marie. *Symbol and Sacrament: A Sacramental Reinterpretation of Christian Existence.* Translated by Patrick Madigan and Madeleine Beaumont. Collegeville, MN: Liturgical Press, 1995.

———. *The Sacraments: The Word of God at the Mercy of the Body.* Translated by Madeleine Beaumont. Collegeville, MN: Liturgical Press, 2001.

———. *Du Symbolique au Symbole: Essai sur les Sacrements.* Paris: Les Éditions du Cerf, 1979.

———. "The Broken Bread as Theological Figure of Eucharistic Presence." In *Sacramental Presence in a Postmodern Context*, edited by Leiven Boeve and Lambert Leijssen, 236–62. Louvain: Peeters, 2001.

———. "Parole et Sacrement." *Recherches de science religieuse* 91, no. 2 (April 2003): 203–22.

———. "Causalité et efficacité: enjeux mediévaux et contemporains." *Transversalités* 105 (January 2008): 31–51.

———. "Are the Words of the Liturgy Worn Out? What Diagnosis? What Pastoral Approach?" *Worship* 84, no. 1 (January 2010): 25–37.

Cipolla, Richard G. "Selvaggi Revisited: Transubstantiation and Contemporary Science." *Theological Studies* 35, no. 4 (1974): 667–91.

Cooke, Bernard J. *The Distancing of God: The Ambiguity of Symbol in History and Theology.* Minneapolis: Fortress Press, 1990.

Crowe, Frederick E. *Christ in History: The Christology of Bernard Lonergan from 1935 to 1982.* Ottawa: Novalis Press, 2005.

Dadosky, John D. "Sacred Symbols as Explanatory: Geertz, Eliade, and Lonergan." *Fu Jen International Religious Studies* 4, no. 1 (Summer 2010): 137–58.

Daly, Robert J. *Sacrifice Unveiled: The True Meaning of Christian Sacrifice.* New York: T & T Clark, 2009.

Doherty, Cathal. "The Language of Identity and the Doctrine of Eucharistic Change." *Irish Theological Quarterly* 72 (2007): 242–50.

Doran, Robert M. *Psychic Conversion and Theological Foundations.* Milwaukee: Marquette University Press, 2006.

———. *Subject and Psyche.* Marquette Studies in Theology. Vol. 3. Milwaukee: Marquette University Press, 1994.

———. *Theology and the Dialectics of History.* Toronto: University of Toronto Press, 1990/2001.

Downey, Michael, and Richard N. Fragomeni. *Promise of Presence.* Washington, DC: Pastoral Press, 1992.

Fields, Stephen M. *Being as Symbol: On the Origins and Development of Karl Rahner's Metaphysics.* Washington, DC: Georgetown University Press, 2000.

FitzPatrick, P. J. *In Breaking of Bread: The Eucharist and Ritual.* New York: Cambridge University Press, 1993.

Fortuna, Joseph J. "Two Approaches to the Role of Language in Sacramental Efficacy Compared: Thomas Aquinas in the 'ST' and Louis-Marie Chauvet." STD dissertation, The Catholic University of America, 1989.

Gelineau, Joseph. *The Liturgy Today and Tomorrow.* Mahwah, NJ: Paulist Press, 1978.

Grisez, Germain. "An Alternative Theology of Jesus' Substantial Presence in the Eucharist." *Irish Theological Quarterly* 65, no. 11 (2000): 111–31.

Happel, Stephen. "Sacraments: Symbols That Redirect Our Desires." In *The Desires of the Human Heart: An Introduction to the Theology of Bernard Lonergan,* edited by Vernon Gregson, 237–54. New York: Paulist Press, 1988.

———. "Whether Sacraments Liberate Communities: Some Reflections upon Image as an Agent in Achieving Freedom." *Lonergan Workshop* 5 (1985): 197–217.

———. "Sacrament: Symbol of Conversion." In *Creativity and Method: Essays in Honor of Bernard Lonergan,* edited by Matthew Lamb, 275–90. Milwaukee: Marquette University Press, 1981.

Hefling, Charles C., Jr. "Lonergan's *Cur Deus Homo*: Revisiting the 'Law of the Cross.'" In *Meaning and History in Systematic Theology: Essays in Honor of Robert M. Doran, SJ,* edited by John D. Dadosky, 145–66. Milwaukee: Marquette University Press, 2009.

————. *Why Doctrines?* Chestnut Hill, MA: The Lonergan Institute, 2000.

————. "A Perhaps Permanently Valid Achievement: Lonergan on Christ's Satisfaction." *Method: Journal of Lonergan Studies* 10, no. 1 (1992): 51–76.

Heidegger, Martin. *Basic Writings.* Edited by David Farrell Krell. San Francisco: Harper, 1977/1993.

————. *Being and Time.* Translated by John Macquarrie and Edward Robinson. New York: Harper and Row, 1962.

————. *Identity and Difference.* Translated by Joan Stambaugh. Chicago: University of Chicago Press, 2002.

————. *Ontology: The Hermeneutics of Facticity.* Translated by John van Buren. Bloomington: Indiana University Press, 1999.

Hemming, Laurence Paul. *Worship as a Revelation: The Past, Present and Future of Catholic Liturgy.* New York: Burns and Oates, 2008.

————. "Transubstantiating Ourselves." *Heythrop Journal* 44 (2003): 418–39.

————. "After Heidegger: Transubstantiation." *Heythrop Journal* 41 (2000): 170–86.

Hütter, Reinhard. "Transubstantiation Revisited: Sacra Doctrina, Dogma, and Metaphysics." In *Ressourcement Thomism: Sacred Doctrine, the Sacraments, and the Moral Life; Essays in Honor of Romanus Cessario, O.P.,* edited by Reinhard Hütter and Matthew Levering, 21–79. Washington, DC: The Catholic University of America Press, 2010.

Irwin, Kevin M. *Models of the Eucharist.* Mahwah, NJ: Paulist Press, 2005.

Jasper, R. C. D., and G. J. Cuming, eds. *Prayers of the Eucharist: Early and Reformed* Collegeville, MN: Liturgical Press, 1990.

Jeremias, Joachim. *The Eucharistic Words of Jesus.* London: SCM Press, 1966.

John Paul II. *Ecclesia de Eucharistia.* AAS 95, no. 7 (2003): 433–75.

Jordan, Mark. *Rewritten Theology: Aquinas after His Readers.* Malden, MA: Blackwell Publishing, 2006.

Kavanaugh, Aidan. *On Liturgical Theology.* Collegeville, MN: Liturgical Press, 1992.

Kelleher, Margaret Mary. "Liturgy as an Ecclesial Act of Meaning: Foundations and Methodological Consequences for a Liturgical Spirituality." PhD dissertation, The Catholic University of America, 1983.

————. "Liturgy: An Ecclesial Act of Meaning." *Worship* 59 (1985): 482–97.

————. "Liturgical Theology: A Task and Method." In *Foundations in Ritual Studies: A Reader for Students of Christian Worship,* edited by Paul Bradshaw and John Melloh, 220–22. Grand Rapids, MI: Baker Academic, 2007.

Kerr, Fergus. "Transubstantiation after Wittgenstein." *Modern Theology* 15, no. 2 (April 1999): 115–30.

Kereszty, Roch. *Wedding Feast of the Lamb: Eucharistic Theology from a Historical, Biblical and Systematic Perspective.* Chicago: Liturgy Training Publications, 2004.

Kidder, Paul E. "The Relation of Knowing and Being in Lonergan's Philosophy." PhD dissertation, Boston College, 1987.

Kilmartin, Edward. *The Eucharist in the West: History and Theology.* Edited by Robert J. Daly. Collegeville, MN: Liturgical Press, 1998.

Kocik, Thomas M. *The Reform of the Reform? A Liturgical Debate; Reform or Return.* San Francisco: Ignatius Press, 2003.

Kodell, Jerome. *The Eucharist in the New Testament.* Collegeville, MN: Liturgical Press, 1991.

Lafont, Ghislain. *Eucharist: The Meal and Word.* Translated by Jeremy Driscoll. New York: Paulist Press, 2008.

Laverdiere, Eugene. *The Eucharist in the New Testament and the Early Church.* Collegeville, MN: Liturgical Press, 1996.

Lawrence, Frederick. "Expanding Challenge to Authenticity in Insight: Lonergan's Hermeneutics of Facticity (1953–1964)." *Divyadaan: Journal of Philosophy and Education* 15, no. 3 (2004): 427–56.

————. "The Fragility of Consciousness: Lonergan and the Postmodern Concern for the Other." In *Communication and Lonergan: Common Ground for Forging the New Age*, edited by Thomas J. Farrell and Paul A. Soukup, 173–211. Kansas City, MO: Sheed and Ward, 1993.

————. "Gadamer and Lonergan: A Dialectical Comparison." *International Philosophical Quarterly* 20 (1980): 25–47.

————. "Language as Horizon?" In *The Beginning and the Beyond: Papers from the Gadamer and Voegelin Conferences; Supplementary Issue of Lonergan Workshop 4*, edited by Frederick Lawrence, 13–34. Atlanta, GA: Scholars Press, 1984.

————. "Lonergan: The Integral Postmodern?" *Method: Journal of Lonergan Studies* 18 (2000): 95–122.

————. "Lonergan and Aquinas: The Postmodern Problematic of Theology and Ethics." In *The Ethics of Aquinas*, edited by Stephen J. Pope, 439–41. Washington, DC: Georgetown University Press, 2002.

————. "Lonergan's Postmodern Subject: Neither Neo-scholastic Substance Nor Cartesian Ego." In *In Deference to the Other: Lonergan and Contemporary Continental Thought*, edited by Jim Kanaris and Mark J. Doorley, 107–20. New York: SUNY Press, 2004.

Levering, Matthew. *Sacrifice and Community: Jewish Offering and Christian Eucharist.* Malden, MA: Blackwell, 2005.

————. "Aquinas on the Liturgy of the Eucharist." In *Aquinas on Doctrine: A Critical Introduction*, edited by Thomas G. Weinandy, Daniel A. Keating, and John P. Yocum, 183–97. New York: T & T Clark, 2004.

Lothes-Biviano, Erin. *The Paradox of Christian Sacrifice: The Loss of Self, The Gift of Self.* New York: Crossroad Publishing, 2007.

Macy, Gary. *Treasures from the Storeroom: Medieval Religion and the Eucharist.* Collegeville, MN: Liturgical Press, 1999.

Marion, Jean-Luc. *God without Being: Hors-Texte.* Translated by Thomas A Carlson. Chicago: University of Chicago Press, 1991.

———. "Thomas Aquinas and Onto-Theology." In *Mystics: Presence and Aporia,* edited by Michael Kessler and Christian Sheppard, 38–74. Chicago: University of Chicago Press, 2003.

Mazza, Enrico. *The Celebration of the Eucharist: The Origin of the Rite and the Development of Its Interpretation.* Translated by Matthew J. O'Connell. Collegeville, MN: Liturgical Press, 1999.

McCabe, Herbert. *God Still Matters.* Edited by Brian Davies. New York: Continuum, 2002.

McDermott, John M. "The Sacramental Vision of Lonergan's Grace and Freedom." *Sapientia* 50 (1995): 115–48.

McGrath, Sean J. *The Early Heidegger and Medieval Philosophy: Phenomenology for the Godforsaken.* Washington, DC: The Catholic University of America Press, 2006.

———. "Heidegger and Duns Scotus on Truth and Language." *Review of Metaphysics* 57 (December 2003): 339–58.

McInerny, Ralph. *Aquinas and Analogy.* Washington, DC: The Catholic University of America Press, 1996.

McKenna, John H. "Eucharist and Sacrifice: An Overview." *Worship* 76 (2000): 386–402.

———. "Eucharistic Presence: An Invitation to Dialogue." *Theological Studies* 60 (1999): 294–317.

McNamara, Brian. "*Christus Patiens* in Mass and Sacraments: Higher Perspectives." *Irish Theological Quarterly* 42 (1975): 17–35.

McShane, Philip, "On the Causality of the Sacraments." *Theological Studies* 24, no. 3 (1963): 423–36.

Miller, Vincent J. "An Abyss at the Heart of Mediation: Louis-Marie Chauvet's Fundamental Theology of Sacramentality." *Horizons* 24, no. 2 (September 1997): 230–47.

Mitchell, Nathan. *Real Presence: The Work of the Eucharist.* Chicago: Liturgy Training Publications, 2001.

Moloney, Raymond. *The Eucharist.* Collegeville, MN: Liturgical Press, 1995.

———. "Lonergan and Eucharistic Theology." *Irish Theological Quarterly* 62 (1996/97): 17–28.

———. "Lonergan on Eucharistic Sacrifice." *Theological Studies* 62 (2001): 53–70.

———. "Lonergan on Substance and Transubstantiation." *Irish Theological Quarterly* 75, no. 2 (May 2010): 131–43.

Morrill, Bruce T. *Anamnesis as Dangerous Memory: Political and Liturgical Theology in Dialogue.* Collegeville, MN: Liturgical Press, 2000.

Ormerod, Neil. "The Four-Point Hypothesis: Transpositions and Complications." *Irish Theological Quarterly* 77, no. 2 (2012): 127–40.

———. "Transposing Theology into the Categories of Meaning." *Gregorianum* 92, no. 3 (2011): 517–32.

Osborne, Kenan B. *Christian Sacraments in a Postmodern World: A Theology for the Third Millennium.* Mahwah, NJ: Paulist Press, 1999.

Pattison, George. "After Transubstantiation: Blessing, Memory, Solidarity and Hope." In *Deconstructing Radical Orthodoxy: Postmodern Theology, Rhetoric, and Truth,* edited by Wayne J. Hankey and Douglas Hedley, 149–60. Burlington, VT: Ashgate, 2005.

Paul VI. *Mysterium Fidei.* AAS 57 (1965): 753–74.

Pius XII. *Mediator Dei.* AAS 39 (1947): 521–600.

Pivarnik, R. Gabriel. *Toward a Trinitarian Theology of Liturgical Participation.* Collegeville, MN: Liturgical Press. 2012.

Power, David Noel. *The Eucharistic Mystery: Revitalizing the Tradition.* New York: Crossroad, 1992.

———. "Postmodern Approaches." *Theological Studies* 55, no. 4 (December 1994): 684–93.

———. *Sacrament: The Language of God's Giving.* New York: Crossroad. 1998.

———. *The Sacrifice We Offer: The Tridentine Dogma and Its Reinterpretation.* New York: Crossroad, 1987.

Powers, Joseph M. *Eucharistic Theology.* New York: Herder and Herder, 1967.

Rahner, Karl. *The Church and the Sacraments, Questiones Disputata 9.* Translated by W. J. O'Hara. New York: Herder and Herder, 1963.

———. "The Theology of Symbol." In *Theological Investigations* 4. Translated by Kevin Smyth. Baltimore: Helicon Press, 1966.

———. "The Presence of Christ in the Sacrament of the Lord's Supper." In *Theological Investigations* 4. Translated by Kevin Smyth. Baltimore: Helicon Press, 1966.

Reichmann, James. "Scotus and Haecceitas, Aquinas and Esse: A Comparative Study." *American Catholic Philosophical Quarterly* 80 (2006): 63–75.

Sala, Giovani. "Transubstantiation oder Transignifikation: Gedenken zu einem dilemma." *Zeitschrift fur Katholische Theologie* 92 (1970): 1–34.

———. *Lonergan and Kant: Five Essays on Human Knowledge.* Edited by Robert M. Doran. Translated by Joseph Spoerl. Toronto: University of Toronto Press, 1994.

Sauer, Stephen J. "Naming Grace: A Comparative Study of Sacramental Grace in Edward Kilmartin and Louis-Marie Chauvet." STD dissertation, The Catholic University of America, 2007.

Schillebeeckx, Edward. *Christ the Sacrament of the Encounter with God.* New York: Rowan and Littlefield, 1987.

———. *The Eucharist.* Translated by N. D. Smith. New York: Sheed and Ward, 1968.

Schmemann, Alexander. *Introduction to Liturgical Theology.* Crestwood, NY: St. Vladimir's Seminary Press, 1996.

Schoonenberg, Piet. "The Real Presence in Contemporary Discussion." *Theology Digest* 15 (Spring 1967): 3–11.

Sokolowski, Robert. *Eucharistic Presence: A Study in the Theology of Disclosure.* Washington, DC: The Catholic University of America Press, 1994.

———. "The Eucharist and Transubstantiation." *Communio* 24 (December 1997): 867–80.

Stebbins, Michael. *The Divine Initiative: Grace, World-order, and Human Freedom in the Early Writings of Bernard Lonergan.* Toronto: University of Toronto Press, 1995.

———. "The Eucharistic Presence of Christ: Mystery and Meaning." *Worship* 64 (1990): 225–36.

Thomas Aquinas. *Summa Theologica.* Translated by the Fathers of the English Dominican Province. New York: Benziger, 1948.

Tillard, Jean-Marie. *Flesh of the Church, Flesh of Christ: At the Source of the Ecclesiology of Communion.* Translated by Madeleine Beaumont. Collegeville, MN: Liturgical Press, 2001.

Turner, Denys. *Faith, Reason, and the Existence of God.* New York: Cambridge University Press, 2004.

Vonier, Anscar. *A Key to the Doctrine of the Eucharist.* Westminster, MD: Newman Press, 1956.

Walmsley, Gerard. *Lonergan on Philosophic Pluralism: The Polymorphism of Consciousness as the Key to Philosophy.* Toronto: University of Toronto Press, 2008.

Walsh, Liam. "Liturgy in the Theology of Saint Thomas." *The Thomist* 38 (1974): 557–83.

Wandel, Lee Palmer. *The Eucharist in the Reformation: Incarnation and Liturgy.* New York: Cambridge University Press, 2006.

Witczak, Michael. "The Manifold Presence of Christ in the Eucharist." *Theological Studies,* 59 (1998): 680–702.

Index

Happel, Stephen, xvi n
Hefling, Charles C., ix, 153n, 160n, 194,
195n, 197n, 225n, 226–28
Heidegger, Martin, xii n, xiv, xvii, xx,
1–3, 5, 10–14, 16–24, 35n, 36, 38,
39, 41, 43, 57n, 58n, 77n, 94, 96, 100,
101n, 109n, 111, 119, 123, 125, 128,
130, 131, 133, 145n, 183
Hemming, Laurence Paul, xii n, 229n
heuristic, xvii, xviii, 6, 48, 52n, 79, 94,
95, 104, 106, 108, 131, 154, 162, 163,
164n, 183; heuristic structure of
proportionate being, 54, 104, 107,
109, 113, 183
Holy Spirit, 136, 167, 168, 171, 176, 183,
185, 187, 206, 207, 214, 215, 222,
226–28, 230, 231
Hütter, Reinhard, 28n

identity, 13n, 16; of cross and
altar, 197–99; *see also*
— unity-identity-whole
insight, 32, 42n, 47, 48, 52–56, 75–76,
82, 84–88, 91, 93, 110, 112–13, 152;
and dramatic bias, 70–71; oversight
of, 32, 44; reflective i., 53–54, 75,
86–87, 149
instrumental causality. *See* causality
intelligibility, 45, 51, 56–58, 75, 77, 81,
93, 113, 116, 148, 149, 176, 193, 200,
209n, 213, 214, 216, 224; and being,
51, 104; and the cross, 193–96, 198,
200, 201, 202, 216, 225; and doctrine, 121, 175
intentional/intentionality, 90n, 144,
145, 157, 158, 178, 185, 188, 190,
195, 203, 219–21, 223, 224, 229; and
being, 95, 96, 98, 140; intentionality
analysis, 49, 59, 60, 94, 104, 119,
122, 129n, 140, 141

interiority, xix, 90n, 128–29, 137, 139,
156, 157–58; religious interiority,
142, 158
intersubjective/intersubjectivity, 41, 72,
143, 219, 222; *see also* meaning

Jeremias, Joachim, 164n
John Paul II, 73n, 171, 176, 178n
Jordan, Mark, 207n

Kant, Immanuel, 41n, 43, 45, 78n, 93n,
134n, 154, 186n
Kereszty, Roch, 181n
Kidder, Paul, 39n, 99n
Kilmartin, Edward, xvii n, 135n, 163n,
165n, 198n, 205n
knowing, xvii, 19n, 21, 32, 36–37, 55,
58–59, 62–65, 69, 71, 75–76, 82,
84–94, 97–99, 103, 104, 109, 113,
123, 132, 141, 158, 166, 192, 196,
215; and being, 95, 98, 99, 102, 104,
116, 140; Chauvet on, 2, 4, 5, 21, 24,
36, 98, divine knowing, 199, 207,
208–9, 210n; and objectivity, 103,
139; and self-appropriation, 54,
136, 157; as taking a look (picture-
thinking), 43, 45, 51, 55, 60, 78–79,
101, 110, 112, 135, 153, 176; *see also*
Lonergan, and desire to know
Kodell, Jerome, 164n

Langer, Susanne, 144n
language, 96–97, 124–25, 131, 142, 145,
182, 218; and being, 21–22, 111; and
the body, 30; as carrier of meaning,
145; of doctrine, xi, xii n, 163–68,
172; as house of being, 21–22, 96,
219n, *see also* Chauvet, and language; as instrument, 14–15, 21–22,
24, 97–98, 218; ordinary l., 145, 158;